BOXES

the secret life of
howard hughes

Douglas Wellman

Mark Musick

Published in the United States by WriteLife Publishing
(An imprint of Boutique of Quality Books Publishing Company)
www.writelife.com

Printed in the United States of America

978-1-60808-139-4 (p)
978-1-60808-140-0 (e)
Library of Congress Control Number: 2015951093

Book design by Robin Krauss, www.bookformatters.com
Cover design by Ellis Dixon, www.ellisdixon.com

DEDICATION

A loving thank you goes to Susan, my wife, and Bradley and Michelle, my children, for not thinking I was crazy as I worked over a decade on this history-changing story.

Also, to Eva McLelland for trusting me enough to tell me about the secrets she had kept for over thirty years.

Mark Musick

To my beloved wife Deborah, who has spent over a decade watching me dash from place to place working on one thing or another. She doesn't always know what I'm doing, but at least she knows where I am. I lovingly appreciate her unending patience and support.

Douglas Wellman

FOREWORD

Boxes is the story of Eva McLelland's husband, Nik, a famous man in the twentieth century, who spent the waning years of his life hiding from the international spotlight of his former life.

The first time I heard Eva's story, it was hard to understand and even harder to accept. It was like a fairytale, albeit bittersweet. Without knowing where it would lead, I began to research her story and her husband's previous identity. Piece by piece, Eva's tale checked out and, strange as it was, aligned with many of the books written about this man.

When we were able to visit, personally, I relayed to Eva how her stories wove into her husband's public life. She had never heard these aspects of his life before, yet they answered countless questions she'd held in her heart for many years. During a visit with her in the summer of 2006, it finally hit me; her crazy stories were absolutely true.

After nearly a decade researching and chronicling Eva's life, many aspects remain a mystery. Maybe they will always remain unknown, or someone, who also knows the truth, will come forward and fill in the gaps.

Not everyone will believe the story that follows. Nevertheless, it is an intriguing tale. Not long ago, I asked Eva if Nik would approve of this story becoming public.

She replied, "Yes, he would be proud. After all, he fooled the world."

Mark Musick

PREFACE

Had Elizabeth Taylor, Ava Gardner, or Katharine Hepburn wished for this dream, it would have been granted to them, but I was the chosen one!

Just imagine a combination of all the multiple personalities a person can possess, switching rapidly and seamlessly from one to the next. During my thirty-one years of marriage to Nik, I saw them all, hundreds of times, sometimes all at once. He was a hidden, naked recluse, and I fronted for him in business dealings, socially, and in every way that might necessitate a personal appearance. I seemed to be the only person alive who was able to understand his personality.

My insight had its inception at the beginning of our relationship. During our courtship, I was struck by his winning traits. The very next day after our wedding, in a shocking and unexpected outburst of temper, he exclaimed that I did not love him and snatched the wedding and engagement rings right off my finger!

Even though I was aware of Nik's shortcomings at the time I married him, I thought he was as near the presentation of the "second coming" as any earthly human could be. I fell in love with his humility and gentle ways and very quickly learned to love his genius. It was quite obvious from the beginning of the marriage that I was to become enslaved by his possessiveness. For years, his true identity was a mystery to me, but slowly everything became clear.

Despite frequent stormy times in the marriage, there were numerous occasions of merriment when we had veritable laughing parties, and Nik seemed unable to stop giggling hysterically about something I said or told him. Some of his childhood stories were quite amusing. Many times, I saw him laugh so hard he ended up crying.

I loved and respected him and never revealed his true identity to anyone. I felt it my duty to front for him with true loyalty. As my husband is now long since gone, and I myself am very near the end of my time, I feel it would be a grave injustice to the world for me not to share the long-kept secret of my experiences with him. Therefore, I give my permission to publish this true story and its secrets, which I loyally guarded for him. It is my duty to inform the world of the truth about this great man.

I expect no financial gain through the release of this book. Many times, Nik expressed grave concern about his insufficient financial resources to support himself. I always responded by telling him if I could hold on to my own small retirement benefit, I would be okay. I really was not worried about what he would or would not leave me.

I feel blessed and honored to have dedicated nearly half of my life to the love, care, and companionship shared between us. I shall always treasure the wisdom he relayed to me from his ninety-six years of life. I helped him keep his secret for years, never revealing the truth to anyone prior to his death. Now I feel justified in sharing with the world the honor it was to be married to the most brilliant and knowledgeable man I have ever known. If I had my life to live over, I would take care of him to the end, again.

Many times, I asked Nik, "Do you think they will ever believe me?"

His consistent response was, "No, they never will."

Eva Renee McLelland

Eva in 2003, at the time her book of poetry, *Restless Winds*, was published.

Eva Renee McLelland died in 2009 at age ninety-three while living in the southeastern United States. Just prior to her passing away, she spoke of her excitement to finally tell the story she kept secret for so many years.

INTRODUCTION

If you set out to write a controversial book about a controversial figure you have to expect to encounter a certain amount of skepticism, particularly if that book appears to stick its finger in the eye of the historical record. The authors were fully prepared for this. They expected their critics to pose three possible alternative theories. The first theory is that the authors are lying opportunists. This isn't a bad theory in the sense that the book is about a deceased person unable to speak out against anyone who might distort the facts about his life. Since the subject is Howard Hughes, it becomes even easier to create a fantasy life for him because he did half of the work himself. The entire latter part of his life is obscured by his self-created matrix of false trails, rumors, and outright deception. One more lie would likely be as plausible as any of the others.

Then there is the theory that Eva was mentally unstable. Critics could point to the fact that Eva was in her late 80s when she told her story to Mark and that it's not uncommon for elderly people to have faulty memories or some form of mild to severe dementia. This theory is easily dismissed, however, since Eva had friends that not only attest to her sanity, but to her high intellect. She spent her last years in an assisted living facility because she could no longer live on her own, but the staff can verify that she had neither signs of dementia nor a propensity to lie. Both authors grilled Eva at various times about her story and it never wavered one bit. On a few occasions, Mark would be discussing something with her and if he made the slightest mistake in the details, she would stop him immediately and correct him. Two weeks prior to her death she was still answering questions exactly as she had five or six years earlier. There was most certainly nothing wrong with her memory.

The third theory is that Eva was the victim of a manipulative husband who wrapped his bizarre behavior in a concocted, or delusional, intrigue of false identity and mystery to the point that his poor wife was psychologically battered into believing him. Many of us know of women who have been emotionally abused and bend to the actions of their abusers as a means of self-defense. There is no doubt that Eva was emotionally abused. She admitted it and left Nik several times. Eva was not one to bend, however. For better or worse, she did love Nik, and she always came back. The marriage resembled a truce that was periodically violated by Nik, and Eva would retreat until it was safe to return to the front. Abused, yes. Delusional, no.

Stories are easy to make up and counter theories are a dime a dozen. What slices through the fiction and anchors this story to reality is evidence. Evidence—particularly independent evidence—is hard to fake, usually impossible. What follows is evidence.

The problem with looking for evidence in the life of a character like Howard Hughes/Nik Nicely is that you don't always know what you are looking for until you find it. Facts, lies, and physical evidence are scattered around like leaves in the wind. Even when you manage to catch a piece of it, you have to question whether it's genuine or a deliberately planted deception. It can be like trying to solve a jigsaw puzzle in which the pieces of many puzzles have been combined into one huge, frustrating pile. The process is time-consuming and sometimes pieces are still missing in the end. As we closed in on publication of the first edition of this book, we thought we had all of the information available. We were wrong.

Once the book was published, the authors conducted numerous speaking engagements and the book was discussed in print and on the radio. Then, a curious thing happened. Evidence began to come to us. People who were connected to Howard came forward. People who knew Nik and Eva came forward. These were people who knew things that hadn't made sense to them until they read the first edition of this book. Suddenly they had a context to understand.

Information from many new people is the core of this second edition.

TABLE OF CONTENTS

ONE

THE ASHES

Dothan, Alabama, June 2002

Life is filled with awkward moments. Sometimes the right words are hard to find. Sometimes, there are no right words at all and silence is the only option. Mark Musick chose silence on this particular afternoon, as he tried to preserve the dignity of the task at hand. An elderly woman stood quietly nearby, as he pried the lid from a metallic gold box and removed a plastic bag of ashes from within. Inside, a charred medallion identified the ashes as the remains of one Verner Nicely, husband of Eva, the woman at his side. Mark understood Mr. Nicely to be a long-retired government employee who had lived in modest means with Eva for thirty-one years. Little did he know when he opened the metal container, that he was unleashing a secret that was to become his obsession for years. Were these the ashes of a retired government servant or the final chapter in a story of espionage and identity manipulation that allowed one of the wealthiest and best-known figures of the twentieth century to quietly disappear into obscurity?

Mark wasn't looking for a mystery, and he certainly didn't need a six-year research project. It was through his employment that he had met Eva. Mark had been working for a nonprofit foundation for the past three years. Eva had several acres of wooded land in Alabama that she bequeathed to the foundation. His first contact with her was in 1999, when he called her on behalf of the foundation to thank her for her generosity. In the course of their conversation, she mentioned that she had a disabled husband and wanted to see if Department of Veterans Affairs would pay to have a ramp built to replace the stairs at their home. Mark told her that he was a brigadier general in the Air National Guard, and he would be happy to contact the VA and inquire about how to get the process started. The VA subsequently built the ramp, but Mark never met Eva in person until January 2002, two months after her husband died from cancer. He had spoken with Eva over the phone many times in the previous three years. They had become friendly, so she turned to him to assist in the final act of her marriage, the spreading of her husband's ashes. Mark liked Eva and was honored that she came to him at this emotional moment in her life. He packed a bag and set out for the steamy southeastern United States.

Dothan, Alabama, is the self-proclaimed Peanut Capital of the World, a thriving community of business, agricultural, and local pride, steeped in Southern hospitality, eighty miles southeast of the capital, Montgomery. Eva and Verner, who everyone knew as Nik, moved to their Fieldcrest apartment in 2000, after what Mark would soon learn had been a semi-nomadic lifestyle. He drove the rental car to the address on the south side of the Highway 210 loop to pick her up, and then Eva and Mark drove to the nearby Waffle House at the intersection of South Highway 231 and the 210 loop.

They had a substantial breakfast as they excitedly discussed their upcoming journey. It would take about two hours to travel from Dothan to the place where Eva and her late husband had enjoyed a wonderful vacation. She cherished the memories of the happy winter in 1975 that they spent in Navarre Beach, Florida, on the Gulf of Mexico. She wanted to return to this site one last time, and it was there that she intended to spread the ashes of Nik in her last act of devotion to her husband.

They drove southwest on Alabama Highway 52, eventually going through Laurel Hill, Florida. The conversation was slightly superficial, since this was a new friendship, but it was not mournful. Though in her mid-eighties, Eva was remarkably sharp. She impressed Mark as a woman of intellect who was as self-sufficient as her years would allow. The effects of age that were beginning to attack her body had thus far spared her mind. The conversation quickly turned to Nik. Thirty-one years is a very long time to spend in someone's arms, only to have death pull them apart. It was not a shock, because he had been going slowly. Nevertheless, thirty-one years is a very long time, and the parting hurt.

As they neared the Gulf at Navarre, Mark could sense Eva's excitement. She pointed out local landmarks and told him stories. Sometimes, she smiled to herself. Finally, they came to their former neighborhood, a row of beach houses baking in the summer sun. Mark found a parking place, and they set out on foot over an old, weatherworn bridge and down to the broad, sandy beach. They kicked off their shoes, stood barefoot in the soft, warm sand, and began the ritual.

Mark struggled with the lid for a moment until Eva spoke up.

"Here, Mark. I brought this," she said in a quiet but firm voice as she handed him a well-worn screwdriver.

Mark took it gently from her trembling hand and pried off the lid. Inelegant, but effective. He started down to the water, but Eva didn't move.

"You go ahead," she whispered into the wind. "I think I'll stay here by the bridge."

Mark nodded and walked down to the shore, the warm Gulf water lapping over his bare feet. He had just begun distributing the ashes when a passing jogger stopped beside him.

"Hi, what's in the bag?" he asked with friendly curiosity.

"A man's ashes," Mark replied.

The jogger had an awkward moment. After a respectful pause, he quietly stepped back and resumed his jog.

For the next few minutes, Mark worked in silence, distributing Nik's remains. It was a spiritual and moving moment for him, standing in the warm sun on a beautiful beach, returning a man for eternity to a place that had given him joy. He retained a small quantity of ashes in the bag as Eva had requested. Then he walked back and handed her the box. They shared a long look then put their shoes back on, quietly returned to the car, and started the drive back north.

Eva was silent, and Mark understood. This was an emotional moment, and she was obviously lost in her thoughts. Finally, she spoke.

"Mark, there is something I'd like to tell you. I have been keeping a secret for a very long time, and I need to confide in someone. You've been good to me and I feel I can confide in you."

"Certainly, Eva," Mark said with some surprise.

"Those ashes . . . my husband was not Verner Nicely."

"Really?" he asked. "Who was he?"

"I was married to Howard Hughes."

Mark wished he had a picture of the stunned, bewildered look on his face when Eva shared her secret. In all of his dealings with her, he'd found her to be sharp and in possession of her mental faculties. This was a new wrinkle. Howard Hughes? Why not Santa Claus? Everyone likes Santa Claus.

"When you say Howard Hughes, you don't mean the Howard Hughes, do you?"

"That's exactly who I mean."

"But Eva, Howard Hughes died over twenty-five years ago."

"Yes, that's what everyone thinks. That is what they were supposed to think."

Mark had an awkward moment. He liked Eva very much and would do nothing to hurt or offend her, but this was too much. Should he play along? Should he change the subject? Mark shifted uncomfortably in his seat.

"I'm sorry, Eva, but that's kind of hard to believe."

"Yes, I know, but it's the truth. I can explain."

And that explanation became the story that changed Mark's life, and that will change history.

TWO

HOWARD, BEFORE EVA

A man like Howard Hughes draws biographers like a magnet attracts iron shavings. He was larger than life and a magnetic figure in a literal sense to those driven to uncover what it is that makes such a man tick. All of the volumes written about Hughes would occupy a significant amount of library shelf space. Curiously, the "facts" about Hughes in these books are frequently inconsistent, the result of the man's successful efforts to hide his personal life. Probing into these inconsistencies has opened a door that leads to what may be the most successful identity swap in modern times.

A detailed history of the reclusive millionaire is unnecessary, since much is widely known. However, a quick overview is important to put our story into perspective. The focus of this story is on Howard's later life; in fact, the most intriguing part of his life occurred after he was "dead."

The mystery of Howard Hughes began long before he became a household name. It began on the very day he was born. As was frequently the case with rural births of this period, Howard's birth was not officially recorded with a birth certificate. The most common date given for Howard's birth is December 24, 1905. However, baptismal records in Keokuk, Iowa, the hometown of his father's parents, record his birth date as September 24, 1905, in Humble, Texas (Higham 13). The December date was provided by Howard's Aunt Annette, his mother's sister, for a notarized replacement birth certificate in 1941, which Howard needed as documentation for his government work during World War II. Later in her life, when she was asked why she gave that conflicting date, Annette could not give an explanation (Hack 21–2).

Whatever Howard's correct birth date may be, he was born about a year and a half after his parents, Howard Hughes Sr. and Allene Gano, were married on May 24, 1904, in Dallas, Texas (Barlett and Steele 30). The paternal grandparents were Felix and Jean Hughes of Iowa. Felix was a superintendent of schools, and later a judge and mayor in Keokuk, Iowa (Hack 22). The maternal grandparents owned a ranch in Irving, Texas. His maternal grandmother died the year he was born, but his maternal grandfather lived until 1913, giving young Howard ample opportunity to get to know him (Barlett and Steele Appendix E).

Young Howard seems to have inherited some of the worst characteristics of each parent. The son of a prominent Iowa judge and nephew of a famous, even notorious, novelist, Howard Sr. was tall, tough, and brutal. As a child, he doled out beatings to any of his peers, boys and girls alike, who dared to displease him. Incorrigible and just plain mean, he was expelled from school after school (Higham 14). However, the American West of the late nineteenth century was still very much the Wild West of legend. Howard Sr., with a Winchester rifle and sturdy wooden club attached to his saddle, rode through the southwest looking for ways to make a dollar by any means that presented itself. For a man who wasn't afraid to brutally impose his will, the West offered opportunities. One of those opportunities was in the relatively new oil exploration business. Howard became a wildcatter with two partners, Walter Sharp and Walter's half-brother, Jim Sharp. The three men, uninhibited by ethics, cheated some business partners, administered beatings to others, and ended up with a few dollars in their pockets. In the case of Howard Sr., the money didn't stay in his pocket long before it was squandered on gambling and prostitutes. Howard Sr.'s iron will, lack of regard for business ethics, and love for chasing women seems to have been passed on to his son (15).

Howard's mother, Allene Gano, was very, very different from her husband. She came from a wealthy society family, prominent in Dallas, Texas. Allene was sensitive, nervous, and a hypochondriac. She was fearful of small animals, bugs, and germs, but not the charming oil field roustabout that she met in 1903. Her parents had reservations about the tough young man, but since Howard had such a prominent father and uncle, they decided there must be some good in him and blessed the marriage. After a lavish ceremony and honeymoon, Howard took his young bride, and soon, his baby boy, on a phobia-challenging tour of some of the filthiest and most disreputable oil towns in turn-of-the-century Texas and Louisiana. In one town, Oil City, Louisiana, near Shreveport, Howard Sr. became the deputy sheriff and postmaster. He used his power to manifest his true character, or lack of it, by chaining prisoners to trees and pilfering from the post office coffers. Meanwhile, Allene, terrified of the ghastly, unhealthy environment of oil towns, fretted endlessly, apparently passing her obsession about germs and cleanliness to young Howard, who was delicate and nervous (Higham 13–9).

Since Howard and his father shared the same first name, Howard Jr. was called Sonny (Hack 25), a name he promptly discarded after his father's death. Unfortunately, young Howard was handed down something else that he could not discard: a hearing loss. The Hughes family suffered hearing loss through several generations. This characteristic was passed on to young Howard at an early age, and it would plague him for the rest of his life (Magnesen 26).

It is possible Howard Sr. and Allene were something less than enthusiastic about having a child so soon in their marriage. Allene has been characterized as being somewhat hard to get along with but she apparently did her best to be a mother. Unfortunately, her phobias about germs and cleanliness grew more intense and were passed on to the boy, where they grew exponentially as he aged.

The mechanically-minded Howard Sr. spent enough time with Sonny to whet the boy's appetite for the world of engineering. Sonny was only eleven when he built his own radio transmitter and received a federal license with the call sign 5YC. At twelve, he built a motorized bicycle powered by a small steam engine donated by his father. This created some local attention when a picture of him with his motor bike was published in the newspaper. Perhaps the most life changing event of his youth occurred when he was fourteen and his father took him for rides in a seaplane. From that point on the boy was hooked on aviation. He immediately began to take flying lessons and was on his way to being a world renowned aviator.

Sonny's paternal grandmother gave him an enormous amount of love and affection. Trips to Keokuk, Iowa, were ones Sonny looked forward to. Besides the love showered on him by Grandmother Jean Hughes, there was always something new to experience in the social circle of the small Midwestern town. Trips to his grandparents' house had the added bonus of train travel. Jean Hughes was originally from the South and took Sonny with her on train trips to that area. Depot stops were frequently long enough for Sonny and his grandmother to see a part of the local town, including several stops in Eva's hometown of Troy, Alabama. Sonny loved his grandmother and never forgot her. Later in his life, Howard bought large areas of Nevada, including the Husite property, which encompassed 27,000 acres of desert north of Las Vegas. Just before he left that city, Howard decided to honor his grandmother, whom he loved so dearly, by using his grandmother's maiden name, Summerlin, to rename the Husite property (Fischer 200).

Life back in Texas wasn't entirely lonely for Sonny, despite a growing, manipulative tendency to avoid certain social and scholastic activities by claiming illness. He developed an interest in the saxophone and practiced obsessively, somewhat to the dismay of his parents (Barlett and Steele 36). He also had a best friend named Dudley Sharp, who was the same age. Dudley was the son of Walter Sharp, Howard Sr.'s partner in the oil drilling tool business, until his untimely death in 1912. The boys spent their idle hours together, and in the summer of 1917 they journeyed for a month to Pennsylvania to attend Teedyuskung Camp, a camp for boys (Higham 22).

If there was anything that the Hughes family had in sufficient quantity, it was money. After years of want, chasing a dream of wealth through uncivilized oil towns, Howard Sr. finally stumbled onto success. In 1908, tired of using fishtail drilling bits that broke or couldn't cut through rock, he purchased the patents for three new drilling bits, and he and Walter set out together to improve them. Howard Sr., while visiting his parents in Iowa, finally had the inspiration for what became the two-cone-roller bit, and he received a patent for it in 1909. This bit revolutionized the oil drilling business in the United States and around the world. Soon, the Sharp-Hughes Tool Company (they used Walter Sharp's money to capitalize the company, since Howard had gambled his away) struck its own gusher in the form of sales revenues (Hack 27). The millions of dollars earned by the Sharp-Hughes Tool Company and later by Hughes Tool, after the original company was acquired by Howard Sr. following a series of battles with his partners, would be the financial foundation on which Howard Jr. would later build his empire.

In an effort to provide a first-class education for their son and create some privacy for themselves, Sonny's parents shipped him off to a number of boarding schools, including the prestigious Fessenden School in West Newton, Massachusetts, in 1920 at the age of fourteen. Years later, his classmates would remember him primarily for his tendency to sit in the front of the room, a habit he likely developed to compensate for his poor hearing. Sonny was not an extraordinary scholar, but neither was he an academic slouch. He graduated from junior high school in June 1921 and returned to his family in Houston (Barlett and Steele 46–8).

His feet didn't stand on the soil of Texas very long. Empowered by their new wealth, the family began to divide its time between Houston and Los Angeles, where the nascent film industry was creating a fantasy land called Hollywood. Howard Senior's brother, Rupert, was a successful writer and director of silent films and he introduced the family to the community of screen royalty. Whatever exciting social opportunities this created for Sonny's parents were nothing compared to the impact it had on him. When Sonny first drove onto the Goldwyn studio lot in Uncle Rupert's fancy Cord automobile he knew his future was in the film industry. (Higham 25-7).

When his Hollywood summer vacation ended in the fall of 1921, fifteen-year-old Sonny was packed off to the Thacher School, the equivalent to a high school, in Ojai, California, where he experienced the first of a series of life-altering events. On March 28, 1922, his mother, Allene, died suddenly at the age of thirty-eight during a medical procedure in Houston (Hack 44–5). She suffered a hemorrhage in her womb, and the combination of surgery and the anesthetic was too much for her weak heart. Sonny rushed home where Allene's thirty-one-year-old sister, Annette, accompanied him to the funeral.

Distraught by the death of his wife and the challenge of raising the boy on his own, Howard Sr. asked Annette to move to Los Angeles for one year to be closer to his son. This was quite a disruption to Annette's plans, since she was engaged to a prominent Houston physician at the time, and it meant a delay of their wedding. Nevertheless, Annette agreed to take care of her nephew for a full year. Sonny returned to the Thacher School in the fall of 1922, but a few months later, seventeen-year-old Sonny was withdrawn from school by his father, who suddenly, and uncharacteristically, couldn't bear to be separated from him. Sonny returned to Los Angeles and his loving aunt. He was very close to Annette, so the arrangement worked very well. By the end of the year, the life of the Hughes family was more settled and Annette returned to Houston to marry Dr. Frederick Rice Lummis.

The fact that Sonny's education had repeatedly been disrupted was apparently not lost on Senior. He somehow managed to get him into some classes at the California Institute of Technology, which was no small accomplishment, since Sonny was too young and lacked a high school diploma. Whether Howard Sr. pleaded his case convincingly or quietly distributed a little extra cash to facilitate the process is unknown, but records show that Sonny did attend an extramural class in solid geometry at Cal Tech. There is, however, no official record of his ever being a matriculated student (Higham 29).

By his late teens, it was readily apparent that Sonny displayed a strong aptitude for engineering. The elder Hughes exhibited his persuasive skills— or checkbook—once again later that same year at the Rice Institute in Houston, where the lack of a high school diploma did not prevent Sonny from enrolling that fall (Hack 47–8).

Whatever Sonny's attitude toward formal higher education may have been, the experience did not last long. In January 1924, Howard Sr., suffered a fatal heart attack, leaving Sonny an orphan (Barlett and Steele 52). Since his father's will had not been updated after his mother's death, young Howard received only 75 percent of the massive estate that included the Hughes Tool Company (53). Young Howard's business acumen was immediately apparent. When he turned nineteen years old, he had himself declared an emancipated minor and fought for the remaining 25 percent of the estate, eventually buying out the other heirs, including his paternal grandparents. A year after his father's death, with his financial fortune ensured, young Howard married

Ella Rice, granddaughter of the founder of the Rice Institute (57). Dudley Sharp, his best friend from childhood, returned from Princeton to be the best man at the service (Higham 32). Howard, no longer Sonny, dropped out of Rice and set out to Hollywood to make a name for himself as a filmmaker, and the Howard Hughes legend began.

The news that Howard had arrived in Hollywood to set the motion picture business on fire was greeted with indifference by the studio heads. He was considered nothing more than a rich dilettante. Perhaps, but he was an exceptionally determined dilettante. His first two films, *Everybody's Acting* (1927) and *Two Arabian Knights* (1928), were very successful at the box office. *Two Arabian Knights* even earned an Academy Award for director Lewis Milestone. While film grosses are essential to the business reputation of a producer, critical acclaim is equally important to his status as a filmmaker. *Hell's Angels* (1930), *The Front Page* (1931), *Scarface* (1932), and *The Outlaw* (1943) brought good notices along with solid box office takes. A producer who makes good money on good movies can't be ignored.

His three-decade presence in the motion picture capital was marked by an obsessive micromanaging of his creative personnel and some well-publicized romantic affairs with starlets. This latter character flaw was not unnoticed by his young wife who saw the writing on the wall early in the marriage and departed for Houston to file for divorce in 1929. Howard's motion picture career culminated with the purchase of RKO studios in 1948. Far from being a creative asset, Hughes's petty interference virtually killed all filmmaking for some time, and battles with RKO shareholders created legal woes. In 1954, he sold the crippled studio and bitterly left the film business for good.

After the demise of his first marriage, his romantic interests did not take long to blossom. Howard's first known trip to Nevada was in 1929, when the twenty-four-year-old was accompanied by the silent film star Billie Dove, whom he hoped to marry. They chose Nevada so they could establish residency and Billie could obtain a divorce from director Irvin Willet, her current husband. Howard and Billie took a train to a remote farm community outside Las Vegas. Under the aliases of George Johnson and his sister, Marion, they worked on the farm as laborers. The couple lived in a shed with a dirt floor. After two weeks of farm labor, Howard's lawyers informed him the shed would not qualify as a residence under Nevada's divorce laws. A few days later, they returned to California. Later in life, Billie recalled that during the two-week experience, Howard seemed happier working as a farmhand than he ever did in the city (Schumacher 30).

Concurrent with his development as a Hollywood mogul, Howard retained his passion for aviation and launched a second career developing and flying aircraft. He made certain that wherever he was, he had ready access to aircraft and the appropriate hangar facilities. The Houston Airport, now known as William P. Hobby Airport, was even briefly named after him in 1938 until the Federal Aviation Administration informed the facility that they could not provide support funds for an airport named after a living individual. The assets of the Hughes Tool Company provided the financial basis for his continual aircraft research and construction through the Hughes Aircraft Company, launched in 1932, as a division of Hughes Tool. During March 1933, Howard and Glenn Odekirk took off from Glendale, California, in an S-43 and flew to Houston to visit Aunt Annette (Higham 64). The route of flight went directly through the Grand Canyon, providing the opportunity for a little sightseeing. In 1935, flying an aircraft of his design, the H-1, Hughes set an air speed record in California (Barlett and Steele 81–3). The following year, in an updated version of that aircraft, he set a transcontinental speed record, flying nonstop from Burbank to Newark, NJ (Brown 96). His streak of records continued in 1938, when he completed a flight around the world in just ninety-one hours. Howard's aviation achievements drew worldwide acclaim and earned him the Harmon Trophy twice, the Collier Trophy, and the Congressional Gold Medal.

Besides being a source of personal enjoyment for Howard, the aircraft manufacturing business was successful and profitable. In 1947, Hughes began manufacturing helicopters through the Hughes Helicopter Division. The next year, the Hughes Aerospace Group was launched. The Hughes Space and Communications Company was consolidated from other existing companies in 1961 in time to establish itself at the dawn of that era of space exploration and satellite communication. This also brought him into contact with the CIA, as spy planes were replaced with spy satellites. In

1953, Hughes gave all of his stock in the Hughes Aircraft Company to the Howard Hughes Medical Institute in Maryland, which opened a branch in Miami in 1959. This meant the aircraft company was suddenly tax exempt, a situation that launched Howard into still another legal fray, this time with the Internal Revenue Service, his longtime archenemy.

For all of Howard's flying achievements and developments, two aircraft experiments stand out. The first was the enormous Hughes H-4 Hercules transport aircraft that Howard designed and sold to the U.S. government on an experimental basis. The key selling point was that it was constructed of birch wood using a special laminating process called Duramold that Hughes Aircraft developed. Metal was in short supply during World War II, and a metal-free aircraft was an attractive proposal. The massive aircraft quickly earned the nickname "The Spruce Goose," much to Howard's annoyance. Howard designed several configurations of the aircraft for troop transport, heavy equipment such as tanks, and general cargo. Unfortunately, the aircraft was not completed by the war's end. He was later called before the Senate War Investigating Committee to explain why the government received nothing for its money. Howard successfully defended his business and aircraft construction practices, and later, he flew the aircraft briefly over Long Beach harbor in California on November 2, 1947. The aircraft never flew again.

The results of the second aircraft experiment remained with Howard for the rest of his life. He was piloting an experimental United States Army reconnaissance aircraft of his design, the XF-11, when an oil leak caused a malfunction in one of the propellers. The Los Angeles Country Club golf course was close enough to provide the space for a safe emergency landing, but the aircraft came down seconds short of the fairway. Howard struck three houses, and the XF-11 erupted into flames. A passing Marine sergeant, Bill Durkin, pulled Howard from the flames moments before the aircraft exploded into a raging fireball. Howard had been spared from being cremated alive, but just barely. He sustained burns over 78 percent of his body including second and third-degree burns on his left hand, second-degree burns on the left side of his chest and on his left buttock. His left hand was burned so extensively that it required a skin graft. What wasn't burned was smashed. He suffered twelve broken ribs, a broken collarbone, massive internal bleeding, and innumerable lacerations. He drifted in and out of consciousness as he endured the long ride to the nearest major hospital capable of dealing with such extensive injuries.

By the time Howard's charred, broken body was wheeled into the hospital emergency room, the smart money was betting on an imminent celebrity funeral. With their patient screaming in agony, the doctors reached for the biggest hammer in their pain relief tool kit: morphine. The drug was administered intravenously and frequently to make Howard's presumed last hours as comfortable as possible. However, Howard surprised everyone. He lived.

As Howard's recovery progressed and his pain began to subside, his doctors substituted codeine for morphine and began to reduce the dosage. Somewhere in the process, the plan to wean him off narcotics went wrong. Drug addiction is a cruel master and has subjugated some of the strongest. Whether Howard couldn't beat the problem or he chose not to is unknown, but the results of his prolonged usage were predictable. He required increasingly larger dosages to achieve the result he desired. He reportedly also used large dosages of Valium, Librium, and Empirin (Drosnin 46). The good news for Howard was that he had the financial resources to buy all the narcotics he wanted as well as the doctors to write the prescriptions. The bad news was that he would live the rest of his life in the cold shadow of drug addiction.

Manufacturing and flying aircraft were not enough to satisfy Howard's passion for aviation. In 1939, he decided to go into the airline business by purchasing a controlling share of Trans World Airlines (TWA). Federal antitrust law prohibited Howard from owning an airline and building his own planes for that airline, so he made a deal with the Lockheed Aircraft Company to make an airliner to his specifications. This creative marriage resulted in the Lockheed Constellation, an extremely successful aircraft. All was not perfect, however. With a fleet of forty of the advanced aircraft, Hughes was ready to take on the international market, a plan that pitted him against Pan American World Airways' pending legislation that would ensure Pan Am as the sole, government approved, transoceanic air carrier. The result was a bitter and public battle. Howard won, but at the cost of his already shaky tranquility. Creditors forced him to relinquish control of TWA in 1960, and a federal court forced him to divest the rest of his shares in 1966 on charges of a conflict of interest between TWA and Hughes Aircraft. However he may have felt about this forced sale, it netted him $546 million, which would soon come in handy for his desert real estate adventures (Drosnin 49).

On July 17, 1966, a train left Los Angeles for Boston carrying Howard Hughes and his entourage of assistants and aides, most of whom were members of the Church of Jesus Christ of Latter-day Saints, commonly known as Mormons. The media rumor mill worked overtime speculating on the possible reason for this mass relocation. The number one guess was Howard had some sort of "eye trouble" and was going to a hospital in Boston, where he would receive specialized treatment (Barlett and Steele 276). In fact, the treatment was extremely specialized. It is speculated that Howard learned of a hospital that was experimenting in changing a person's eye color. Howard was preparing his deception by having his dark eyes altered to blue. Howard holed up in Boston for several months, presumably to recover from the surgery. Around this time, Kay Glenn, the supervisor of his aides, saw him for the last time until 1976 (Magnesen 170). Howard was beginning to isolate himself.

The isolation extended to his family. Howard married movie star Jean Peters in 1957, but as with all things in Howard's life, the marriage was unusual. It is interesting to note that for the nuptials, Howard, Jean, and the presiding judge all used aliases (Magnesen 203–4). Howard was absent from Jean much of the time, and like his business, the marriage was primarily conducted over the telephone. As strange as the relationship seemed, it survived for thirteen years with only infrequent personal contact. Howard brought that to an end while he was away in Boston. Although they did not divorce until 1971, Howard and Jean never saw one another face-to-face after the Boston trip. He was protecting the beginning of his disguise.

By the time Howard moved from Boston to the Desert Inn Hotel in Las Vegas on November 27, 1966, he had been physically absent from the operation of his businesses for a decade. He ran his business over the telephone through his associates, most notably Robert Maheu. In 1966, Howard began to change his method of operation from verbal orders to written orders. From this point on, if Howard had something to say, he dictated it to one of the few aides who still had access to him, and the aide wrote it on a page from a yellow legal pad that was then sent to the person with whom Howard wished to communicate. There was no longer any direct access to Howard. All communications were transmitted through one of five personal aides: Roy Crawford, Howard Eckersley, George Francom, John Holmes, and Levar Mylar (Barlett and Steele 324). The aides were accessible to key people, but Howard was not. This way, Howard could be undisturbed at the Desert Inn. In fact, he could be undisturbed anywhere he chose to be.

Dr. Norman Crane was engaged as his personal physician. He would spend nearly all of his time at the Desert Inn responding to Howard's beck and call. Living in virtual captivity began to take its toll on the doctor, and he began to drink heavily as a result. The smell of liquor on his breath and his shaking hands did not instill confidence in Hughes (Hack 296).

Although Howard was known for spending vast sums of money to make a motion picture or build an aircraft, his willingness to part with his money did not extend to the taxman. Hughes was notorious for thinking up clever ways to retain possession of his money at the expense of the government. He went so far as to live in hotels in different states for brief periods of time to avoid establishing legal residency anywhere and avoid the bite of the state tax dogs. This was one of the more dramatic exhibitions of his obsessive nature. There was no battle too large or too small to fight.

Howard's aversion to giving his money to the government did not apply to politicians. He financially supported numerous candidates whom he felt would be supportive of his business and personal agendas. This backfired prior to the 1960 election when it was revealed that Howard loaned $205,000 to Richard Nixon's brother, Donald (Barlett and Steele 204). To what degree this impacted Nixon's loss to John F. Kennedy is a matter of speculation, but the matter was an embarrassment to the presidential candidate and confirmation for Nixon's detractors that he couldn't be trusted.

The Nixon/Hughes relationship surfaced again during the Watergate scandal in 1972. Richard Nixon feared the Democrats had harmful information about his relationship with Howard. Insiders in the Watergate investigation later speculated the desire to find out exactly how much the Democrats knew was a motivating factor in the Watergate break-in. By this point, Howard's relationship with Nixon was already stressed.

In 1966, Howard's itinerant hotel lifestyle finally ended when he landed in Las Vegas, where he moved his personal and professional headquarters into the ninth floor of the Desert Inn Hotel. After an extended stay, the hotel owners, lacking adequate rooms to house high-roller gamblers, suggested he might try living somewhere else for a while. Unwilling to endure the inconvenience of moving, he purchased the entire hotel with a portion of his TWA windfall profits. There was only one small glitch remaining in his living arrangements. The government was testing nuclear bombs in the Nevada desert, and Howard was deathly afraid he would come in contact with nuclear fallout. A man phobic about germs on a doorknob will most certainly react negatively to vast amounts of atomic radiation scattered randomly outside his home. Howard called in his favors to Nixon with a request to solve this problem by cancelling the tests, but Nixon did nothing.

The acquisition of the Desert Inn Hotel for $13.25 million barely put a dent in Howard's half-a-billion-dollar airline sale (Schumacher 52). Howard had a vision of Las Vegas as a sophisticated entertainment mecca. His timing was, excuse the expression, "right on the money." The Justice Department and the Internal Revenue Service took note of the unsavory influence of the Mafia in Las Vegas and the amount of untaxed money leaving town in paper bags and overstuffed satchels. It was clear the mobsters had lost their license to steal money and needed to get out of town. Howard was more than willing to buy them out. In the space of two years, between 1966 and 1968, he acquired the Castaways for $3.3 million, the Frontier for $14 million, and the Sands for $14.6 million (53). After moving into the Desert Inn, Howard became fixated on the Silver Slipper Hotel across the street, which had a 65-foot high sign with a large, rotating silver slipper on top of it. Howard became obsessed with the idea that there was a photographer in the slipper taking pictures of him. The result was his purchase of the Silver Slipper for $5.4 million, and the slipper was sealed, so no one could enter it (Fischer 215).

Buying casinos from the mob is a bit more complicated than your average real estate transaction. Since the real power and muscle of the casino industry lived in the shadows, a shadowy guy was needed to facilitate the deal. Fortunately, Howard had an old friend, Johnny Roselli, who was perfect for the job. Roselli will be dealt with in more detail later in this book, but for the time being we'll just say that he was a mobster with his fingers in a lot of pies. That, and he was complicit in one of the most heinous murders of American history (Drosnin 120).

Like most things in Howard's life, his connection to Johnny Roselli was strange and filled with bizarre coincidence. The first Hughes–Roselli connection came through Archie MacDonald, who ran the Hughes operations in Los Angeles dating back to the 1920s. MacDonald was a genial, but shrewd, businessman who kept the West Coast Hughes ship on course. He was a prominent figure in Los Angeles society, but the marriage of his son, Bob, sent a branch of the family tree from the upper crust of society into the lower depths of the underworld. Bob's new mother-in-law, Gaynell, was married to an L.A. mobster, Nick Moretta, who worked for L.A. mob boss Jack Dragna. Johnny Roselli worked for Chicago mob boss Sam Giancana and was assigned to cover Los Angeles. In the late 1940s, the happy extended family frequently met at the Moretta residence for Sunday dinner, and a frequent guest was Howard Hughes (John MacDonald interview).

More coincidence. At the time of the casino deals, Robert Maheu was Howard's key employee at a fairly sturdy salary of $10,000 per week. For ten grand a week you expect to get something, and in the case of Maheu, it was connections. Maheu was a former FBI agent and a CIA operative. His CIA dealings included oversight of the failed Bay of Pigs Invasion of Cuba, as well as a plot to assassinate Fidel Castro. Appealing to civic pride— with a likely hint that they might get back the Havana casino business that Castro confiscated—Maheu enlisted the aid of Roselli and the Giancana organization to conduct the hit. The hit never happened, but Maheu kept the mob connection. When Howard needed a go-between for his casino purchases, Roselli was the perfect candidate (Drosnin 73).

Howard's interest in buying out the mob caught the attention of Nevada Governor Paul Laxalt. The corrupt casino ownership was a black eye on the face of Las Vegas, and Laxalt viewed anyone who was willing to clean up the adult playland as an ally. Giving the mob the boot was good for Nevada, which, by extension, would also be good for Laxalt's political future.

The fact the mob was under pressure to divest themselves of these properties was not reflected in the price. It is generally believed that Howard overpaid for these hotels, but he became much more careful with his money after he took possession. He performed only routine maintenance on the properties, made no improvements to them, and built no new hotels.

Howard avoided the public, especially the news media, for years, but he was not yet a complete recluse. He no longer drove flashy cars. Instead he traveled in nondescript, mid-priced automobiles. He kept a fleet of Chevrolet sedans stashed at his Los Angeles headquarters at 7000 Romaine Street in Hollywood, and even left cars parked at airports, sometimes for years, waiting for the unlikely moment when he might appear. At one point, he had a mundane-looking Chrysler sedan equipped with a special air purifying system that filled the trunk of the vehicle (Drosnin 103-4).

He certainly did not dress like the richest man in the United States, either. Quite to the contrary, he dressed like a bum. He would walk through his casinos in an old, wrinkled, seersucker sport coat, open neck shirt, and tennis shoes (Magnesen 24). He looked like a local who wandered in from his trailer in the desert to play the nickel slots. The only clue to his importance was the small cadre of bodyguards who stayed close enough to discourage the overly curious.

These "Howard Sightings" bring up a very large question. Was this shabby man the real Howard Hughes? He was known to use doubles to throw the curious off of his trail, so there is some speculation about whether these sightings were the real Howard or an orchestrated act with a body double to divert attention from his real activities. We will discuss one of these doubles, Brucks Randall, in Chapter Twenty-Two.

Howard was now the largest casino owner in Nevada. However, he still had a lot of money left, so he focused his shopping spree elsewhere. His love of aviation soon moved him to open his checkbook for the North Las Vegas Airport and Alamo Airways (Real 59). The airport purchase allowed him to have his airplane on standby whenever he wished without drawing any attention, and the airport had no control tower to record his comings and goings. Howard's personal pilot, Guido Robert Diero, frequently received instructions from Howard's aide, Howard Eckersley: Have a plane fueled and ready at a certain time, be ready to depart at such a time, there will be one passenger, and don't file any flight plans (Magnesen 233). Howard rarely showed up for the flight.

Since he spent an extraordinary amount of time in his hotel rooms, Howard ensured he would have a ready source of entertainment by purchasing a local television station, KLAS-TV. He also purchased gold and silver mines near Virginia City, Nevada, and thirty-four mines in the Las Vegas area that would soon become the launching site for one of the biggest Howard Hughes controversies.

This mystery started after 9:00 p.m. on Friday, December 29, 1967, when a twenty-three-year-old man, Melvin Dummar, allegedly picked up a man who was lying near Highway 95, north of Las Vegas. Dummar stated the man was about sixty-five years old, tall, about 150 pounds, with a five- to six-day growth of beard, and long, shaggy, gray-brown hair. He wore a long-sleeved, light brown shirt, dress slacks that looked too large for him, and tennis shoes. The man was not in good physical condition and had dried blood on his left ear. Dummar claimed that he drove the man to the back door of the Sands Hotel. As they drove, the man told him that he was Howard Hughes (Magnesen 113–21). This episode would take center stage a decade later when the fight for the Hughes estate began and Dummar was named in the so-called Mormon Will.

That, in a very small nutshell, takes us to Howard's life in the late 1960s. What does it all mean? The picture is not pretty. Howard Hughes was a wealthy, phobic, friendless man, hiding in his hotel room behind a cadre of Mormon aides who managed his numerous interests while deflecting his wife, the IRS, and a steady stream of lawsuits. Howard was looking for just one thing. He needed a back door through which to escape into a new life.

Notes

Barlett, Donald, L., and James B. Steele. *Howard Hughes: His Life and Madness*. New York: W.W. Norton, and Company, 1979.

Brown, Peter Harry, and Pat H. Broeske. *Howard Hughes: The Untold Story*. Cambridge, MA: De Capo Press, 2004.

Drosnin, Michael. *Citizen Hughes*. New York: Broadway Books, 1985.

Fischer, Steve. *When the Mob Ran Vegas: Stories of Money, Mayhem and Murder*. Boys Town, NE: Berkline Press, 2005.

Hack, Richard. *Hughes: The Private Diaries, Memos and Letters*. Beverly Hills, CA: New Millennium Press, 2001.

Higham, Charles. *Howard Hughes: The Secret Life*. New York: St. Martin's Griffin, 2004.

MacDonald, John. Interview with the authors. June 4, 2014.

Magnesen, Gary. *The Investigation*. Fort Lee, NJ: Barricade Books, 2005.

Real, Jack. *The Asylum of Howard Hughes*. Bloomington, IN: Xlibris Corporation, 2003.

Schumacher, Geoff. *Howard Hughes: Power, Paranoia, and Palace Intrigue*. Las Vegas, NV: Stephens Press, LLC, 2008.

THREE

EVA MEETS "NIK"

On the road, 2002

Mark was perplexed. Eva's claim to be the widow of Howard Hughes, and that they had lived a secret life together until only months before, seemed perfectly absurd. It was actually disturbing to him, because it indicated a problem in Eva that was totally counter to everything he had learned and felt about her in their brief relationship. In his long military career, Mark had come to be a pretty good judge of character, and everything told him that Eva was an intelligent, knowledgeable woman in complete charge of her mental faculties. In every way, she seemed to be an especially sharp, lucid woman. In every way, apparently, except that she thought she had been married to Howard Hughes.

Mark now faced the classic "elephant in the room" problem. He couldn't ignore it, and frankly, he didn't want to. If this was a delusion, it was a unique one, so he might as well hear it.

He didn't have to wait long. Eva was ready and she began her strange story.

Panama, 1967–1969

In March 1967, Eva told him, she packed her clothes, a few personal belongings, and a pet parakeet, and set out from Georgia to a new life in the Panama Canal Zone. Her final destination was Howard Air Force Base, which operated from 1942 to 1999 near Balboa, Panama, on the west side of the canal's south end. She found herself in a culture far different from her rural American roots.

In many ways, the Canal Zone was unique. For centuries, sailors and merchants longed for a water route linking the Atlantic and Pacific oceans through Central America. Prior to the canal, all shipping had to be directed around Cape Horn on the southern tip of South America, a journey that added many weeks to a trip. Canals were proposed through Nicaragua and Panama, which was then part of Colombia. The French attempted to build a canal in the current location in the latter half of the nineteenth century, but delays caused by construction difficulties and disease forced the company into bankruptcy. United States President Theodore Roosevelt purchased the assets of the bankrupt French company in 1904 and gave tacit approval to a Panamanian revolution that separated the area from Colombia. The United States received the right to build the canal and control a zone around the canal for ninety-five years until 1999 when it was returned to Panama. The canal went into service in 1914.

Since the United States operated the Panama Canal and the Canal Zone, there was a U.S. administrative and diplomatic staff to manage the U.S. holdings, as well as a strong military presence to guarantee the security of the canal and the administrative personnel. Eva had a strong civil service background that secured her a job with the Department of State as an executive secretary. She was assigned to work for Lt. Colonel Wood and the Air Commandos, a group easily recognized by their distinctive hats with brims curled up on one side. Shortly after she joined this organization, it was separated from the State Department and attached to the Air Force. The Air Commandos then became the Air Force Special Operations Unit. The stated mission of the unit in Panama was to assist with the training of the Panamanian Air Force and to assist with U.S. aircraft movements in and out of Panama. The unstated mission of this special operations unit in Central America is left to the reader's imagination (http://www.pancanal.com/eng/history/history).

The U.S. government provided housing for military and civilian employees of Howard Air Force Base within and near the actual base compound. They were simple, military structures that conformed to the theme of utility over beauty, but they were convenient and had the advantage of creating something of a family atmosphere among the civilian employees. Even though she was far from family and friends, Eva was comfortable in this environment. She had spent her entire adult life on military bases and took comfort in the unique bond that military families share. You are never a stranger on a military base, and Eva quickly fit in.

Eva knew most of her neighbors in the small community, so new arrivals were quickly noted. Consequently, when the tall, handsome, blond-haired man with the deep blue eyes arrived, he drew a fair amount of attention, particularly among the single women. Eva and her friend, Lucille, were no exceptions.

Eva had worked at Howard Air Force Base for two years when she noticed the new arrival. He sparked her curiosity, not simply because of his good looks, but because he was always surrounded by a group of aides. Civilians who live in government housing on military bases are not typically surrounded by assistants with whom they conduct conversations in hushed tones. This was something quite different than what Eva witnessed before. She didn't speak to the man, but she kept an eye on him. So did Lucille.

Two weeks later, in October 1969, Eva had her first conversation with the tall stranger. After working late one night at her civil service job, she returned home to her apartment on the base to find that lights in the stairwell of her building did not work. It was totally black. She went back outside and saw that the lights in Lucille's building were working, so she dashed over and shouted to her friend from the stairs, asking for a flashlight. She got a response, but not from Lucille. The new stranger's head popped out of one of the adjacent apartments, and he asked what the trouble was. Eva told him, and he came out to join her.

"I'd better go up to your apartment with you and make sure everything is all right," he said, as he gently escorted her back toward her building. There was a presence about him that was special. Eva thought that he was the most perfectly mannered, humble human being she had ever met.

The thin man, well over six-feet-tall, entered Eva's apartment, checked to see that all was well, and fixed the connection to the lights. Eva remembered later that he casually adjusted something on a pole outside the apartment before they went in, as though he knew exactly what the problem was. Eva thanked him for his courtesy, and he headed back down the stairs, but neither of them was ready to end the conversation. He stood at the foot of the stairs and spoke to her for over an hour, as she leaned over the second floor railing. She was transfixed and perfectly willing to stand there listening for as long as he might talk. *Even forever*, she thought at the time. Everything he said fascinated her, especially the way he said it. He used expressions specific to ships and aircraft, like aft, fore, deck, and bulkhead. Even though she had lived on the air base for two years, Eva was not used to this, and sometimes she had to stop and think about what he said. The whole experience put Eva on an emotional high, and she knew she wanted to get to know this gentleman better.

Eva would be the first to admit that she suddenly felt like a schoolgirl again, and it had been a long, long time since she felt that way. She had grown up in hard circumstances and had responsibilities to her family. She had married young and had obligations to her children, her husband, and to the United States Army, which dictated much of the circumstances of their lives. For the first time Eva was truly free. She could focus on herself for a change. She could even fall in love.

When the conversation ended, Eva was vaguely aware that the man had spoken long and eloquently while revealing practically nothing about himself. Nik was the only name he went by, and for some strange reason, he spelled it without the letter C. He arrived in Panama about a month earlier in September 1969 and worked on the base as an aircraft maintenance supervisor. This seemed logical enough in the early days of their relationship, although Eva couldn't help but notice that his comings and goings seemed irregular for someone in that position, and he would never take her to the place he worked. Still, the air of mystery made him all the more exciting.

The stairwell conversation was the springboard for a full-fledged courtship. Nik, who by now had revealed his full name, Verner Nicely, (pronounced NICK-e-ly), was clearly different from any man she had ever met. His gentlemanly manners gave her a feeling of safety and security. He called her Miss Renee, using her middle name, like she was a Southern belle. Everything about him indicated that he was a man who had a proper upbringing. In addition to being a gentleman, Nik was also generous. He lavished gifts on her, but it was his humility and gentle ways that won her heart. She had wanted to meet him from the first time she saw him and was thanking her good fortune for the lights failing that night. Later, remembering him fiddling with the pole outside her apartment, she began to wonder how much good fortune had to do with the incident.

One day, Nik confessed, "I had my people following you because I wanted to meet you. I wanted to find out where you lived. You look like Liz Taylor."

It had already occurred to her that Nik may have had a quick solution to the electrical problem in her building because he caused it. It was flattering that he might have gone to such lengths to meet her. Whether it was fate or cunning, they were both happy with the result. The only one who wasn't happy was Lucille. She and Eva were soon ex-friends.

As they spent more time together and their relationship grew, Eva discovered much about this man, Verner, who called himself Nik, which was unusual. She was fascinated by his eyes. Eva always believed that the eyes were the window to a person's soul. If so, Nik's windows were closed. Nik had brilliant, midnight-blue eyes like she had never seen before. "They were the bluest of blue," she remembered. Her image would reflect in his eyes as though they were mirrored glasses, but they were impenetrable to her. At first, she thought he wore special contact lenses, but she later learned that he didn't. Those blue mirrors were his real eyes, and they didn't work very well. When Eva first met him, he could hardly see anything. He needed bifocals with very thick lenses to read any sort of printed matter, and even then, only if he held it very close to his face. As she got to know him better, she noticed he would always turn his head to the left when he read, as though he needed to favor his right eye.

Nik had another ailment that caused him trouble and embarrassment. From the evening she first spoke to him, it was immediately apparent to Eva that he was very hard of hearing. For some reason, he chose not to acknowledge this problem. Instead, if he didn't hear something correctly he had a tendency to get angry. This was especially difficult on the many occasions when he would "mishear" her and think she said something that she didn't. They would then end up arguing over something she hadn't said.

Despite the sensitivity over his hearing problem, the relationship grew for a couple of months, as they got together regularly. Eva was clearly enamored with the tall, handsome gentleman with the mirror-blue eyes. Then, in late November 1969, Verner Nicely, the man known as Nik, disappeared.

Eva at her desk in Panama. Her resemblance to actress
Elizabeth Taylor got Nik's attention.

Just who was Verner Nicely? Like Howard Hughes, the end of his life is shrouded in mystery, but public records and family members provide a broad sketch of its beginning.

Verner Dale Nicely (pronounced NICE-ly) was born in Franklin, Ohio, on July 7, 1921. He was named after his father who gave up an unsuccessful attempt at farming to become a particularly skilled baker at a local bakery. With his wife, Hazel Roush Nicely, they settled into the community and raised four children, one girl and three boys. Verner's childhood was, apparently, typical of other young people of this era. He displayed a youthful energy that earned him the nickname "Speed," because he was always seen dashing and biking around Franklin, running errands and just being a boy. His enthusiasm and energy spilled over at his high school commencement ceremony in 1939, when his brother, Donel, revealed that he was so excited to graduate that he danced across the stage to receive his diploma.

Immediately out of high school, Verner took a job that was well suited for a young man who liked to keep moving. He became a mail carrier. He remained in the job until the outbreak of World War II when, like so many other brave young men, he stood up to defend his country by enlisting in the United States Army Air Corps in 1942. He immediately distinguished himself by displaying exceptional intelligence on the Army evaluation tests. In fact, he came within one point of the highest possible score. The Army also saw that he had an aptitude for mechanics, a very useful characteristic.

Verner arrived at Patterson Field, Ohio, on September 10, 1942, to prepare for assignment as an Airplane and Engine Mechanic, Specialty Code 747. Records from Patterson indicate that he had hazel eyes, blond hair, and was five feet eleven inches tall. Verner adapted well to the military, and the life seemed to suit him.

His training completed, Verner was sent off to war in the Pacific Theater of Operations. As a mechanic, he was not subjected to the dangers of enemy fire, but the Japanese were not the only danger in the South Pacific. Verner contracted several lingering diseases on the airbase including malaria, intestinal infections, hepatitis, and psychogenic musculoskeletal reactions, a condition in which pain is perceived to be more intense due to psychological stresses. To add to the miseries of his many diseases, he was bitten by a dog and contracted rabies. All in all, his tour in the Pacific was not tremendously enjoyable.

Fortunately, in the midst of all these diseases, there was one ray of sunlight. While in the hospital, he met a beautiful Australian nurse, Aileen Anne Powell, and they struck up a relationship that culminated in their marriage on July 27, 1949, in Ontario, Canada. The union was witnessed by Verner's brother, Donel, and Donel's wife, Lois. Verner and his new bride settled into the lifestyle of a military family and soon became the proud parents of two boys: Paul, born in 1950, and Gary, who arrived in 1952. After several reenlistments and a number of physical and emotional problems, Verner decided to leave the military, and on September 30, 1955, in San Antonio, Texas, Verner retired.

Verner Nicely's enlistment documents dated September 10, 1942

PHYSICAL EXAMINATION

1. Eye abnormalities.......... None
2. Ear, nose, throat abnormalities. None
3. Mouth and gum abnormalities. None

	Right	(Examiner's)	Left	
4. Teeth	8 7 6 5 4 3 2 1		1 2 3 4 5 6 7 8	(Strike out those that are missing; circle those that
	16 15 14 13 12 11 10 9		9 10 11 12 13 14 15 **E**	may be restored)

5. Skin .... Normal
6. Varicose veins .... None
7. Hernia .... None

8. Hemorrhoids .... None
9. Genitalia .... Normal
10. Feet .... Normal

11. Musculo-skeletal defects .... None

12. Abdominal viscera .... Normal

13. Cardiovascular system .... Normal
14. Lungs, including X-ray, if made .... No significant pathology, qualified

15. Nervous system: reflexes, pupillary .... Normal   patellar .... Normal

16. Endocrine disturbances .... None

17. Results of laboratory examinations, when made .... Negative Kahn

18. Remarks on defects not sufficiently described above .... —

19. Summary of defects in order of importance, impression of physical fitness .... —

Vision:
Right eye 20/.......... 20
Left eye 20/.......... 20
Hearing:
Right ear .... 20 .... /20
Left ear .... 20 .... /20
Height .... 71 .... in.
Weight .... 143 .... lb.
Girth (at nipples):
Inspiration .... 38 .... in.
Expiration .... 35 .... in.
Girth (at umbilicus) .... 27 .... in.
Posture .... Good
Frame .... Light
Color of hair .... Blond
Color of eyes .... Hazel
Complexion .... Ruddy
Pulse:*
Sitting 79
After exercise 104
2 min. after exercise 80
Blood pressure:*
Systolic 108
Diastolic 60
Urinalysis:
Sp. gr. 1,010
Albumin .... Negative
Sugar .... Negative
Microscopic*.......... —
Other data*.......... —

* When required.

I certify that I have carefully examined the applicant and have correctly recorded the results of the examination; and that, to the best of my judgment and belief, he is mentally and physically qualified for service in the Army of the United States.

Patterson Field
Fairfield, Ohio   Signature ....

Date August 14, 1942   Name typed or stamped: C. K. COOK, Captain   (Grade)   Medical Corps,

ar

FINGERPRINTS—RIGHT HAND

Fingerprint impressions will be made in this space in the case of every man enlisting and reenlisting in the Army of the United States.

1. THUMB	2. INDEX	3. MIDDLE	4. RING	5. LITTLE

Page 2 of Verner's enlistment document identifying physical characteristics.

Verner and Aileen's Marriage Certificate dated July 27, 1949.

Retired may not be the correct term. Verner was clearly not ready for the rocking chair. In 1958, the Nicely family moved to Panama, and Verner was soon given a clean bill of health. At this point, a bit of mystery creeps into Verner's life. His contacts with his family, other than his wife and sons, became sporadic. His brother, Donel, saw him for the last time in 1960 when Verner visited him in San Francisco. Verner told him that he was returning to Panama on a classified operation. Donel felt the trips had something to do with Cuba, which had fallen to the communists under Fidel Castro two years earlier. Future efforts by Donel to contact his brother were fruitless. He tried especially hard in 1966 when their father died, and later in the mid-1970s when their mother passed away. There was never any response. Verner disappeared.

Verner's immediate family was no help either. He and Aileen divorced in 1965, apparently because Verner's medical difficulties placed a stress on the marriage from which it never recovered. The younger son, Gary, last saw his father in the Canal Zone in 1967 prior to Gary's return to the States. In a discussion with Mark, Gary stated in November 2007 at that time his father was working with the CIA in Panama, assigned to counter the drug smuggling traffic from South and Central America. Once in the States, Gary lost contact with his father.

Social Security # 274-12-8132

CHARACTER OF SEPARATION	REPORT OF SEPARATION FROM THE ARMED FORCES OF THE UNITED STATES	DEPARTMENT
HONORABLE		AIR FORCE

1. LAST NAME — FIRST NAME — MIDDLE NAME	2. SERVICE NUMBER	3. GRADE — RATE — RANK, AND DATE	4. COMPONENT AND BRANCH OR CLASS
NICELY VERNER DALE	AF 15 327 117	T/Sgt(P) Nov 48	USAF

SEPARATION DATA

5. QUALIFICATIONS		EFFECTIVE DATE OF SEPARATION	6. TYPE OF SEPARATION
SPECIALTY NUMBER OR SYMBOL	RELATED CIVILIAN OCCUPATION AND D.O.T. NUMBER	DAY MONTH YEAR	Permanent
		30 Sep 1955	Retirement

| 8. REASON AND AUTHORITY FOR SEPARATION | 9. PLACE OF SEPARATION |
| Removed from TDRL, AFM 35-4 & Par 10, SO #172, DAF dtd 2 Sep 55 | San Antonio, Texas |

10. DATE OF BIRTH			11. PLACE OF BIRTH (City and State)	12. DESCRIPTION					
DAY	MONTH	YEAR		SEX	RACE	COLOR HAIR	COLOR EYES	HEIGHT	WEIGHT
7	July	21	Franklin, Ohio	Male	Caucasian	Brown	Grey	72"	160

SELECTIVE SERVICE DATA

| 13. REGISTERED | | | 14. SELECTIVE SERVICE LOCAL BOARD NUMBER (City, County, State) | | 15. INDUCTED | | |
| YES | NO | SELECTIVE SERVICE NUMBER | | | DAY | MONTH | YEAR |

| 16. ENLISTED IN OR TRANSFERRED TO A RESERVE COMPONENT | |
| YES | NO | COMPONENT AND BRANCH OR CLASS | COGNIZANT DISTRICT OR AREA COMMAND |

SERVICE DATA

| 17. MEANS OF ENTRY OTHER THAN BY INDUCTION | | | | 18. GRADE — RATE OR RANK AT TIME OF ENTRY INTO ACTIVE SERVICE |
| ENLISTED | [X] REENLISTED 3 Yrs | COMMISSIONED | CALLED FROM INACTIVE DUTY | |

| 19. DATE AND PLACE OF ENTRY INTO ACTIVE SERVICE | 20. HOME ADDRESS AT TIME OF ENTRY INTO ACTIVE SERVICE (St., R.F.D., City, County and State) |
| DAY | MONTH | YEAR | PLACE (City and State) | 702 East Elm St, Urbane Ill (Champaign) |

STATEMENT OF SERVICE FOR PAY PURPOSES	A. YEARS	B. MONTHS	C. DAYS	25. ENLISTMENT ALLOWANCE PAID ON EXTENSION OF ENLISTMENT, IF ANY
				DAY MONTH YEAR AMOUNT
21. NET ( ) SERVICE COMPLETED FOR PAY PURPOSES EXCLUDING THIS PERIOD				
22. NET SERVICE COMPLETED FOR PAY PURPOSES THIS PERIOD	4	2	0	
23. OTHER SERVICE (Act of 15 June 1942 as amended) COMPLETED FOR PAY PURPOSES	8	10	22	26. FOREIGN AND/OR SEA SERVICE
24. TOTAL NET SERVICE COMPLETED FOR PAY PURPOSES	13	0	22	YEARS MONTHS DAYS

27. DECORATIONS, MEDALS, BADGES, COMMENDATIONS, CITATIONS AND CAMPAIGN RIBBONS AWARDED OR AUTHORIZED

| 28. MOST SIGNIFICANT DUTY ASSIGNMENT | 29. WOUNDS RECEIVED AS A RESULT OF ACTION WITH ENEMY FORCES (Place and date, if known) |
| None | |

30. SERVICE SCHOOLS OR COLLEGES, COLLEGE TRAINING COURSES AND/OR POST-GRAD. COURSES SUCCESSFULLY COMPLETED	DATES (From-To)	MAJOR COURSES	31. SERVICE TRAINING COURSES SUCCESSFULLY COMPLETED

INSURANCE AND PAY DATA

GOVERNMENT INSURANCE INFORMATION: (A) Permanent plan premium must continue to be paid when due, or within 31 days thereafter, or insurance will lapse. (B) Term insurance not under waiver same as (A) above. (C) Term insurance under waiver — premium payment must be resumed within 120 days after separation. Forward premiums on NSLI to Veterans Administration Office having jurisdiction over the area shown in item 47. Forward premiums on USGLI to Veterans Administration, Washington 25, D. C. (See VA Pamphlet 9-3) When paying premiums give full name, address, Service Number, Policy Number(s), Branch of Service, date of separation. Contact nearest VA office for information concerning Government Life Insurance.

32A. KIND & AMT. OF INSURANCE & MTHLY. PREMIUM	32B. ACTIVE SERVICE PRIOR TO 26 APRIL 1951	33. MONTH ALLOTMENT DISCONTINUED	34. MONTH NEXT PREMIUM DUE
	YES NO UNKNOWN		
35. TOTAL PAYMENT UPON SEPARATION	36. TRAVEL OR MILEAGE ALLOWANCE INCLUDED IN TOTAL PAYMENT	37. DISBURSING OFFICER'S NAME AND SYMBOL NUMBER	

AUTHENTICATION

| 38. REMARKS (Continue on reverse) | 39. SIGNATURE OF OFFICER AUTHORIZED TO SIGN |
| No active military service performed since 31 July 1951. Retired (Permanent Disability) effective 30 September 1955. Auth: Par 10, SO #172, DAF dtd 2 Sep 55. 9004 Schizophrenic reaction | NAME, GRADE AND TITLE (Typed) F B HELMS MAJOR USAF ASST AIR ADJUTANT GENERAL |

PERSONAL DATA

40. V. A. BENEFITS PREVIOUSLY APPLIED FOR (Specify type) COMPENSATION, PENSION, INSURANCE BENEFITS, ETC.			CLAIM NUMBER
41. DATES OF LAST CIVILIAN EMPLOYMENT	42. MAIN CIVILIAN OCCUPATION	43. NAME AND ADDRESS OF LAST CIVILIAN EMPLOYER
FROM TO		

| 44. UNITED STATES CITIZEN | 45. MARITAL STATUS | 46. NON-SERVICE EDUCATION (Years successfully completed) | |
| YES NO | MAR | GRAM. HIGH COL. DEGREE(S) SCHOOL LEGE | MAJOR COURSE OR FIELD |

| 47. PERMANENT ADDRESS FOR MAILING PURPOSES AFTER SEPARATION (St., R.F.D., City, County and State) | 48. SIGNATURE OF PERSON BEING SEPARATED |
| c/o Mrs. Aileen A. Nicely 590 Francisco Street, Apt 239, San Francisco, Calif. | |

DD FORM 214 1 JUL 52 EDITION OF 1 JAN 50 IS OBSOLETE

HEADQUARTERS COPY (ARMY & AIR FORCE: ATTACH TO SERVICE RECORD. NAVY: TO BUREAU OF NAVAL PERSONNEL, WASHINGTON, D. C. MARINE CORPS: TO CMC. TR TO INACTIVE DU FWD TO CMC (DGH). COAST GUARD: TO HQ. COAST GUARD, WASH.)

Verner Nicely's discharge document, dated September 30, 1955.

Did Verner abandon his entire family to marry another woman in the Canal Zone, aging fifteen years, changing his eye color, and growing five inches taller in the process? Or did he lose his life in a covert CIA operation that left his identity conveniently available to be assumed by someone who wanted a new life? All we know for certain is that in the late fall of 1969, Eva McLelland was in Panama, fascinated by a mysterious, tall, blue-eyed man who was always shadowed by a cadre of aides. He gave his name as Verner Nicely, but his physical characteristics did not match the physical description of Verner Nicely's United States government documents. This is most curious.

Howard Hughes, 1969

Where is Howard Hughes? That was a very popular question in 1969. In his determined efforts to disappear from the public eye, Howard managed to engage the curiosity of people who would not otherwise be interested. "Where's Howard?" became a question that inquiring minds wanted to know. Even the president of the United States didn't know what to think (Hack 316).

The confusion over Howard's whereabouts was fed by the best efforts of his staff. The last picture of Howard available to the public was snapped in 1954. His aides later admitted that they employed more than one body double, and one in particular, Brucks Randall, was used specifically because he looked not so much like the aging Howard of the period, but like the Howard that people remembered from the pictures and newsreels of the 1940s (Phelan 43). They moved Randall around as a diversion to allow the real Howard to move freely in peace. Eva did not connect the old, but handsome man with whom she was falling in love to the twenty-year-old pictures of Howard in the media.

Rumor and speculation about Howard ran rampant, largely fueled by information leaked about his physical condition. He was said to be a six-foot four-inch stack of bones, topped with a long mop of gray hair, and a beard that trailed down over his colorless skin. A description of him during this period, which appeared in a lawsuit filed by the Hughes estate against several Mormon aides and Hughes's doctors, states he was almost totally lacking in personal hygiene. He was said to never brush his teeth, giving him atrocious breath, and to rarely bathe. He suffered from chronic, severe constipation, often going for long periods of time without a bowel movement, and requiring frequent enemas. When he did go to the bathroom, he often spent as much as twelve hours there. He reportedly took large amounts of drugs and stared blankly ahead when he wasn't sleeping (Real 272). To deal with these numerous medical issues, a Dr. Buckley was hired to attend to him. This was no easy task, since Howard's aides would not allow the doctor to examine him personally (Barlett and Steele 428). All of this is a curious description of Howard, considering what else was going on in his life during this period.

By the end of 1969, Howard Hughes had been living in Nevada for several years and acquired a string of hotels and casinos that included the Desert Inn, Sands, Castaways, Landmark, Silver Slipper, and the Frontier. He also owned Harold's Club in Reno (Schemmer 21–5). His Las Vegas headquarters was high in the Desert Inn Hotel, but he had ceased making personal appearances in his business dealings back in the 1950s, the same period in which he was last photographed. His public business surrogate was ex-FBI agent and CIA operative Robert Maheu, who had control of the hotels and casinos. The relationship was not as warm and cozy as it once was. The Nevada operations were not performing up to Howard's financial expectations. The strain between Howard and Maheu increased proportionately to the decrease in cash flow (Barlett and Steele 435).

The poor financial performance of the casinos was an insult added to the previous financial injury inflicted on him by the mob. Presumably, without his knowledge at the time, the mob scammed him for millions of dollars through inflated real-estate values. The richest man in America had his pocket picked by the mob. Making matters worse, Robert Maheu took a step beyond executing Howard's orders. By this point, he was not only making his own independent decisions, but they were decisions with which Howard did not agree. Howard was not about to abide this insubordination forever and began to try to pull Maheu in line. As Maheu slipped from his position of trust, Howard's Mormon aides stepped in to fill the gap and took on increasing amounts of authority. Howard placed an unusually high degree of trust in Mormons because of their extreme loyalty to him. He had formed the opinion that Mormons could keep secrets, something that rated very high on his personal checklist. They were also not drinkers. Howard was very much against alcohol consumption, perhaps because he'd witnessed the effects of it on his alcoholic aunt, Adelaide Hughes (Higham 26). Generally speaking, he found Mormons to be of superior moral character, and senior aide John Holmes won his position and trust, because he exemplified all that Howard demanded in an employee.

Howard began receiving memos from aides Bill Gay, Nadine Henley, and his attorney, Chester Davis, implying things were not being conducted appropriately on Maheu's watch. They implied, very strongly, he was engaging in financial improprieties. Whatever the cause, the effect was obvious to all; the casinos were losing a great deal of money. The one-time cash machine of the mob lost Howard $3 million in 1968 and nearly three times that in 1969 (Hack 332-33).

Business wasn't the only thing on which Howard and Maheu disagreed. In late 1969, Robert Maheu contacted Howard and indicated he wanted to dismiss John Meier, the man who was in charge of the Hughes mining operations. Howard disagreed. He believed that Meier did good work and did not want to let him go. The direct order from his boss not to fire Meier was not enough to keep Maheu from doing it, and in November 1969, Meier was cut loose (Magnesen 209). This presented still another problem for Howard. It is quite possible Meier was the man who held the notorious Mormon Will that was to later become the centerpiece of years of legal wrangling. Howard had to recover that will, and he did. Gary Magnesen, a former FBI agent and author of *The Investigation*, speculated that John Meier might have been the holder of Howard's will for several years between the time Howard wrote it in 1968 and when it was given to LaVane Forsythe in the late summer of 1973 (224). Exactly how Howard recovered it is open to speculation, but the fact remains that he found a new caretaker for his wishes.

Richard Nixon won the 1968 presidential race and was inaugurated in January 1969. Howard had been a staunch supporter of Nixon for many years and looked forward to the numerous favors he assumed he would be granted by the White House. On September 10, 1969, Maheu called Howard and told him that the Atomic Energy Commission was about to announce a new Nevada nuclear blast, a big one. Howard implored the president to stop this test. Nixon declined. His refusal to suspend atomic testing in Nevada was Howard's first clue that money couldn't necessarily buy everyone. At least, not all of the time (Hack 357).

Howard had another problem with his neighborhood, as he lived high atop the Desert Inn. The social change and activism that boiled through the mid-1960s surfaced in Las Vegas, but not in a positive way. As African Americans stood up for their rights all over the country, some chose peaceful demonstrations, and some were not so peaceful. Racial violence broke out in Las Vegas, and Howard didn't like that one bit. He didn't want civil conflict on his doorstep, so in September 1969, Howard began looking for an alternative place to live (176-79).

During the holiday season of 1969, Howard had two pieces of business that were significant enough to require his personal attention. The first was the acquisition of Air West Airlines. There were few things in Howard's life that rivaled the passion he held for aircraft and airlines. An airline purchase would be a significant enough event to require his active participation. The second piece of business was the planned acquisition of the Dunes Hotel and Country Club. This drew his personal attention because another hotel purchase in Las Vegas would increase the possibility of an antitrust investigation. If Howard wanted this hotel, he was going to have to work for it and call in a favor. Nixon would get a second chance (Higham 236-39).

Clearly, Howard Hughes was a private man, so private that his supervisor of aides, Kay Glenn, said he didn't actually see him face-to-face between 1966 and 1976. However, Howard did have one friend who remained loyal to him, and vice versa, for many years. Jack Real, a longtime executive with the Lockheed Aircraft Corporation, never saw Howard for the entire time he lived at the Desert Inn, but they spoke on the telephone weekly, sometimes, daily. In September 1969, Howard told Real that he intended to leave Las Vegas and go to the Bahamas for a very long stay (Real 78).

Real was one of the few people to remain in telephone contact with

Howard. Up to this point, Howard directed his activities over the telephone to the appropriate subordinate employees. Even more strangely, this impersonal approach to his employees extended to his wife, Jean Peters, who had not seen him for three years. She was not allowed to visit him. He told her that he was searching for the perfect house for them. Understandably upset, Peters started to speak of divorce. At that point, all communication from her went unanswered. On January 15, 1970, Peters got word to Robert Maheu she was through with this charade of a marriage. She intended to bring this bizarre, thirteen-year relationship to a close. She did, and in typical Howard Hughes fashion, he had her followed after the divorce, just as he had all through their marriage (Hack 331-32).

As if things weren't entertaining enough for Howard during this period, it was at this point that the CIA entered the picture, hoping for a little favor from him. They approached him through their former colleague Maheu. They had a challenge that was right up Howard's alley. A Soviet submarine had sunk in the Pacific Ocean, and the CIA was anxious to raise the vessel surreptitiously to evaluate the state of its nautical and weapons technology, and find a few interesting documents, such as code books.

An obvious vessel recovery operation was out of the question. It would most certainly trigger an international incident. Something innocent, something that looked like a deep sea mining vessel, but was really designed for submarine recovery could accomplish the job without pushing the Cold War to hot. Howard loved a good engineering problem. He also stated many times he was a fan of the CIA. Under the code name Project Jennifer, Howard agreed to build the vessel that was to become known as the *Glomar Explorer*. If he helped the CIA, perhaps they might help him sometime, maybe sometime soon. Possibly, he could even make it part of the deal.

During the holiday season of 1969, the reclusive Howard Hughes bought a hotel and an airline, battled with the man to whom he delegated the oversight of his empire, sought favors from the president of the United States, spoke to his close friend over the telephone regularly, and built a spy ship for the CIA. Not bad for a long-haired, smelly, emaciated, drugged up, incoherent, somnolent shell of a man with six-inch fingernails.

Unless . . . maybe that shell of a man wasn't Howard Hughes.

Notes

Barlett, Donald, L., and James B. Steele. *Howard Hughes: His Life and Madness.* New York: W.W. Norton, and Company, 1979.

Hack, Richard. *Hughes: The Private Diaries, Memos and Letters.* Beverly Hills, CA: New Millennium Press, 2001.

Higham, Charles. *Howard Hughes: The Secret Life.* New York: St. Martin's Griffin, 2004.

Magnesen, Gary. *The Investigation.* Fort Lee, NJ: Barricade Books, 2005.

Phelan, James. *Hughes: The Hidden Years.* New York: Random House, 1976.

Real, Jack. *The Asylum of Howard Hughes.* Bloomington, IN: Xlibris Corporation, 2003.

Schemmer, Benjamin F. "What Happened to Howard Hughes?" *Look.* 1 June 1971: 21–25.

FOUR

NIK RETURNS

Florida, 2002

It was about 2:30 p.m., as they approached Interstate 10 from Florida Highway 87, but Mark barely noticed the miles or the scenery. This had become a much more interesting drive than he anticipated. Mark was prepared for some pleasant conversations with a woman that he had grown to like very much. He was not prepared to have his understanding of one of the most significant historical figures of the twentieth century completely altered. This was a story that was hard to believe, but Eva told it with great conviction, and it was beginning to sound plausible. He was hooked.

"How long was he gone, Eva?" Mark asked. "Did he give you a reason for leaving so suddenly?"

"He left in November 1969 and didn't return until late January 1970," she responded. "I asked him, 'What's up with this disappearing act?' He told me that he needed to handle some entertaining in the States over the holidays."

"Hmm."

"Right, that didn't really sit well with me. I'd only known Nik for a few months by then and everything had to be so mysterious. When I told him that I had a feeling I was being followed all the time he was gone, he said to me, 'You were.'"

Mark could feel Eva watching him from her side of the car.

"Then later, I learned that he not only had people following me, but he had them investigating my background and my family."

"Wow, Eva. That's intense."

She nodded and went on with her story, telling her intriguing tale of Nik's peculiarities and how, despite them, she found herself falling in love with the mystery man. Among his many quirks was a fascination with the name Howard, which was her birth name. After they were married, he spent several years trying to get her a Florida birth certificate in that name. Why he wanted it she never knew, but compared to his other idiosyncrasies that one was pretty harmless.

"Do you think you were being followed by the mysterious aides?"

"Probably."

The person Eva described certainly did not sound like the average aircraft maintenance supervisor. Mark had to admit to himself that it sounded a lot more like the Howard Hughes he read about.

"And he stayed in Panama after that?"

"Not exactly." She smiled and continued her story.

Panama, 1970

Nik was private, secretive, and sometimes even rude, Eva told Mark, but for all of his annoying characteristics, he had one overwhelmingly positive characteristic. He was charming! He was unique in this sense, someone entirely different from any man she had ever met. His intellect and broad range of knowledge was engaging, but when he turned on the charm, he could melt hearts. His special smile and his gentle touch revealed a man who understood how a woman desired to be treated. Whether this tender side was natural or contrived remains a question. What is certain is that it was effective.

Nik had a distinctive wardrobe for special occasions that Eva referred to as his "courting clothes." She thought they were glamorous. He wore either navy blue or black suits with high top shoes that laced up the front. When he was all dressed up, Eva thought he was the most handsome man she ever saw. When he was not dressed to the hilt, Nik's favorite clothes were khaki-colored shirts and slacks. He asked Eva to alter his shirts, remove the tails, and leave them straight at the bottom, so he could wear them loose and not tucked into his pants. Everything about him exuded class and quality. Later in their life together, Eva would think back on that handsome sophisticate and wonder how he turned into the naked man running through the woods of Alabama, erecting voodoo icons on stakes by the trees that they planted on their property, but that comes later.

Nik had few predictable characteristics. One was his charm when he was courting Eva. The other was his reaction to news stories. If the story was not true, or something was said that didn't meet his approval, Nik would yell, "Damn liar," and start ranting and raving. On the other hand, if it was true, he would just smile from ear to ear. As the years went on, Eva found this to be a very accurate barometer of the truth.

Everything else with Nik was a surprise. One day, early in 1970, Nik asked Eva a question. "Which will hold the most liquid, a cube or a sphere?" Eva was getting used to unusual questions, so she gave it a moment's thought.

"A cube," she replied. Nik smiled broadly, grabbed her, and "hugged her to pieces." Years later, on a television documentary, Eva learned that Howard Hughes asked Robert Maheu the same question during Maheu's job interview.

Shortly after he returned, an apartment became free in the housing area of the Howard Air Base that was directly across the hall from Eva's. The convenience was too much for Nik to pass up, so he rented the unit. This was good, but also perplexing. Eva frequently heard deep male voices coming from the apartment, discussing some business or other, but she never managed to see anyone enter or leave. Although she couldn't hear clearly enough to understand what they were discussing, Nik's voice stood out to her from the rest. She was familiar with his normal tenor voice and the way he would deepen it when he wanted to make sure the listener did not miss his point. She didn't have to hear the words to know when he was talking about something of importance.

After some time passed with these muffled meetings taking place across the hall, Eva's curiosity got the better of her. She was dying to know what was going on. Finally, she asked Nik if she could meet his friends, but his answer was as mysterious as his guests.

"That is not a good idea, and it is best for you to stay out of the picture. It would be too dangerous for you to know what we are doing." He made similar comments many times during their stay in Panama until Eva left in 1972. The context was always the same. Eva could not meet the aides because it would be dangerous for her personally, and potentially damaging to his work.

What business could they be conducting that was too dangerous for her to know about, she wondered, and how could this aircraft maintenance supervisor afford to have all of these aides?

To further confuse matters, Eva saw a letter addressed to Colonel Nicely. Nik never said that he was a colonel, and he never indicated that he held any military position, active or reserve. It was quite unusual for a person employed as an air maintenance supervisor in the civil service to be hobnobbing with colonels, although he did indicate that his business was done with high-ranking colonels and generals, actually mentioning them by name. Since the real Verner Nicely spent his entire career as a noncommissioned officer, the odds of him suddenly becoming a colonel are zero. Howard, on the other hand, was never in the military, so the odds of him suddenly becoming a colonel are also zero. Nik never seemed to have an office or real job, so the chances of any of this being true are again zero. It's likely that all of this was something concocted by Nik and the aides to further obscure his identity in the eyes of Eva.

When he wasn't having mystery guests, mystery conversations, mystery mail, or just being mysterious in general, Nik was a delightful companion, and he and Eva had wonderful times together. Throughout the early months of 1970, Nik continuously offered to assist Eva in her apartment with anything that needed to be fixed or adjusted. They talked as they spent this time together and got to know one another better. Several times, Nik asked Eva to go with him to see interesting sights in the Canal Zone he wanted to show her. She would drive her Volkswagen bug on these trips. Nik had a Jeep but never drove it; in fact, he really preferred to walk if it was feasible.

Eva lounging in Nik's Jeep in Panama.

The Volkswagen Eva drove in Panama.

Nik was the most unusual man Eva had ever met. As if his mysterious lifestyle wasn't enough, he came up with the strangest questions and tests for her. One time he asked her to perform the "dime test." He concocted this unique ritual as a test to see if a woman had, in his opinion, perfect legs. The objective of the exercise was to be able to hold a dime in a fixed position just below the knees while standing. Apparently, he felt that the diameter of the female knee should not be too much greater that the diameter of the leg. It didn't make any sense to Eva, but throughout their many years together he continued to challenge her with strange tests and she continued to put up with them. In the dime test challenge, Eva succeeded in keeping a grip on the dime and passed the test. This made Nik beam. He took almost childish pleasure in her success. Another time, he asked her what she would do if she had a lot of money. She told him that she would buy a good home, invest the remainder of the money, and live off the interest. Once again, this was the right answer, and he grinned with glee.

Even though he never actually showed Eva where he worked and his hours were irregular at best, Nik appeared to be a federal civil service employee, and he was able to attend union meetings with Eva. At one meeting, an individual indicated he knew Nik when he was a colonel. Eva did not understand this at all. She mentioned it to him, as she had done with the letter.

"The military always tends to foul things up," he replied, not really providing an answer.

Nik was always a generous man, but in the late winter and early spring of 1970, he became particularly insistent about taking Eva shopping. Finally, one Saturday in March, he asked her to accompany him into town. They ended up at the classiest jewelry store in Panama, Mercurio S.A., at 120 Via España. Nik was exceptionally fond of Italians for some reason; he called them "eye-ties," so ending up in an Italian store was no surprise. It was the fact that it was a jewelry store that caught her off guard.

"Why are we going to a jewelry store?" she asked. His only reply was a smile.

Nik firmly told the jeweler what he wanted to see, and the accommodating man wasted no time bringing out a tray of the most brilliant diamonds Eva had ever seen. Nik told her to pick one, whereupon she selected the smallest one on the tray. Nik scoffed and picked up a beautiful stone over two carats in weight. "That's the one," he said, "and make sure you mount the highest quality diamond of that carat size you can get in a solitary mounting of platinum, hardened with iridium, and don't try to fool me about the quality, for I know something about these rocks."

"But, Nik, honey," Eva pleaded in shock, "we can't afford that much, can we? This smaller one is very nice." Nik and the jeweler exchanged glances. Suddenly, Nik broke down and cried. That was too much for Eva. She began to cry, too. Before the day was over, Nik had purchased a beautiful two carat diamond ring for just under $5,000. That was a substantial sum in 1970, especially for an aircraft maintenance supervisor who would have made roughly $9,000 per year.

A portion of envelope from the jewelry store Nik favored in Panama.

This whole experience was all the more stunning because Nik consistently and insistently stated that he didn't want to get married. Eva was in perfect agreement with that, so this surprise shopping trip really caught her off guard. That night, Nik's attitude toward marriage took a dramatic reversal.

"Do you want me to get down on my knees and beg you?" he asked.

"No, you don't need to do that," replied the elated Eva, "I will marry you." The surprise and emotion got the better of her, and the tears flowed again.

"Oh, my darling, I never realized you cared this much!" She continued to gush words of love until a little voice inside told her she was getting carried away.

A few days after Eva received the ring, she proudly wore it to the office to show it off. A diamond of that size would garner attention anywhere, but it was a real showstopper in a civil service office in Panama. Employees with that kind of money in their pocket could buy a very nice car. Actress Elizabeth Taylor recently had been gifted with an enormous diamond by her husband, Richard Burton, so the comparison to the actress was drawn once again. Her friends started calling her Liz Taylor. Eva received enormous pleasure from this affectionate teasing by her friends, because Nik said that she actually looked like Liz Taylor when the actress was sixteen years old. Nik clearly had an eye for beautiful women and specifically for Miss Taylor. Besides, what woman wouldn't want to be compared to a beautiful movie star?

In the spring of 1970, Nik retired from the aircraft maintenance supervisor job at Howard Air Force Base that had the strangely flexible hours. He used his new free time to have meetings with his shadowy staff and dote on Eva. He made a 180-degree turn from the man who insisted he wanted nothing to do with marriage. As the days flew by and their bond became stronger, Nik spoke of "showing Eva off" at a big church wedding. Strangely, for as happy and excited as she was about becoming the wife of this unique man, she was plagued by doubts. Was he putting her on about a big wedding, or was this another test? At one level, it really didn't matter. Eva didn't want publicity or a big wedding. She told this to Nik, and he started concocting something different. He came up with something that was perfect, but it was secret.

May 13, 1970, was the big day. That morning when they headed to the judge to perform the marriage, Eva noted Nik had an extremely worried look on his face. "Nik, we do not have to get married today, if you are so worried. We can get married at a later date," she told him. Nik took a few seconds to think about his response and replied, "Oh, no! We will get married today."

In Panama City, Panama, a Spanish-speaking judge performed a small ceremony that united the couple as man and wife. By now, Eva had lived in Panama long enough to acquire just enough Spanish to appreciate the beauty of the service. This resulted in another embarrassing flood of tears. Nik was not embarrassed or ashamed of his new bride in any way. In fact, he was very touched by this display of emotion.

"Now I know I've married an angel," he told her affectionately after the nuptials.

"And I, too, have married an angel," she replied. "Yesterday, I called my mother to inform her that I found the perfect man, godly and saintly!"

For all the tenderness and beauty of the small ceremony, it was not without the imprint of mystery that surrounded all things Nik. There were no wedding pictures. Nik refused to be photographed, if it was within his means to prevent it. Even the wedding certificate, written in Spanish, mysteriously disappeared for many years.

Nik and Eva's Marriage Certificate in which Verner's name is spelled wrong, his parents are not listed, and Eva has her age incorrectly written as thirty-five.

Their ship of matrimonial bliss hit its first storm shortly after the ceremony. Eva always kept herself looking young and fit and, as some women did in those days, she kept her actual age to herself. Consequently, it came as a great surprise to Nik when she finally told him she was actually fifty-four years old. This did not go over well at all. Nik assumed that she was in her thirties and was angered to learn he didn't have the young bride that he thought he had. He accused her of misrepresenting herself. To make matters worse, he didn't let it go. He brought it up several times during the first years of their marriage to the point that Eva suggested he file for divorce if he was that unhappy. Apparently, his unhappiness did not run that deep, and the matter was dropped.

The newlyweds decided to continue to make the American housing area in the Canal Zone their home, and Nik moved into Eva's apartment. This was very convenient for him, since it was directly across the hall from the apartment he was still renting for his office, but Nik didn't immediately give up the apartment that was his residence. He continued to rent it for the remainder of 1970 to conduct his private business. The exact nature of that business remained a mystery to Eva. It was understood that this area was out of bounds to her, and the muffled male voices that penetrated to the hallway were indecipherable. Eva violated the no trespassing rule one day when she was in need of an envelope and went into Nik's apartment to find one. Nik was livid and yelled at her to never do it again.

"Don't you trust me?" she demanded, upset.

"It's not that I don't trust you; if you knew the whole story, you might get interrogated," he explained with some indignation. The answer was not only unsatisfying, but unnerving. Living with this man was not going to be dull.

Now freed by retirement from whatever responsibilities he presumably had in his civil service job, Nik expanded the locations for his business meetings to include boats and yachts. Although Eva was still working, she was aware of his ever-increasing shadowy activities. Again, she asked to be allowed to meet his associates. Again, she was firmly told, "No."

Still struggling to adjust to her mystery man spouse, Eva was confronted by a new problem. The generous, refined, gentleman who courted her seemed to have an evil twin. The "saint" Eva married had a dual personality like

Jekyll and Hyde. Occasionally, returning home from her job, she found herself confronted without provocation by a husband primed for attack. He unleashed a torrent of invective, cutting her to ribbons with the cruelest form of verbal abuse imaginable. The attacks were infrequent, but totally uncalled for and inexcusable. To be sure, Eva knew she was marrying a man with a variety of secrets and quirks. She was prepared to accept that, since the kind nature he had previously displayed in her presence put him as close to a real life "perfect man" as she thought was possible. He had always retained his self-control in her presence, so these verbal assaults were unexpected. This was not at all what Eva signed up for, and the experiences left her hurt, angry, and perplexed.

Eva had not been living some delusion before the wedding. Nik was unquestionably a strong personality, a dominant figure who intended to dominate her. That was acceptable to her and, to a degree, even desirable. She had long craved a strong man who would take care of her, and Nik clearly fit the bill. For the most part, her vision of him was correct. He was basically gentle and kind, but when he became cruel, he was heartbreaking.

Strangely, this evil side did not evolve slowly. The first temper tantrum occurred on the second night of their marriage. For some reason, known only to him, he flew into a rage yelling that she didn't love him. He tried to jerk the wedding band off her finger, but she snatched her hand away from him.

"Don't tear my finger off! I'll give the ring to you," she yelled back, as she pulled the wedding band from her finger and flung it across the room. He leaped out of bed after it and found it on the floor. Frightened and afraid, she ordered him out of the room, and he complied.

It didn't take long for his other personality to regain control. He stood outside the bedroom all night tapping on the door and pleading to be allowed back in. When she opened the door in the morning, she found the child-like nature back, this time penitent and humble. He was either an Academy Award class actor or two personalities struggling for control of one body.

Nik's emotional seesawing played a role in Eva's decision to keep her own last name. She had to consider the possibility that this marriage, as wonderful as it was sometimes, might end in divorce. When he went into a rage, he frequently threatened to leave. Maybe they were idle threats, maybe not. Eva also considered her retirement was coming soon, and all of her records were in the name of her first marriage. Attempting to change all that paperwork now might very well result in a delay of her benefits.

Between rages, Nik acted very much like the man with whom she had fallen in love. For the first year they were married, he gave her an anniversary gift each month. Unlike some of his more ostentatious gifts, these items were strictly of a practical nature. They were usually something useful for the kitchen, like a mixer, spoons, or utensils of some sort, not terribly romantic perhaps, but thoughtful, nevertheless. They had always kept their finances separate, and Nik contributed to their living expenses sporadically. This was possibly another of his strange and frequent tests of Eva's loyalty. He may have wanted to see if Eva would complain about not receiving any money. Whatever may have been on his mind, Eva said nothing and life went on.

For her part, Eva took on the responsibilities of a nurturing, caring wife. She noticed and was appalled by his poor diet long before they were married. She resolved to fix him nutritious meals and start him on a program of vitamins. She learned that, for some unknown reason, he constantly took dosages of over-the-counter cold medications, primarily Coricidin. Whether it was physical or psychological, the Coricidin habit was tough for Nik to kick. It took Eva two years to break him of this odd addiction. At first, she assumed that he took the medication under the direction of a doctor. Her assumption was woefully incorrect. For over a year following their union, he would frequently lapse into attacks of severe trembling, nervousness, sweating, and chills. He was clammy to her touch. It wasn't until years later that Eva realized that these were symptoms of drug addiction, and the cold medication was not the real problem. Eventually, the symptoms went away, something Eva attributed to good food, vitamins, and her gentle patience. An added bonus was that his temper tantrums became less severe.

Theirs was far from a storybook marriage in paradise. Still, when he was good, he was very good. The rest of the time was the problem.

Howard Hughes, 1970

Back in the Nevada desert, the mystery and speculation surrounding the health of Howard Hughes continued to whirl like a desert sandstorm. Stories abounded that Howard was gravely ill, lying in a trance-like state in his self-imposed exile, high above Las Vegas in the Desert Inn (Barlett and Steele 434). The implication was his mental health and physical condition continued to degenerate in the late 1960s, when he was first reported to be a long-haired, long finger-nailed, shell of a man (Hack 297, 306).

Whatever questions there may have been about the state of Howard's personal condition, there was one thing certain about his business affairs; a definite and permanent frost had fallen upon the once warm relationship between Howard and Robert Maheu. By 1970, the Mormon aides were wielding more power in the Hughes Empire than the man who was supposed to be in charge. This was due largely to the efforts of the aides themselves, particularly Bill Gay, who constantly undermined Maheu behind his back, telling Howard that Maheu couldn't be trusted and was dishonest.

The fact that Howard's assets in Nevada were in a serious downturn no doubt added support to the argument that Maheu was not a competent executive. In fact, the operations under Maheu's aegis had not only been profitless, but they actually showed steady and alarming losses. From 1967 to mid-1970, the Maheu operation was $18,570,000 in the hole, with another $7,000,000 in losses projected by the close of the year (Drosnin 393–94). This was partially caused by Maheu's well-known tendency to be very free with the way he spent Howard's money. A very good argument could be made that Maheu was not earning his $10,000 per week base salary (393). Changes had to be made, and Howard decided to begin by changing the way he communicated with his chief operating officer.

"Bob," wrote the billionaire, "I've decided not to ask you to write me any more messages in long hand and sealed envelopes. I know this is time consuming for you, and my men think I don't trust them. So, in the future, except in rare instances, I prefer you to dictate your reply to my messages via telephone to whichever of my men happens to be on duty. I shall continue to send you most of my messages in writing, simply because it is much quicker and more accurate" (394).

The chasm between Howard and Maheu continued to widen. Maheu soon found himself confronted by the Mormon aides who came to retrieve all written correspondence previously issued to him by Howard (394). This obvious loss of trust in him sent Maheu into a rage. With his direct line of communication to Howard severed, Maheu was slowly being marginalized as a force in the Hughes organization. Howard could call Maheu on the telephone, but Maheu could only call the Mormons, who more and more frequently told him that Howard was busy and refused his calls. Communication from the other side also dwindled. Howard's frequent phone calls slowly diminished and then stopped altogether (396–97).

In October 1970, Howard suffered a health crisis that became widely known, eventually even making the pages of the popular *Look Magazine*. According to Dr. Norman Crane, Howard suffered a case of viral pneumonia that nearly killed him (Real 275). Things got worse. On November 5, 1970, Dr. Harold L. Feikes administered several transfusions using blood from Mormons. He reported Howard had a heart condition, pneumonia, and anemia. He listed his weight as ninety-seven pounds (Schemmer 21–5). His use of Codeine and Valium was prodigious, as later documented in a 1978 memo by the Food and Drug Administration.

On November 25, 1970, a one-hundred-pound, six foot four inch tall skeleton of a man was lifted on a gurney into a Lockheed JetStar Aircraft to be flown to the Bahamas. Howard was said to be suffering from shrinking, deteriorating kidneys, and a tumor was forming on his head. Totally disheveled, his hair had not been cut for four years and was nearly two feet long. It, along with a scraggly beard, tumbled down over blue pajamas. A snap brim fedora, typical of the one he wore in his youth, was propped on his head (Drosnin 401–2). In characteristic fashion, the move was pulled off in secrecy and under cover of night. A man named LaVane Forsythe (a name that will also arise later) was paid $500 to stand guard in the Desert Inn parking lot after midnight while a man dressed in a "topcoat or a rain coat or a bathrobe" was helped by two men down nine floors of the Desert Inn fire escape. They placed him in a car and disappeared (Hack 346). The destination was the Britannia Beach Hotel on Paradise Island in Nassau. The entire operation was accomplished without the knowledge of Bob Maheu.

The next day, a coherent, forceful Howard called friend Jack Real and thanked him profusely for arranging the use of the aircraft. He would later attempt to buy the plane, eventually settling for another that was fitted with a custom interior (Real 80).

On December 3, 1970, Robert Maheu was terminated from his position at Hughes Tool. Howard called the governor of Nevada, Paul Laxalt, at one o'clock in the morning on that day to inform him personally of the dismissal. He spoke with the governor for an hour, assuring him that, among other things, he intended to return to Nevada (Maheu 238). He stated, "I directed everything that has taken place. I gave the proper instructions to the proper persons to terminate them." Hughes, who initiated the call, denied that he had left Las Vegas for good. "I'll be home shortly. I intended to go on a vacation fourteen months ago [October, 1969] and will return to Las Vegas and spend the rest of my life there." Howard was reported to have said that he was "in good spirits and in good condition" (Laytner 78).

"He was very concerned," Governor Laxalt said, "about speculation that he had been kidnapped and that he was not going to return here." The governor added that Hughes sounded in good humor and confirmed that he was staying at the Britannia Beach Hotel on Paradise Island. The question arose as to where the call originated. It was arranged by Mr. Gay, and there was no way of checking where it originated or how Howard was connected (78).

The media reporters did their best to chronicle every moment of Howard's life, and they were now anxious to chronicle every moment toward his death. Piecing together the information the reporters received, they typically reported his condition as that of an emaciated man confined to a hotel room bed and occasionally relocated to a chair. Reports stated that his bedsores got so bad that surgery was needed to repair them (Drosnin 413). In fact, the bone of his right shoulder blade was exposed through the festering sores. His kidneys continued to malfunction due to his limited intake of fluids, and his rotting teeth were abscessing, causing his upper jaw to swell and drain. Despite his obvious pain, Howard refused medical treatment. Instead, he relied on massive doses of Codeine that affected his mind as well as his body (Hack 346–47).

Business continued in 1970, particularly in the area of technology and Howard's cozy relationship with the CIA. As Hughes's satellites circled the globe, they provided the platform for high-resolution cameras that snapped countless images of the Soviet Union, China, Vietnam, and any other country that piqued the intelligence agency's interest (Higham 250). In addition to being at the helm of his vast business operations, Howard continued to keep up friendly relationships in the world of politics. Howard had a tendency to equate friendship, and pretty much everything else, with money. In this spirit, in July 1970, Richard Danner delivered $50,000 to Nixon associate, Bebe Rebozo, in San Clemente, California. A further wave of friendship engulfed Howard in August of that year, when he had Danner deliver an additional $50,000 to Rebozo (Higham 243).

Throughout all of this, Howard's constant nemesis, the Internal Revenue Service, was still hot on his trail. For Howard, the IRS was harder to get rid of than a tattoo. They just wouldn't go away, but they, too, sensed something was up. One agent reported to headquarters, "It is my belief that Howard Hughes died in Las Vegas in 1970, and the key officials running the empire concealed the fact in order to prevent catastrophic dissolution of his holdings." The speculation of Hughes's death reached IRS Commissioner John Walters, who then launched an investigation, but it turned up nothing (Drosnin 454).

In the constant churning of the Hughes machine, one event stands out as unique in the fall of 1970. One of Howard's favorite customers, the CIA, had an idea to launch an intelligence coup right under the nose of their opposition. Howard was asked to pull off an enormous espionage feat, code named Project Jennifer, which could only be plausibly concealed by someone with his reputation and assets. On April 11, 1968, a Soviet Golf-II class ballistic missile submarine had sunk 17,000 feet to the floor of the Pacific Ocean. The submarine could be an intelligence gold mine, if it could be raised without incurring the wrath of the Soviets. Howard's mission was to raise the sub while pretending to be engaged in a commercial venture.

Hughes agreed to build a ship, the *Glomar Explorer*, to operate under the program name, Deep Ocean Mining Project (DOMP). Naturally, the ship would focus its mining operations directly over the hull of the sunken Soviet sub. By agreeing to the CIA proposal, Howard was committing himself to a $200 million or more project.

In 1970, the perception of Howard Hughes varied based on who a person talked to. He was unable to care for his most basic personal needs, yet he was capable of fighting the federal government with one hand, while partnering with it on the other. He was seen as a critically ill, emaciated, drug-addled shadow of a man, but he was heard, to those who spoke to him on the telephone, as the same dynamic and charismatic man they'd always known. Curious. There appeared to be two different personalities.

Or maybe . . . there were two completely different people.

Notes

Barlett, Donald, L., and James B. Steele. *Howard Hughes: His Life and Madness*. New York: W.W. Norton, and Company, 1979.

Drosnin, Michael. *Citizen Hughes*. New York: Broadway Books, 1985.

Hack, Richard. *Hughes: The Private Diaries, Memos and Letters*. Beverly Hills, CA: New Millennium Press, 2001.

Higham, Charles. *Howard Hughes: The Secret Life*. New York: St. Martin's Griffin, 2004.

Laytner, Ron. *The True Story of Howard Hughes in Las Vegas*. BookSurge. 2nd Printing, 2009.

Maheu, Robert, and Richard Hack. *Next to Hughes*. NY: HarperCollins Publisher, 1992.

Real, Jack. *The Asylum of Howard Hughes*. Bloomington, IN: Xlibris Corporation, 2003.

Schemmer, Benjamin F. "What Happened to Howard Hughes?" *Look*. 1 June 1971: 21–25.

FIVE

EVA, BEFORE NIK

Mark assumed that Eva had always lived in the South, so the fact that her story started in Panama took him completely by surprise and added another layer to an already thoroughly surprising story. He wasn't ready to believe that Eva had been married to Howard Hughes, but he was willing to listen.

It was apparent that it was going to take Eva longer than the drive back to Alabama to tell this story, so he made a mental note to find out more about her at a future date. When he did, he discovered her life before Nik was also fascinating.

Eva was a true daughter of the rural South. She entered the world on May 4, 1916, in Laurel Hill, Florida, the seventh of eight children born to William and Dora Howard. Like many poor children in those days, Eva's arrival lacked the formal documentation of a birth certificate. This is significant only because Howard was not the name her father used after moving to Alabama. It was Campbell. Among William Howard's many skills was a knack for making moonshine. At this time in Florida, the local authorities spread the word that anyone caught making moonshine would be sent directly to prison. William had a family to take care of, so his entrepreneurial venture ended abruptly, and the family was compelled to make a hasty move from Florida to Alabama. The surname change from Howard to Campbell provided an additional layer of protection from anyone in law enforcement who might consider following them.

The economically disadvantaged did not own automobiles in 1919. Three-year-old Eva, her parents, and seven siblings endured the trip to Goshen, Alabama, in a wooden wagon pulled through the dust and mud by a mule. The uncomfortable trip finally ended at the small cabin of Nan Graves, William's cousin. The family soon found a local place of their own, but they didn't sit still long. In 1923, the family moved to new quarters in Pike County, Alabama, just northwest of Troy. They had barely settled in when they moved again around Christmas of that year to an unpaved road between Troy and Elba in Coffee County, Alabama. The area was secluded and offered few opportunities to mingle with strangers, but their sunbaked property was only a short, dusty walk from the small country school where Eva would enjoy her first taste of education. She loved to study, dance, and participate in the youth programs at the local church where she also developed an interest in public speaking.

Eva's beloved mother, Dora, later in life.

The early 1920s was a pleasant time for the Howard family, and Eva enjoyed a childhood that was typical for that place and time. Although she was not particularly close to her father, who was a stern man, she did have respect for him and his talents. He was quite accomplished on the violin and earned the nickname "Fiddling Bud" from the locals. Eva inherited this talent and, with her father's coaching, became quite an accomplished violinist. Later in life, when she and her first husband were stationed at Fort Benning, Georgia, she earned a chair with the Columbus, Georgia Symphony. For all of his talents, William Howard wasn't a particularly strong man. In fact, an early attempt at farming failed because he lacked physical endurance. What he excelled at was carpentry. He built a log house just west of Troy, Alabama, that is still standing and remains occupied today.

There was always a bit of work available for a master carpenter, and William kept his family fed. Eva's relationship with her mother was quite different. Eva adored her mother, and the two were extremely close. William's sternness was balanced by Dora's kindhearted generosity. She was an excellent cook and more than willing to share the family's limited resources with the occasional hobo who passed by looking for a meal. Most important to Eva, her mother had more than enough love to lavish on her eight children.

The house Eva's father built was located west of Troy, AL.

For some reason, the Howard family just couldn't sit still, and in 1925 they packed up and moved again. They remained in Coffee County but put two miles between the Troy-Elba highway and their log cabin home, further insulating themselves from strangers and neighbors. This home didn't last long, either. In 1926, the family moved back to Pike County, then quickly moved again to a home in the Oak Grove area, about five miles west of Troy. The Oak Grove house was included with William's new job as a caretaker of the local amusement park. This time everything seemed right, but it wasn't.

In 1927, William's weak constitution deteriorated to full disability, and he died in 1930. The family moved to a cotton farm where Eva's three grown brothers stepped up to bear the responsibility for supporting the family. Eva was only thirteen years old and somewhat frail, but she had a talent for mathematics, and she became the farm "accountant." Her office was an overstuffed gunnysack, where she sat recording the quantities of cotton that each individual farm laborer picked. The job provided a unique fringe benefit: beautiful music. The farm laborers sang to pass the long hours in the hot sun, and Eva was an appreciative audience, mesmerized by the beautiful, rhythmic lyrics. She would slip off her perch and walk out into the field where the sweet harmonies of one hundred field hands surrounded her. She would actually join in and sing with the beautiful melodies. When she left the farm, she never again heard anything like those voices, but they remained fresh in her memory for seven decades.

Despite hardship and poverty, Eva managed to complete her high school education. She left the farm in 1935 and went to work for the Rural Electrification Administration in Troy. The job suited her well enough, but a chance encounter at the local bus station catapulted her into a world she barely knew existed. William Starling McLelland Jr. was a career military man en route from his base at Fort Benning, Georgia, to visit family in Andalusia, Alabama. His stopover in Troy was brief, but long enough to get a mailing address from the dark-haired beauty named Eva, whose path he was fortunate to cross.

Courtships were frequently brief in the uncertainty preceding World War II, and the relationship of Eva and William was no exception. They were married in December 1940 and on their way to starting a family. Their son, William Starling McLelland III, was born in 1942. William Sr. was sent to several locations within the United States to train soldiers going to the European Theater, before returning to resume life with his family in Georgia. The family grew when twin daughters, Michele Denise and Eugenia Diane, were born in 1947. The threat of being uprooted by a change of assignment loomed over them, as with all military families, but a nomadic life was certainly nothing new to Eva.

When William's new orders finally came, the move was much more than Eva's usual experience of crossing the county. This time, she would cross the Pacific Ocean. Early one day in October 1948, half dead from seasickness, she crept down the walkway of a military ship with three children in tow and set foot in the war-torn remains of the Philippine Islands. Damaged buildings were everywhere, and unusual odors came from every direction. To further complicate matters, the government was not stable. The Republic of the Philippines had been established two years before, and few natives were politically savvy. The result was an internal political struggle in which competitors used violence instead of the ballot box. The Philippine constabulary was constantly engaged in battles with the communist guerrillas, known as Huks, who were hiding in the mountains. Where Eva once slept surrounded by cotton fields, a protective wall of sandbags and soldiers with rifles now surrounded her. Hardly the ideal environment for raising young children.

Despite the danger and inconvenience, the family adapted to their new, if somewhat hostile, home. Eva took the children to Manila occasionally, and they were delighted to see the unusual sights such as the "house with legs" that William gleefully pointed out one day. Many of the houses were constructed of palm fronds and were quite light. Since plumbing consisted of a hole in the floor, it was necessary for the local men to get together frequently and move the neighborhood to a more sanitary location. The house with legs that gave William such delight was the Filipino version of a mobile home.

Eva grew up in a family with little means, but the lifestyle in the post-World War II Republic of the Philippines was primitive, even by her standards. Washday for the country women meant a trip through the rice fields down to their river where they pounded wet clothing on the big rocks along the riverbank. The pounding loosened the dirt in the fabric, making it easier to rinse out. Wet clothing was spread out on the growing rice plants and wet foliage to dry in the sun. Eva marveled to see the hard-working Filipino women toting baskets of soiled clothing, as they balanced suckling babies on their hips. Communications with gardeners and houseboys was done with extreme care, since the locals had an unnerving tendency to settle cultural misunderstandings with machetes.

Female domestic help was another problem. Eva found that the house girls were uniformly excellent in all tasks, except ironing. For some reason, that was a skill they couldn't quite master, which resulted in a multitude of scorched garments. The most egregious assault on the family wardrobe was perpetrated on a Scarlett O'Hara style, orchid dotted, Southern Belle gown that Eva purchased for formal events. In the process of smoothing out a few wrinkles, the house girl managed to "burn those pretty dots right off" and leave scorch marks everywhere else. Eva considered borrowing a machete.

Every day in the Philippines was a mini-adventure, but days that involved public transportation were particularly exciting. A train trip through the countryside was reminiscent of a circus, and the arrival in town was worth the purchase of a good camera. All passengers brought their goods with them to sell, and these wares were frequently alive. Imagine sharing a train coach with bleating goats, cackling hens, and grunting pigs, while dodging bunches of bananas tossed over the shoulders of the farmers. The jitney bus, another colorful mode of travel, was a converted Jeep, usually liberated from an unattended military motor pool. The vehicles were painted in wild colors and decorated with flags, tassels, and anything else that struck the drivers as artistic. To add to an already bizarre spectacle, the capacity was limited only by the imagination of the commuters. If there was a place to wedge a foot or grip a hand, it counted as a seat. Passengers, dragging a foot on the street, or waving an arm, indicated departure points. Chaotic as it sounds, it worked.

As crude as local transportation was, military transportation was only marginally better. It was somewhat less breathtaking, in that all of the passengers were actually inside the vehicle. Once a month, the United States government provided bus service across the island to Clark Air Force Base, so military families could do their shopping.

A volcano later destroyed Clark, but in those days the Post Exchange was the next best thing to a modern Walmart. On shopping days, dependent families boarded the bus at 7:00 a.m. for a kidney-wrenching ride over roads still unrepaired from World War II wartime shelling. The uncomfortable, one-hundred-mile trip took a large part of the day, but there were no options. Even something as mundane as a shopping trip could bring danger.

On one trip, Huks attacked the bus Eva was on. The leader stepped through the door brandishing a rifle and shouting something in the Tagalog language that one did not need to be multilingual to understand. He wanted their money, he wanted their groceries, and he wanted them fast. Eva and the passengers began quickly to comply, but the guard jeep that was trailing behind arrived in time. The submachine-gun-toting GIs took two of the Huks captive and turned them over to Philippine authorities. The rest of the gang escaped. A few days later, the same gang attacked an American dairy facility, and all of the Americans were killed. It was a sobering moment.

Of all the memories of her time in the Philippines, the hardest for Eva to shake occurred on a Friday afternoon when she returned from the Post Exchange. On her buffet, a folded piece of paper from her children's school principal informed her that seven-year-old William had been bitten by a rabid dog. They administered the first series of rabies shots, but the only serum available was so old that they didn't know if it was still effective. Eva had to stand by helplessly every twenty-one days, while six men held down her screaming child as the painful injections were administered into his spine. This torture was made all the worse because the effectiveness of the vaccine was still unknown. But they were lucky. It worked.

Despite the frequent hardships and dangers, the Philippine Islands of the late 1940s offered an exciting mixture of old and new, traditional and modern cultures. For a young woman from rural Alabama, this was a new and exciting world. Horse racing was popular, and Eva could spend the entire day watching jai alai, a sport that was entirely new to her. The upper classes and the military families also had access to the Filipino social scene.

The hot spot for dancing was the Santa Ana Cabaret. At the time, it was the largest such establishment in the world and drew top talent. Eva saw the Benny Goodman Band perform there and even danced with some of its members when they were on a break.

On another occasion, the American Consul and his wife hosted a reception in downtown Manila and invited Eva. The American ambassador, Paul V. McNutt, and the president of the Republic of the Philippine Islands, Elpidio Quirino, were in attendance for this high point of the social season, with the finest entertainment and food for the guests who filled the building and the spacious grounds. This was in stark contrast to Eva's excursions to the battlefields of Corregidor, Fort Drum, and her trip down the path of the Bataan Death March. For a young woman and her family, the Philippine Islands were a monumental cultural and historical experience.

After five years, William completed his assignment, and the family was transferred back to Fort Benning, Georgia. Eva was filled with conflicting emotions as she walked up the gangplank of the ship and waved at her friends who were staying behind.

"Don't look back," she told herself. "America, here I come!"

As it turned out, the move from the Philippines back to Fort Benning was little more than a rest stop in the frequent relocation that is part of military life. Still, the years of 1953 and 1954 allowed the McClellands to get reacquainted with their families and the children reintroduced to their native land. The family settled into an American lifestyle, and Eva was even able to get her old job back at their Rural Electrification Administration. Just when their lives became routine, Uncle Sam came knocking with new orders for William, and his next stop was Heidelberg, Germany.

Eva loved Heidelberg. It was the United States military headquarters for Germany at the time, and she thought it was the best city in the country. William had a great assignment, and Eva got a job as a civilian worker on the base. She worked in the publications department, editing and proofreading publications for final typing. The job had a certain amount of prestige, since it involved handling classified documents. Eva particularly enjoyed her coworkers, especially a wonderful woman from Latvia who was a translator.

Germany and the German people suffered terribly during the war, but the western sectors recovered rapidly with the influx of money, technology, and personnel from the conquering countries. Unlike the territories governed by the Soviet Union, the British, French, and American sectors were cleared of the debris of war, and many new buildings were under construction. The Germans are well known for being hardworking, and the resurrection of their country from the ashes was a testament to their determination. These combined factors created a stable social environment that allowed for the growth of culture and the arts. Eva and her family took advantage of this. With her long-standing love of art and music, Eva was excited to hear young, piano prodigy Van Cliburn when he played a concert near their home, and a local artist painted her portrait in oil. Wearing her favorite green dress, she felt that she looked like a princess in the painting and cherished it for the rest of her life.

A portrait of Eva, age 34, was painted in her favorite green dress.

There were plenty of opportunities to see Europe from their base in Germany. The family attended the World's Fair in Brussels, Belgium, and took a trek up to see Berchtesgaden, Hitler's mountain lair. They ventured into the salt mines in Salzburg, Austria, where they attended a church service in the subterranean cathedral. Then they traveled to England to visit Oxford University, the Kings and Poets' corner of Westminster Abbey, the changing of the guard at Buckingham Palace, and the beautiful pastoral English countryside. It was an exciting experience for Eva and a unique educational experience for the children.

There was another unique experience that was not pleasant. One day, Eva's Latvian friend confided in her that she had the gift of reading palms and could tell what the future had in store for individuals. This was too intriguing for Eva to ignore, so she thrust out her hands. It was not good news. The woman told her that her husband was running around with other women and that her marriage would end in divorce. There was more. The palmist told her that she saw something else so astonishing that she didn't even want to talk of it. Years later, when her second husband was shrouded in mystery, Eva believed the palmist saw her future.

In 1956, the family returned to Fort Benning, Georgia, where they stayed until 1967. While she was waiting for a secretarial job to open up on base, Eva took a temporary position as a receptionist at the local Arthur Murray Dance Studio. At the time, a group of Iranians was training at Fort Benning, and they frequented the studio for dancing lessons and female companionship. There was one young man who chose not to take dancing lessons but would accompany the other men when they came into town. He took an interest in Eva and spent his evenings at the receptionist's desk in conversation with her. He was interested in establishing correspondence with her when he returned to Iran, but Eva felt this was improper and discouraged it. Eva later learned that the young man had urgent business to attend to in his homeland; he was a prominent member of the Iranian government.

By the mid-1960s, Eva was working at Fort Benning as a temporary secretary for the provost marshal, which was followed by a stint in the Criminal Investigation Corps and the Criminal Investigation Division. By this time, Eva learned the palmist's vision of her future had been accurate. William was, indeed, seeing other women, and the marriage was on the rocks. The couple divorced in 1965, and William died shortly thereafter.

Single and with grown children, Eva's nomadic spirit took charge. Through coworkers at Fort Benning, she learned there were civil service jobs available in the Canal Zone in Panama. It sounded like a new adventure, so off to Panama she went.

SIX

EVA, NIK, AND A "DAMN LIAR"

Florida, 2002

Mid-afternoon sun glared down on Interstate 10 as Mark and Eva neared the Crestview exit. Mark listened with rapt attention as Eva continued her story of a thirty-one-year rollercoaster of a marriage.

"Nik was a strange mixture of arrogance and humility," she told Mark. "He was gentle, and he was cruel. He was generous, and he was frugal. Surprises were common, though some were more surprising than others." Eva lapsed into a brief silence, but Mark could tell she was thinking, so he waited for the rest.

"Like, one day out of the blue, Nik tells me he neglected to mention he was married before." Eva eyed Mark for a reaction, her eyebrows raised.

Unsure what to say, Mark tried for humor, "What, like that small detail slipped his mind?"

Eva huffed, "Right. Well, you can imagine I wasn't pleased. Seemed like a fairly fundamental bit of information I might have liked to know before going into our marriage . . . but that was nothing compared to the letter."

"The letter?" Mark couldn't hide the curious tone in his voice.

"Mhm. I intercepted a letter addressed to Nik from a woman who claimed to be his present wife. I know . . . I know I shouldn't have opened it," she told Mark, "but my curiosity got the better of me."

Mark couldn't help thinking that—given the number of mysteries in

Nik's life and the way he doled out information in small, stunning bits, like this ex-wife he'd sprung on her—a little snooping was probably forgivable.

"So who was she? Where did it come from?" Mark asked.

"It was postmarked from Ohio. The woman called herself Dorothy. Said she was happy living alone and didn't want to be married to him anymore. She wanted a divorce. Well, you can imagine I was livid. So, I confronted Nik. I said, 'What's this about being married to another woman when you are married to me?' He was angry. 'You don't know what is going on, so you better mind your own business!'"

Eva told Mark she felt that the possibility of being married to a bigamist was very much her business. Weeks later, another letter came, which she opened and read as well. This time she mailed it back to Ohio with an enclosed note telling the woman that Nik was married and to leave him alone.

"When I told Nik what I'd done, he was furious. 'You shouldn't be sticking your nose into my business! It is to your benefit that you shouldn't have done that. You have messed everything up!' How's that for an answer? Well, time passed, there were no more letters, and things finally blew over. But I never stopped wondering about it."

Years later, in 2009, in an attempt to add clarity to the situation, Mark asked Verner's son, Gary Nicely, if he knew of a woman from Ohio named Dorothy who his father associated with, and the answer was, "No."

There was an Ohio woman in Howard's life at this point, though. Her name was Jean Peters.

Panama, 1970s

Living with an anti-social curmudgeon can be difficult. Eva liked going to the movies, but it was a real challenge to get Nik to go with her. He would struggle against it, occasionally giving in because he knew it would make her happy. He hated the whole experience. He would grumble throughout the film and try to get her to leave early. If she wouldn't, he would eventually get up and leave alone. He firmly told Eva that Hollywood was a terrible place.

Nik's idiosyncrasies were endless. On the rare occasion when Eva was allowed to venture into his apartment, she noticed that he always had a cup placed under the kitchen faucet, and the water from the tap was slowly trickling into it, overflowing into the sink. She would walk over and turn the water off, but Nik would always turn it back on before they left. Eva never figured out why he wanted the water constantly running. Nik was also careful to leave as few traces of his existence as possible. He had a bank account at the Canal Zone branch of the Chase Bank that he opened shortly before they were married. Both before and after the marriage, Nik refused to sign checks. Eva had to write all of his checks for him. He seemed very reluctant to have any samples of his signature or writing available where any outsiders may be able to access them. If it was leaving the house, it was in Eva's handwriting. This quirk was harmless, as far as Eva could tell, particularly when compared to all of his other quirks. Although she signed the checks, Eva never knew how much money was in Nik's account. She didn't bother to ask, but if she had, she knew he would tell her it was none of her business. Fortunately for Eva—and their marriage—she was never a very material person. She didn't require much and had the resources to care for her own needs. She didn't need Nik's money and she wasn't interested in it.

His secret meetings continued, and he had a real knack for stealth. He would slip away from the apartment in the middle of the night, so quietly that he wouldn't wake her. To ensure that he didn't wake her when he returned, he put two sawhorses in the apartment and laid a door across them to use as a bed until Eva awakened. Odd as it was, it fit in nicely with all the other strange things he did. He was strange, but at least he was consistent.

In November 1970, Nik gave her a huge surprise. Eva was in the middle of preparing for a trip to Alabama to see her mother, when Nik dropped the bomb.

"How would you like to go to Las Vegas? I would like you to meet Howard Hughes." Eva was stunned and momentarily speechless, but she finally found her voice.

"I wouldn't know what to do or say, but I would do my best if you wanted me to." She was as excited as a schoolgirl. For a few days, she continued to pack for the trip home, but her mind was on the journey to Las Vegas. She finally pressed him for details.

"When can we go to meet Mr. Hughes?"

"The trip to Las Vegas is off. They said it was not a good idea." As usual, Nik did not elaborate on just who "they" were. Disappointed and bewildered, Eva left for Alabama and her mother. The massive engagement ring made quite an impression.

"You're married to a billionaire, and you don't even know it," her friends teased. The thought of being married to a billionaire amused Eva. Still, that was an awfully big ring for a working class man to buy.

In the middle of all of this unusual behavior, Eva craved something traditional and normal. In December 1970, the Christmas holiday was almost upon them, and she wanted to celebrate the season—so far from her native home—with a Christmas tree. She especially wanted the fun of decorating it. Pine trees are about as common in Panama as snowmen, but Eva set out to find what might be available from the local vendors of Christmas decorations. All the trees were gone, and Eva was bitterly upset. The disappointment was replaced by anger when she peeked into Nik's apartment and saw a Christmas tree lying on its side on the floor. She was hurt, furious, and crying as she demanded to know why he let her look all over town for something he already had. What's more, he did not have the common sense to put it in water! When he saw her tears, he started crying as well. The episode went unexplained, like so many others.

As 1970 drew to a close, the curious life of Eva and Nik had strange similarities to that of Howard Hughes. While Eva was receiving shocking letters from "Dorothy" in Ohio claiming to be Nik's wife and seeking a divorce, Jean Peters, a former farm girl from East Canton, Ohio, who attended Ohio State University, was negotiating a divorce from Howard (Barlett and Steele 138). She filed the divorce papers in February 1970. Howard had been fending her off for quite some time, but now he was forced for the last time to convince her to remain married to him or to negotiate a financial settlement with her. His luck at stalling ran out, and he was forced to cut her a deal. On

June 18, 1971, the Hughes-Peters divorce was final. Howard agreed to pay Jean between $70,000 and $140,000 a year for twenty years, the exact figure to be determined each year by a cost of living index (What could be more Howard-like than that?). She was also given the house that she lived in at 507 North Palm Drive in Beverly Hills (Barlett and Steele 425).

The timing of Nik's offer to take Eva to meet Howard Hughes was also interesting. At that time, Howard, the key to the vast Hughes Empire, was reported to be near death according to the media. His health was failing and he was unable to get out of bed. What would happen to his numerous businesses if the emaciated, shell of a man died suddenly in the Desert Inn Hotel? About the time word got out that he would survive, Nik cancelled the trip to Las Vegas, and taking Eva to meet Howard was not critical anymore. Undercover planning was placed into motion to move the bedridden man from Las Vegas and transport him to the Bahamas. This was another interesting coincidence in the saga of Nik and Eva.

The Christmas tree crisis became just another strange memory, as the calendar turned to 1971. Since Nik was no longer a civil service employee, he was forced to give up the apartment he kept across from Eva's to use as an office. As a consequence, Eva's apartment suddenly became the repository for boxes of files that pertained to whatever Nik was doing in his secret meetings. Nik was big on boxes. They held his files, his clothes, everything he could put in a box was in one. Part of his rationale was the need for secrecy and a desire to shield his belongings—whatever they may be—from prying eyes. The other component was a raging paranoia about some circumstance that would cause him to move, immediately, without time to pack. Eva didn't understand that second component at first, but later, when more facts became apparent, she realized his reason for concern. The result was that for thirty-one years, Eva lived in a house of boxes.

The loss of the office apartment impacted the meetings as well, since Nik wouldn't conduct business in front of Eva. He and his "gang of cohorts," as Eva began to refer to them, started gathering daily on yachts somewhere in the Canal Zone. Ever curious, Eva pressed him for information.

"Why do you go out on boats?" she asked.

"I am needed to calibrate the engines," was the reply. Eva didn't buy this for a moment. Why was an aircraft maintenance supervisor needed to calibrate yacht engines? Why had he never done this before he moved out of his office? What were the cohorts doing out there, helping him? None of this made any sense, but she knew enough to stop asking questions. If she probed him, he would just tell her to mind her own business. Nik made a comment once that the yachts belonged to the "eye-ties." That wasn't very illuminating.

The yacht meetings were mysterious, but as Eva began to piece these individual situations together, like pieces of a puzzle, she began to see a picture. The huge diamond, the aides, the constant secrecy, and the reference to Howard Hughes were beginning to make her suspicious—impossible as it sounded—that Nik might actually be Howard Hughes. Somehow, the notoriously reclusive billionaire had pulled off an incredible identity swap. She did the sensible thing with this theory and kept it to herself.

In addition to wondering whom she was married to, Eva also had to be concerned about how long she would be married. Nik was always talking about leaving, particularly of going to the Philippines. Almost daily, he told her that he would be leaving the next day. When they had one of their numerous arguments, he would pick up the phone and order the person on the other end to, "Prepare the plane, I am leaving tomorrow." He kept his personal items separate from hers in his boxes and navy blue and black footlockers, ready to load onto an airplane at a moment's notice. Eva was never allowed to open the footlockers. They remained there as a silent threat that she could be abandoned at any moment.

In the early summer of 1971, Eva decided she needed a little security and used her own money to purchase some property on the West Indies island of St. Eustatius. Her intention was to live on the island at some point, perhaps when she retired, but the property turned out to be the ideal getaway when Nik's idiosyncrasies got to be more than she could tolerate. She tried to lure Nik to join her there on many occasions when the marriage was going smoothly, but he never did. He pretended he wanted to go but always had a last-minute excuse to stay. His usual reason was that he was guarding the household goods. Later in life, he told Eva that he had never intended to go, because he didn't like the people on the island, but Eva knew he sent his men down there because she saw them poking around on the grounds. She surmised that the real reason was that he and his cohorts couldn't do business from the remote location with its one-room cabin.

Although the story of the marriage between Eva and Nik sounds bizarre, there were also many good times. For all of his quirkiness, Nik could be enormously charming when he wanted to, and it seems that he really did try to make Eva happy when he wasn't absorbed in his own world. Panama was an interesting place for two displaced Americans to explore, and they took advantage of the weekends, when Eva was off work, to visit the parts of the country that sounded appealing. Eva had a Volkswagen bug, and Nik had a Jeep, so they had the ability to travel at will. Eva always drove. Nik enjoyed walking, but he wouldn't get behind the wheel of a car unless absolutely necessary. He had lost his coordination—the result of many accidents over the years, she learned—yet he always insisted that whenever possible they buy vehicles with manual transmissions. Eva never saw his logic behind this, other than it was his way of ensuring that she always had to do the driving.

Bahamas, 1970–72

Meanwhile, back on Paradise Island in the Bahamas, Howard and his empire continued to be a quagmire of contradictions. Incapacitated in his lounge chair in the Britannia Beach Hotel, the surgery on his bedsores was not a total solution. There was a recurrent five-inch wound on his shoulder blade where his thin skin continued to rub on the chair. There was also some question about the fundamental source of Howard's medical problems. In June 1971, Dr. Lawrence Chaffin told Hughes's aides, Chester Davis and Bill Gay, that Howard's primary problem was drugs, and if he could get off them, he could be rehabilitated (Real 281). Was Howard so addicted that he was willing to sacrifice everything for drugs, or was the man in the Britannia

Beach Hotel easier to control if kept addicted? Chaffin was Howard's doctor in 1932 and briefly in 1946. At the time Dr. Chaffin made this diagnosis, he had not seen Howard for thirty-five years.

At the same time, the Hughes organization obtained a new Washington representative, former CIA employee Robert Bennett, and planning continued on Project Jennifer, the scheme to use the Hughes Tool Company as a front to build the *Glomar Explorer* to raise the sunken Soviet submarine. To make matters more interesting, on August 6, 1971, the news broke of Howard's $100,000 contribution to Richard Nixon the year before (Drosnin 419), but the biggest controversy of them all came from a source that no one expected: a book.

Clifford Irving had authored seven books, both fiction and nonfiction, since his first book was published in 1958. He received some critical attention and success in both genres, so in 1970, he decided to combine his artistic skills and write a fictitious, nonfiction book. His subject, or victim, was Howard Hughes. Irving felt Howard was an easy mark. He had been a recluse for years, and rumors of his mental illness, or even death, were numerous. Irving figured he could claim Howard had authorized him to write his autobiography, and Howard wouldn't reveal the lie to protect his privacy, or he couldn't reveal it due to mental or physical incapacity (421).

While Irving's plan may sound foolish, or at least extraordinarily daring, it had a plausible foundation. In 1969, he published *Fake!*, a biography of art forger Elmyr de Hory. Irving went to his publisher, McGraw-Hill, and claimed Howard had read the book, liked it, and chosen Irving to write his autobiography. He supported his claim with letters forged in Howard's supposed handwriting. The forgeries were good enough to withstand the scrutiny of handwriting analysis experts—although it's not certain what they compared them to—so McGraw-Hill committed $765,000 to the book to be divided between Clifford Irving and Howard Hughes, with Howard getting the largest share. McGraw-Hill was confident they had a blockbuster on their hands and followed Irving's instructions to keep quiet about the project until publication.

Irving, along with writer Richard Susskind, delved into the piles of public information and speculation about Howard to research their subject. By using personal connections, they also gained access to research material and files that were not only secret, but the product of other writers intended for their own projects. Irving traveled around the world, supposedly having secret interviews with Hughes, and skillfully wove the research into a believable autobiography, which was delivered to the publisher and announced to the world on December 7, 1971 (421). Hughes "experts" blessed the work as authentic, and the public was wild with anticipation, so Irving and McGraw-Hill were poised to rake in the money. There was only one flaw in the plan. Howard Hughes was neither unable nor unwilling to fight.

On January 7, 1972, the word got out Hughes was going to speak by telephone from the Bahamas to seven journalists who were familiar with him and his voice (Irving 307). Irving got the bad news early. He later commented, "I got the inside word. On Friday night, there was a press conference from the Bahamas to several newspapermen in Los Angeles. I know, McGraw-Hill called me about it. They've already prepared a press release. They figure Hughes was going to deny the autobiography" (307).

On January 9, Howard Hughes spoke by telephone to the seven respected journalists: Jim Bacon, Marvin Miles, Vernon Scott, Roy Neal, Gene Handsaker, Wayne Thomas, and Galdwin Hill (Real 97–8). He informed them he was speaking from Paradise Island, the Bahamas. Jim Bacon, a Hollywood columnist and personal acquaintance of Howard, immediately identified the voice as that of Howard Hughes. It was older and more hesitant, but it was him (Barlett and Steele 469). This would seem to be a significant achievement for a man that the world believed to be a drugged-up skeleton, decomposing somewhere in a lounge chair. The questioning began.

"Did you cooperate with or know a man named Irving who claims to have written this biography with you (Irving 308)?"

"This must go down in history," the voice replied. "I only wish I was still in the movie business, because I don't remember any script as wild or as stretching the imagination as this yarn turned out to be. I'm not talking about the biography itself, because I haven't read it. I don't know what's in it. But this episode is so fantastic that it taxes your imagination to believe that a thing like this could happen. I don't know him. I never saw him. I never

ever heard of him until a matter of days ago when this thing came to my attention" (Irving 308).

The reporters clearly understood this interview with the reclusive Howard Hughes was not an event likely to be repeated. They maximized the opportunity. When they concluded their questions about the Irving book, they held him on the line in the hope of getting some answers to penetrate the fog of rumors and contradictions that enshrouded him for years. His highly publicized ill health and unkempt appearance were at the top of their list. Hughes was surprisingly accommodating. In fact, he talked for over two hours. He was quick to deny reports of being a long-haired, long finger-nailed, one hundred pound skeleton when he left Las Vegas (Barlett and Steele 471–72).

"I keep in fair shape. I have always kept my fingernails at a reasonable length", he maintained (Drosnin 423). Perhaps, to emphasize his physical and mental fitness, he stated that he intended to give up his reclusive lifestyle (Barlett and Steele 472).

Irving claimed the voice was a fake and not Hughes, but enough suspicion was aroused to launch an investigation. Howard Hughes's attorney, Chester Davis, filed suit against Irving, McGraw-Hill, Life Magazine, and Dell Publications, but the mystery was finally solved in Switzerland. Swiss authorities investigated the bank account where Hughes's share of the McGraw-Hill money was deposited in an account for "H.R. Hughes." The investigators turned up the fact that the account was actually opened by one "Helga R. Hughes," who, coincidentally, turned out to be Edith Irving, Clifford's wife, with a forged Swiss passport. The game was up. Clifford Irving's anticipated gravy train was derailed, and he, his wife, and Richard Susskind were on the fast track to prison.

Eva vividly remembered when Nik heard the news about the Irving book in early December 1971. He was irritable, very irritable, and extremely concerned.

"The story is false, full of lies, and none of this is true!" he insisted to Eva.

By now Eva was aware of Nik's reaction to lies and she decided to prod him a bit.

"Well, that's not very fair to Mr. Hughes. If it's false, the public should be told the truth, shouldn't they?" Nik slowly smiled, as he always did, when she said something of which he approved.

A few weeks later, the media was buzzing about the much-anticipated interview with Howard Hughes. Eva was alone and listened to it on the Armed Forces Network broadcast. She got a bigger surprise than the other listeners. The voice was Nik. She confronted him later, when he returned.

"Nik, that was you!" Nik just smiled his special smile. No affirmation. No denial. Just the smile. Another piece fit into the puzzle, and the picture was now becoming recognizable.

Notes

Barlett, Donald, L., and James B. Steele. *Howard Hughes: His Life and Madness.* New York: W.W. Norton, and Company, 1979.

Drosnin, Michael. *Citizen Hughes.* New York: Broadway Books, 1985.

Irving, Clifford. *The Hoax.* New York: Knightsbridge Publishing, 1981.

Real, Jack. *The Asylum of Howard Hughes.* Bloomington, IN: Xlibris Corporation, 2003.

SEVEN

EVA ESCAPES

On the road, 2002

Mark was having quite a time trying to listen to Eva, absorb what she said, and still focus on driving. He couldn't help thinking her story sounded like a child's fantasy, yet she related it with such clarity and conviction that he found himself believing her!

Mark was hooked. He came up with a plan. *I'll have to come back and record her telling these stories and do some research on Howard Hughes to see if these details actually fit.* It occurred to him that this was going to be a lot of work, but he realized he didn't care. In fact, he was suddenly anxious to get started. If Eva was as truthful as she sounded, this was a staggering addendum to the Hughes mythology.

His next question was obvious. "What happened next, Eva?"

Without a pause, she continued the strange and fascinating story.

Panama, 1972

In early 1972, Eva told him, Nik was becoming increasingly anxious to return to the United States. They both felt that Flagstaff, Arizona, would be a good place for them to settle or "land," as he put it. Unfortunately for both of them, Eva was in no shape to travel. She was experiencing a variety of health problems, including infections, kidney stones, and the temporary loss of her eyesight. She was hospitalized several times. The medical problems were serious enough for her to question whether or not she could return to work. She told Nik that she was considering filing for early disability retirement from the Civil Service. Nik was not only supportive of the idea, but he embraced it with the enormous enthusiasm that was characteristic of him when he was in agreement with something. Eva's retirement fit in perfectly with his desire to leave the Canal Zone and return to the States.

Nik's impatience to leave the Canal Zone did not mesh well with the government's glacial pace in certifying Eva's disability retirement. He complained that the government doctors were dragging their feet over the whole thing. If they didn't pick up the pace, he threatened to route her through a medical foundation in Miami. He didn't mention the name of the foundation, although there is one such very well-known facility in Miami, the one funded by Howard Hughes.

The retirement process dragged on, and Eva was not up for traveling to Miami, so the impatient Nik tried to move things along by bringing in a doctor of his choosing from the States. On the night he arrived, Nik made a concerted effort to stay out of the way by parking himself in the kitchen, doing dishes, and keeping himself occupied elsewhere. Other than the fact that the examination was conducted in the living room of their apartment, it was typical of the process that Eva had been through so many times before. At the conclusion of the exam, however, the doctor asked an unusual question. He wanted to know if she would like to go out and have a drink. This seemed highly inappropriate to Eva, and she declined. She later learned that the good doctor went out on the town without her and had a few drinks too many, reminiscent of Howard's physician Dr. Crane, whose virtual imprisonment at the Desert Inn had left him with a drinking problem. Coincidence? Maybe, but then again, maybe not. Whoever the mystery doctor was and wherever Nik had found him, the whole experience seemed strange and unproductive to Eva, but Nik insisted, so she grudgingly played along. The Civil Service machinery turned slowly, but in June 1972, it finally stopped. The process was over, and Eva was granted her disability retirement.

Through two years of marriage, particularly during her period of ill health when she didn't go to work during the day, Eva began to realize that everything was very peculiar about this man. The more she learned, the more perplexed she became, to the point of even being uneasy. She felt that she was living in a mystery movie.

Nik had sandy-colored, blond hair, but as they lived together, Eva realized that he colored it. There was frequently the strange, strong chemical smell after he showered. At times, she could see that the roots of his hair were growing in dark. She finally asked him what color his hair was when he was young. He told her that it was black. Apparently, the physical unlikelihood of a man with black hair becoming a blond didn't occur to him. Maybe, he just didn't care anymore.

When they first met, Nik had a permanent crease in his brow that Eva attributed to suffering and worry. She would massage his forehead to try to bring him some comfort. She asked him what he worried about, but he would always tell her that it was too complicated, and she wouldn't understand. His countenance began to relax over time, and Eva felt that her loving care was the reason.

Nik's furrowed brow could be explained by worry, but the burn scars on his scalp, hands, and feet were clearly not the result of tension. He had to have been in a violent accident. His left hand was scarred much worse than the right, and the left side of his scalp was red with burn scars. Eva asked him about the scars and got the usual answer, which was no answer at all. When it came to talking about his past, Nik's lips were sealed.

Nik's other physical disabilities remained a problem. His hearing certainly wasn't getting any better, and he could only read with the aid of a magnifying glass, turning his head to favor his right eye, although he could see distant objects fine.

On the few occasions Eva saw Nik communicate in writing for his own personal notes or notes to her, he always did it longhand, never with a typewriter. He had a unique style of writing, a combination of printing intermixed with cursive writing. His spelling was also unique, which is to say that it was atrocious. It displayed a lack of basic formal education. He always wrote on a legal pad, and he was passionate about how good Paper Mate ballpoint pens were. He frequently used shorthand codes of his own devising.

A few notable ones were VIP, for very important papers; IK, for Indian Kid, a pet name for Eva that reflected her Seminole heritage; and the code for his own name, Nik. He spelled Nik by dotting the "K" and eliminating the "i." He used a special script on his name that looked like a cattle brand.

One of Nik's paper bag files with his codes.

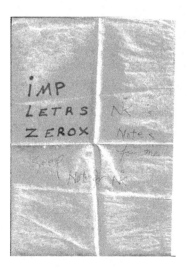

An example of Nik's writing and spelling, which is similar to documents proven to be hand written by Howard Hughes.

Finding samples of Howard's handwriting was never simple, since it is generally reported that he dictated much of his communication to his aides, who wrote his memos longhand on yellow legal pads. This was a critical factor in the trial over the Mormon Will, which will be discussed in Chapter Thirteen. Lawyers for the Hughes family, which was contesting the will, maintained that the handwritten document couldn't possibly have been written by Howard because it was sloppy, with scratch-outs and a plethora of misspellings and grammatical errors. Howard, the family and aides maintained, would never make these types of errors, and as a perfectionist would never let such a poorly written document be distributed. Given the status of the billionaire, this seemed like a very logical argument. It might have held up if it weren't for the fact that the attorney representing the will, Harold Rhoden, and his team, produced several memos that Hughes's aides grudgingly, under oath, acknowledged were personally written by Hughes in the 1960s. John Holmes was the unfortunate Hughes aide on the witness stand when Rhoden began to shred their argument. One by one, he produced fifty-eight different Hughes-written documents with spelling errors such as *payed, Dessert* Inn, *companys, opointees, devided,* and *aircraf.* He didn't do well with names, either. Hubert Humphrey became Hubert *Humphries,* Bob Maheu became Bob *Mahu,* and Howard even got creative with his own name, spelling it *Hughest.* After the spelling test, Holmes was subjected to another pile of documents that featured egregious, and seeming endless, examples of improper capitalization and grammar. Other than being angry and frustrated, Holmes could do nothing but sit and endure the painful presentation of facts (Rhoden 243–48).

Gary Nicely stated that his father, Verner, had no problems with spelling or grammar. However, the court record shows that Howard wrote just like Nik!

Another curious coincidence was revealed on the witness stand. An FBI analysis of the Mormon Will revealed that out of the three thousand brands of ink available at the time, the will was written with a Paper Mate pen with an ink formula only made from 1963 to 1974. A Hughes aide testified that Howard would only write with a Paper Mate pen and that the aide bought them by the dozen (Magnesen 88).

So . . . what are the odds of that?

Time apart, June–December 1972

Once in 1972, Eva indicated she wanted to call her brother, Everis, in Alabama, in the worst way. Nik said he would help. Late in the evening, he took her to a building in a field that had a desk located outside. There was a phone on the desk, and he placed the call to Everis. She specifically remembers looking up at the brilliant stars and moon in the night sky as he made the call. When Everis answered the phone, Eva was amazed at the clear connection. She had never had such a clear contact before when calling Alabama from Panama. Nik explained to her the phone used satellite links. This was the only time Nik took her to this location.

When her retirement became official in June 1972, Eva was a very bewildered woman. She agreed that the time was right to move to Arizona, with one small change in the previous plan; she intended to go alone. Nik was driving her crazy. She said, "This is final, and I am leaving you for good."

He remained in Panama, while she made good her escape to Arizona. In keeping with the trend of her life at this point, even her return to the States was strange. She settled into an apartment in downtown Flagstaff above the Knowles Bakery at 7 East Aspen Avenue. She was free at last. She relaxed, went for walks in the beautiful countryside that surrounded Flagstaff, and even went to a Hopi powwow, where the tribe members were so kind to her that she felt like a queen. Peace returned to her life, but not for long.

"In July 1972, while in Flagstaff, I opened up a letter from Nik and was shocked to find a year's worth of his Air Force retirement checks, all uncashed," Eva told Mark. "Who on earth would not cash their paychecks for over a year?" While in Panama, he had periodically given her his checks, but then suddenly stopped without explanation. Eva said nothing, but absorbed all living expenses until this surprise package arrived. They had not spoken during June and most of July, so Eva thought that the checks were his way of making up. Withholding the checks was likely another of his aggravating loyalty tests. That wasn't the only surprise. Much to her dismay, in late July,

Nik showed up in Arizona. He told Eva that he had been cleaning up some business affairs in Panama and took the first opportunity to join her. As far as Eva was concerned, he could have taken his time. Lots of it. However, he was in Arizona, and he was her husband, so she didn't reject him.

As it turned out, their cohabitation was brief. Shortly after his arrival, he went to the VA Hospital in Prescott for a routine physical. He knew he needed medical attention, and the price at the VA—free—was too good to pass up. The checkup revealed a hyperthyroid condition, and he was moved to the Veterans Administration Domiciliary where he stayed from July until December 1972. The VA Domiciliary, Building 14, a two story, U-shaped, white building was located just north of the VA Hospital, separated by a large traffic circle, so access was easy. It's possible that the drug addiction that had plagued him since his 1946 airplane crash in Beverly Hills was also dealt with at this time. He displayed typical symptoms of opiate withdrawal, such as alternately sweating, being cold, and suffering physical tremors, and this long convalescent period would have allowed him to withdraw slowly and safely from narcotics.

For some reason that was never made clear, he wanted to keep his marriage to Eva a secret during this period, but he had no problem revealing the staff of aides that reported to him. They found accommodations in the area, and business continued as usual. Interestingly, the CIA has a facility between Phoenix and Tucson, and Hughes Helicopter is located east of Phoenix. Both are within driving, or helicopter, distance.

On her increasingly rare visits, Eva occasionally overheard bits of conversation. Once, she heard Nik tell someone that the move to Canada was not a wise move. Eva never found out what that was about either, but she was surprised, since Nik always spoke highly of Canada.

Prescott and Flagstaff are only ninety-one miles apart, but Eva saw little of Nik from July to October. Finally, she packed up her new GMC pickup truck and decided to find an apartment in Prescott, so she could be as close as possible to him. The VA Domiciliary Facility had two stories, and Eva could enter through a back door to a stairwell that led directly to the floor that Nik was on. Her visits weren't entirely welcomed. For a while, he suggested that she time her visits around noon, but he finally came out and said, "I have business to do with my friends, and you are holding me up." He suggested that she not visit so often because, "He and his friends needed to do some business." Eva was as accommodating as Nik was rude. She stopped coming around.

Nik had a reason for limiting her visits. He had been coming and going from the facility as though it were a hotel, and he didn't need to have his comings and goings revealed to his wife when she made a bed check. A man with a private jet can live anywhere there is an airport. He even showed up at her apartment a couple of times in his usual unique fashion. A man in Eva's building was showing interest in her, and word got back to Nik, probably as a result of him having her followed. Suddenly, he cared about Eva very much and showed up in Prescott to explain it to the man in no uncertain terms. The confrontation was unpleasant, but not violent. Another time, she was awakened in the middle of the night by the sound of a rake on the sidewalk. She looked out the window, and there was Nik. Just knocking on the door would apparently have been too simple.

His pattern of lukewarm receptions changed one day in December, when he greeted her with a smile that extended from ear to ear. He told her, absolutely beaming, "Bless your little heart. You are an innocent little girl, and I am going to spoil you rotten." This emotional 180-degree turn made no sense to her at the time, especially since the "spoiling" part never happened. It wasn't until years later, after much research, that Mark pointed out that this period of unbridled elation coincided with the settlement of the TWA lawsuit against Howard Hughes. There's a reason for everything, even with Nik.

In late December 1972, Eva was with Nik as he listened intently to radio reports of the deadly earthquake in Nicaragua. The newscasters sharply questioned why Howard Hughes had not provided financial assistance, since he was living in Nicaragua.

"Why do they think that Howard Hughes should be robbed of his money to pay for those poor people?" Eva asked, "He was not responsible for their welfare, just because he was there." At this point, Eva was pretty convinced as to Nik's real identity, although he had not confirmed it. She waited for his reaction to her comments. He told her he thought it was funny that people thought Howard Hughes was in Nicaragua, and then he smiled that smile.

Howard on the move, 1972

The telephone interview about the Irving affair had done much to dispel the image of Hughes, popular in the press, that he was a drugged shadow of a human being. The reporters recognized his voice immediately and stated Howard spoke lucidly, even articulately. Like most everything in Howard's life, this successful resolution of one problem inevitably created another.

In the course of his lengthy interview, Howard made some seriously derogatory comments about Robert Maheu, who, understandably angry, filed suit for libel, slander, and defamation of character. The court agreed Maheu's reputation had been damaged, and Maheu was awarded a $2.8 million judgment (Barlett and Steele 473).

To make matters worse, the interview also caught the attention of the Bahamian Government, which started asking questions about Howard's immigration status (Hack 350). Howard hated answering questions as much as he hated playing by the rules, so it was time to disappear again for a new official hideout.

Before he left the country he had a meeting with Jack Real in Freeport, Bahamas. Howard wanted to go over the financials for the Las Vegas operations. He had to use a magnifying glass to read the spreadsheets, or anything else, because he was severely farsighted and refused to wear glasses (Real 101). It should be noted that the Bahamas are a short jet flight from Panama.

Eyewitness accounts of Howard's departure from his fourteen-month residence at the Britannia Beach Hotel paint a picture quite contrary to the image of the articulate man in the telephone interview. On February 15, 1972, his aides took him down the back fire escape stairway on a stretcher. He was anything but robust. He was extremely fragile and didn't like to wear clothes. The aides covered him with a bathrobe (107). He was transported by stretcher to a chartered yacht, the *Cygnus*, which was standing by to sail him to Nicaragua. The skipper of the yacht, Bob Rehak, was shocked at the condition of his important passenger (Barlett and Steele 474).

"He didn't have a damn stitch on underneath, no pajamas, nothing, and that's when I noticed his long toenails. They were so long they curled up, never seen anything like that in my life. I had to look twice. Craziest thing I ever saw. He had on sandals" (Drosnin 432).

On February 15, 1972, Howard slipped quietly into Nicaragua. He didn't have a passport, since he refused to be photographed for one (Hack 351), but he had something that was actually better: the blessing and protection of Nicaraguan dictator General Anastasio Somoza. Howard decided to cement the relationship with a little gift—or bribe—to the general. He thought an expensive, rare car ought to do it. Somoza had something a little grander in mind. He wanted Howard to rescue the financially failed national airline, which Somoza happened to own, as well as take a financial stake in a few of Somoza's other failing ventures. When it started to look like he was going to be asked to prop up Nicaragua's entire industrial sector, the Central American country began to seem less attractive to Howard.

His stay in Nicaragua was limited to twenty-five days, but before he left, he came out of hiding, accompanied by aide George Francom, to meet with General Somoza and United States Ambassador Turner Shelton. The meeting was held on Howard's turf, a Grumman Gulfstream II jet aircraft (Barlett and Steele 475). It should be pointed out that Nicaragua is just over an hour's flight from Panama. According to Shelton and Somoza, the men had quite a good time. They reported that they were truly impressed with what a fine, articulate man Howard was. He was charming and mannerly, with a firm handshake at the beginning and end of the meeting (Real 109). When Ambassador Shelton met with the media later, he recounted that Howard had short hair and a short, Van Dyke beard. The whole picture in no way matched the description of the Howard that left Paradise Island a month before (Barlett and Steele 476).

As long as Howard was out of his supposed sick bed, he decided to continue his journey and fly from Nicaragua to Vancouver, British Columbia, Canada. He marched into the Bayshore Inn unassisted and with a confident stride and was recognized by a number of surprised guests. In fact, he lingered in the lobby while the hotel guests watched him. As he arrived in the Penthouse, he watched a seaplane land in the harbor (Drosnin 433). Once again, this was a far cry from the Howard with the long, curling toenails that was carried out of the Britannia Beach Hotel the previous month.

Tourism wasn't all that was on Howard's mind in Vancouver. He had an important appointment with LaVane Forsythe in August. Forsythe was the aide who stood guard in the parking lot at the Desert Inn in 1970, when Howard made his escape to the Bahamas. Howard wanted Forsythe to do him a favor. Howard produced a brown envelope that he said contained the instructions he wanted followed upon his death. He made it quite clear that he had no intention of departing the firmament soon; in fact, he intended to stay around for a while, but someone had to hang on to this document. Howard indicated that the will had been in the hands of someone else until recently, but the man no longer wanted the responsibility. Howard asked if Forsythe would be willing to take over the role of guardian of his testament. Forsythe agreed. The job came with one more strange responsibility. Upon Howard's death, Forsythe was to deliver the will to one Melvin Dummar in Willard, Utah (Magnesen 73–5).

Having dealt with the distribution of his wealth after his death, Howard now needed to skip town to avoid distributing some of it during his life. The clock was ticking down on the 180-day grace period before he would be subject to Canadian income tax, which was at an even higher rate than the taxes he was dodging in the States. On August 29, 1972, Howard saved his assets by moving to the Intercontinental Hotel in Managua, Nicaragua (Real 109).

Howard's desire to keep his money out of the hands of the taxmen was not entirely a matter of principle. He also had a serious potential financial crisis looming in the near future, and he didn't have the money to cover his liability. The TWA dispute had been plodding its way through the courts since the early 1960s. Howard purchased a 21 percent stake in the company in 1939 and boosted his holdings to 78 percent in 1940 (Brown 128). A man like Howard doesn't spend that kind of money for something if he doesn't intend to fiddle around with it, and fiddle he did. Unfortunately, the TWA

Board didn't like his tune, and they sued him for mismanagement, seeking $483 million in damages. Howard fought back, and the battle raged on for years, eventually involving fifteen corporations and fifty-six lawyers. Howard liquidated his TWA holdings in 1966 for $546 million, but the legal battle continued (Barlett and Steele 274). In a classic example of being his own worst enemy, Howard refused to appear in court, even though his attorney, Chester Davis, felt that he stood a good chance of winning the suit if he would just show up. This stubbornness resulted in a judgment against him on February 14, 1970, with triple damages levied for failure to appear in court. Hughes's response was typical. He appealed, all the way to the Supreme Court.

With the very real possibility of receiving a massive financial judgment against him in a matter of months, Howard had a problem that a fast flight out of the country couldn't fix. TWA was going to want its money, and the company wasn't going to take an I.O.U. If Howard was to avoid an even greater financial nightmare, he was going to have to come up with some cash, and the only way to do that was to sell something. Selling Hughes Aircraft Company wasn't an option, since he already gifted it to the Howard Hughes Medical Institute in Maryland and Miami. That left him with one choice; he had to sell the Hughes Tool Company, the business started by his father in 1909 and the springboard that launched all his other ventures. It was no easy decision, but in the end, it was no decision at all. It had to be done.

Howard selected the Merrill Lynch brokerage firm to take Hughes Tool public, and on September 25, 1972, a Mr. Sedlmayr and a Mr. Ivey represented the firm in a meeting with Howard in Managua, Nicaragua. They later reported that Howard looked very much like the Howard of days past, with just a touch of gray in his hair and a closely cropped Van Dyke beard on his chin. Howard scheduled the meeting at a time that was convenient for him, 4:00 a.m. (Barlett and Steele 480). As a result, on December 7, 1972, during normal people's business hours, the privately held Hughes Tool Company became the publicly held Hughes Tool Company in a sale that raised $150 million. Howard's assets, including his Las Vegas hotel properties, KLAS-TV, Hughes Air West, Hughes Helicopters and his mining and real estate investments were grouped in a holding company that was named the Summa

Corporation (Real 114). From this point forward, anyone who had a dispute with Howard would have to go after him through Summa.

In a bitter irony, just twenty-seven days after Howard sold his company to pay the TWA judgment, it was thrown out by the United States Supreme Court. Howard caved in to twelve years of litigation just four weeks early (114).

The TWA victory put Howard's name in the news again, but he was also connected to another big news story where his name was apparently suppressed. On June 17, 1972, several unlucky burglars broke into the Democratic Party offices in the Watergate Hotel in Washington, D.C. Richard Nixon was up for reelection to the presidency, and the group was rummaging through the files to see what they could find in the way of offensive or defensive weapons in the campaign against Democrat George McGovern. More importantly, Nixon's staff had gotten word that Democratic Party operative, Larry O'Brien, had some very damaging information. He supposedly knew that Nixon had received illicit packages containing a significant amount of money from a supporter, and the supporter expected something in return. They needed access to O'Brien's files to see how bad the trouble could be. If the news of the financial shenanigans got out, it could be fatal for the president's reelection campaign. It wouldn't be good news for the person who was slipping him the money, either. The generous supporter was Howard Hughes.

Among their other connections, G. Gordon Liddy and E. Howard Hunt, who were involved with the break-in, turned out to be on the payroll of Robert Bennett, who was on the payroll of Howard Hughes (Drosnin 429). This would shock no one, since Hughes had long supported Nixon. As the investigation progressed on the break-in, it was discovered that President Nixon recorded all of the conversations held in his office. This fact was of particular interest to investigators who wanted to know what Nixon and his associates were discussing about the crime. One recording, specifically on June 20, 1972, drew special interest. Eighteen-and-a-half minutes of it was erased accidentally, according to Nixon's secretary, but few believed this was the truth. Nixon aide, H.R. Haldeman later said the erased portion of the tape dealt with Howard's involvement in the fiasco (430).

As if taxes, litigation, and political intrigue weren't enough, Mother Nature stepped up to the mound and threw Howard another curve. On Saturday, December 23, 1972, a devastating magnitude 6.2 earthquake struck Managua, leaving about 5,000 dead and 20,000 injured. Tens of thousands of structures collapsed leaving over 200,000 people homeless. Howard had to choose which disaster he wanted to be in, natural or financial. He chose to flee first to Fort Lauderdale, Florida, and the potential grasp of the taxman.

On his sixty-seventh birthday, December 24, 1972, Howard set foot on American soil for the first time in two years. Government agents were there ready to extend a welcoming hand. Unfortunately, the hand held a subpoena for tax evasion for the millions of dollars the government claimed he owed. Hughes's aides attempted to block IRS and Customs Agents from boarding the jet, but eventually relented. The agents were stunned when they met the shrewd tycoon in person. They found a painfully thin man with a flowing gray beard and long, greasy hair tumbling below a black hat that was pulled tightly over his ears (Magnesen 40).

"He was emaciated, filthy, and unkempt, like a derelict. He could barely state his own name," one agent reported (40). Serving any legal document on the shell of a man was clearly a waste of time and would never hold up in court. The agents backed off. Shortly after the bizarre encounter, the customs forms were properly stamped and Howard was cleared. Then, as quickly as he had arrived, Howard was gone again. Next stop, London.

Notes

Barlett, Donald, L., and James B. Steele. *Howard Hughes: His Life and Madness*. New York: W.W. Norton, and Company, 1979.

Brown, Peter Harry, and Pat H. Broeske. *Howard Hughes: The Untold Story*. Cambridge, MA: De Capo Press, 2004.

Drosnin, Michael. *Citizen Hughes*. New York: Broadway Books, 1985.

Hack, Richard. *Hughes: The Private Diaries, Memos and Letters*. Beverly Hills, CA: New Millennium Press, 2001.

Magnesen, Gary. *The Investigation*. Fort Lee, NJ: Barricade Books, 2005.

Real, Jack. *The Asylum of Howard Hughes*. Bloomington, IN: Xlibris Corporation, 2003.

Rhoden, Harold. *High Stakes*. New York: Crown Publishers, Inc., 1980.

EIGHT

THE THEORY

By now it should be apparent the only thing clear about the latter years of Howard Hughes's life is that nothing is clear at all. There is no way to avoid facing the fact that the historical record of his life, from the 1960s on, is hopelessly contradictory.

The months from January 1972 through August 1973 stand out as a crystal clear indicator that there had to be more than one Howard Hughes. His friend of many years, Jack Real, met with him in the early part of 1973 to discuss financial issues and reported that he was fine, except for normal signs of aging like his eyesight. Howard refuted the Clifford Irving scam, supposedly from the Bahamas, and people who knew him positively identified the voice and speech mannerisms as those of Howard. Shortly thereafter, an emaciated "Howard" was removed by the Mormon aides from the Bahamas by ship. The captain remarked on his barely coherent, drugged condition and his long, curling toenails. He was taken to Nicaragua where he remained reclusive for twenty-five days until a well-groomed, articulate Howard scheduled a middle-of-the-night meeting with General Somoza and Ambassador Shelton in a private jet aircraft in Managua. Mr. Hughes then flew to Vancouver where he was seen entering a hotel under his own power. In September, back in Managua, Howard arranged the sale of the Hughes Tool Company with Merrill Lynch brokers at a 4:00 a.m. meeting. Interesting that they reported the recluse to be "remarkably unchanged" from how he looked fifteen years earlier. Howard then finished up the year by traveling from Nicaragua to Miami, where he arrived as an emaciated, drugged, incoherent shell of a person with long, curling toenails who was so pitiful the United States Government allowed him to continue on to London, despite the tax hold they intended to put on him. When one can grow, cut, and re-grow four-inch toenails in one year, and inspire pity from the United States Internal Revenue Service, something is clearly amiss.

It should also be noted that "Howard" fell in London in August 1973. Attending physicians reported his muscles and organs were atrophied and barely functioning, and his teeth were rotting away. Even if they were totally concentrating on their commissions, the Merrill Lynch brokers would have noticed something like that in their meeting several months earlier.

From 1969 to 1976, moving from location to location, hotel to hotel, there are numerous descriptions of a 100-pound, long-haired, long-toenailed, drugged Howard, interspersed with stories of business meetings with the articulate, commanding Howard who forced his will on several industries as he expanded the Hughes Empire. So, what is the truth?

For all of his lying, cheating, and "biographical" shenanigans, Clifford Irving might have gotten part of it right. He took the risk of committing his literary fraud because he believed Howard Hughes was dead or, possibly, replaced by a stand-in. We now know Howard wasn't dead when Irving wrote his book, but the idea of a Howard Hughes stand-in fits in very well with the documented facts.

The bon vivant, Hollywood mogul, and airplane daredevil Howard Hughes of the 1920s and 1930s slowly began to withdraw from society in the 1940s. Meetings managing his vast financial empire gradually began to be conducted in nondescript sedans or out-of-the way places in the middle of the night, instead of the boardrooms and offices of power his business peers coveted. Eventually, the face-to-face meetings all but ceased and were replaced by scraps from legal pads delivered by a staff of trusted Mormon aides. The face that was recognized around the world was last photographed with Howard's consent in 1952. He wanted to be left alone.

It's not easy to be left alone when a person is making multimillion-dollar business deals, particularly if he has an unfortunate tendency to annoy people with those deals. Irritating the Internal Revenue Service by refusing to pay his taxes was another surefire way to ensure that his peace and quiet didn't last long. Howard wanted to run his life by his rules, but that didn't work. His life touched too many other people, too many other institutions, and too many other sets of rules. His business intransigence and desire for personal solitude were mutually incompatible.

Howard may have been strange, but he clearly wasn't stupid. He knew hiding might keep people from finding him, but it certainly wouldn't keep them from hunting him. A much better solution to his problem would be to hide, while giving the legion of process servers, lawyers, and litigants a substitute Howard to chase. To make their efforts as futile as possible, the ideal candidate for the fake Howard should be certifiably mentally incompetent. That way, even if they got to him, what could they hope to legally accomplish? While his tormentors tried to figure out that puzzle, the real Howard could live in relative peace and continue to do business through his organization of Mormon aides, who were already central to the operation of the Hughes Empire.

This chapter is entitled "The Theory" because that is exactly what it is, a theory, although we obtained new information after the publication of the first edition of this book that clearly supports it. This second edition has integrated much of that new evidence. The facts dictate that there must be at least two Howard Hughes characters. He simply couldn't transform himself from the drug-addled, ninety-pound, living corpse to the articulate, healthy businessman in a matter of weeks and do it repeatedly. We believe that it was the real Howard who installed himself on the entire ninth floor of the Desert Inn Hotel in 1966. After that, it gets murky. Was the man seen by tourists and locals alike as he walked through the casinos in his distinctively sloppy attire the real Howard or a stand-in? Howard's Las Vegas holdings increased during this period, but so did his legal and tax problems. As the problems increased, his sightings diminished and were replaced by rumors of his insanity. Word got out that the occupant of the ninth floor of the hotel was a drug-addicted madman. Was that the truth, a ruse to keep lawyers at bay, or maybe even an opportunity for Howard to exit his own empire and live his final years in peace?

If one speculates Howard needed a drug-addicted madman to be his stand-in, Las Vegas was probably as good a place as any to find one in the 1960s. Less than twenty years since being a mere speck in the Nevada desert, the city became synonymous with glamour, excitement, and gambling. Whatever corruption that reputation wouldn't attract on its own, the mob supplied through their numerous illegal business ventures. The affluent were attracted to Vegas by the glitz. The desperate and degenerate were attracted by everything else. If one needed to find a homeless derelict without friends or family, a highly skilled and motivated Mormon aide probably wouldn't have any trouble finding one. Easier still, what if one of the Hughes body doubles became disabled and/or drug addicted? More on that later.

The descriptions of the "Howard" who was transported from the Desert Inn in the middle of the night to the Bahamas and on to Nicaragua through Miami all say that the man was poorly cared for. He was kept alive, but not much more. He was malnourished and barely clothed. If this was the real Howard, would his trusted aides who had been with him for years allow him to be in this condition? He was drugged nearly senseless, yet Dr. Crane stated in 1974, when he attended to the man, he did not actually have a medical need for the medications that he was taking. He kept himself drugged, or more likely, he was kept drugged senseless because he was easier to control that way and couldn't ruin the arrangement by deciding to leave or utter a spontaneous statement of truth on those few occasions when he was exposed to outsiders. To make the stand-in scheme work, the fake Howard had to clearly be mentally incompetent and controllable.

If the stand-in was the occupant of the official Hughes residence, where was Howard? Panama, Arizona, and Alabama, perhaps? The evidence leads in that direction as the saga of Howard gets stranger and stranger.

The man who Eva fell in love with and married identified himself as Verner Dale Nicely. He was a man from Ohio who led an average life until World War II, when he enlisted in the United States Army Air Corps. He became an aviation mechanic, married, had children, and left the Air Force in 1955. He moved to Panama, divorced, and began to have sporadic contact with his family. After 1967, before he dropped from sight, he told his son he was assisting on a secret antidrug mission in Central and South America for the CIA. His family never heard from him again. Eva gave Nik's death certificate to Mark. Sometime later, Mark showed it to Gary Nicely, Verner's son, and Gary pointed out it listed his father's birthplace as Texas, when he had, in fact, been born in Ohio.

In October 1969, Eva met Verner Nicely, who referred to himself as Nik. He had grown five inches since he left on his CIA mission two years before, changed his eye and hair color, and forgotten he was previously married. He acquired a staff of aides, a private office apartment to meet with them, and an aircraft maintenance supervisor's job that had no apparent job site or regular job hours. He also was doing very well for himself, since he apparently had unlimited money, was on a first name relationship with high-ranking military officers, and had frequent meetings on yachts. He eventually admitted Verner Nicely wasn't his real name, but he couldn't tell her who he was, because that would be "dangerous" for her. Soon, he would have to give up the mystery.

NINE

THE DRUGGIE DERELICT AND THE ARTICULATE AIRMAN

Florida, 2002

Mark wondered how he might describe his feelings if asked. But how can you explain the feeling of listening to a story that sounds like a complete fantasy, yet hearing it with such clarity and conviction you can't ignore it? Eva's story was unbelievable at first, but she was as credible a storyteller as Mark had ever heard. She was definite about dates and places and unshakably consistent when he would ask her questions about statements that she made earlier. If Mark were a trial lawyer, she would be his ideal witness.

"You know, Eva, I spent thirty-five years in the Air Force, I know a little about Howard Hughes. You don't spend that much time in aviation without knowing a thing or two about a man who had such an impact on aircraft technology and the industry."

"Well, you can certainly see the similarities, then, can't you?"

Mark nodded slowly, "I have to say, I am intrigued. I think, with a bit of research, that we might be able to corroborate these stories."

As it turned out, that was a very naïve assumption, but he was eager to ask Eva more questions. She was just as eager to answer, as though a great burden had been lifted from her. Maybe it was, but the burden was now transferred to Mark.

As they drove from Florida Highway 83 onto Highway 2, heading toward Geneva, Alabama, the oppressive heat and 90 percent humidity escaped Mark's notice, as the strange story forced everything else from his consciousness. Mark pushed Eva for details about everything. She didn't hesitate to answer.

"Now, how long did you and Nik stay in Arizona?"

Arizona, 1973

After several months of living alone in an apartment in Prescott, Arizona, while Nik was at the Veterans Administration Hospital, Eva and Nik moved to a horse ranch in Camp Verde, Arizona before Christmas. The place was called Myer's Ranch, and the couple rented a small house on the property. Nik agreed to be a caretaker for the property when Mr. Myer was away, and the arrangement seemed to suit all of them well. Mr. Myer, in his late fifties, spent quite a bit of time operating the Valley View Restaurant, which he opened in Camp Verde. Eva and Nik spent a substantial amount of time together, although Nik still made frequent trips to the Veterans Hospital at Prescott. As was the case in their relationship from day one, they were never truly alone. One night, the tranquility of their Arizona hideaway was shaken by a loud crashing sound coming from their chicken coop. Nik's cadre of aides decided to venture on its roof for some reason, and the aging wood gave way. Eva was startled, and the chickens let it be known they weren't too happy, either. Eva ran to the window, which drew a sharp rebuke from Nik. "Damn fool! Get away from that window!" he yelled at her. Eva stepped aside, and Nik went out to handle the matter.

The remoteness of living on a horse ranch in Camp Verde probably brought back memories of when Howard and Billie Dove, using false names, resided in a shed, dirt floor and all, working as farmhands in a small community in southern Nevada in 1929.

Eva found their conversations were very much the same as before she left him. If he didn't hear something she said correctly, he would never tell her that he didn't hear her. Instead, he would leap to the conclusion she said something he didn't like, and an argument would ensue. These storms would eventually blow over, while the whispered conversations with the aides over the phone or in person were as mysterious as ever.

Everything with Nik was an adventure. The two of them decided they liked Arizona well enough to buy a place of their own, so they looked at property. As always, Eva drove, and Nik navigated. When Nik wanted to go somewhere, the quality of the road wasn't up for discussion. Consequently, Nik led Eva through canyons and up mountain roads that scared her half to death. She could not stand driving up the side of a cliff, but lumbering up a mountain on a narrow mining road, inches from a steep drop-off meant nothing to Nik. In fact, he got a kick out of the danger. Nik would laugh as he watched Eva drive nervously. Eva, on the other hand, had a much better developed sense of her own mortality. She pled with him to find routes that were less risky, but as always, he was not to be argued with. When these ordeals passed, and Eva's color returned, she thanked God for sending her guardian angels, since she was positive she didn't do the driving alone.

"I'll never understand how any human being could not possibly be afraid of heights," she told Mark. She believed that acrophobia, under these circumstances, was a tendency of a normal person; whereas, the opposite would indicate an abnormality. Nik would probably prefer to be thought of as fearless, rather than abnormal, but whatever the name for it, he did not hesitate when it came to climbing to the most dangerous vistas.

Despite the white-knuckle drives, Eva had to admit that Nik led her to some of the most beautiful scenery she ever saw. They explored Sedona, Jerome, and Copper Canyon, and when they were at the Grand Canyon, with Eva standing safely away from the edge, Nik told her he flew through the massive canyon in one of his airplanes with a passenger on board when he was young. Based on his antics throughout the trip, Eva didn't doubt him one bit. Nik was always interested in the mining towns and was very knowledgeable about the operations. In the picturesque town of Jerome, which bravely clutches a mountainside, they explored some local mines, and Eva got a mini-lesson about the mining industry. This reminded her of something Nik said previously, during an unguarded moment.

She asked, "Didn't you buy mines in Nevada?"

"They were a mistake," he said with a frown, "and you wouldn't want to live there."

One of the highlights of the trip was a stay at Oak Creek Canyon in the beautiful, red rock area of Sedona, Arizona. This was a treat for the nature lovers, since the area blended mountains and forests, and there was plenty of scenery to enjoy. This was a peaceful and romantic change from the life-threatening mountain drives.

For all of the intellect and love he displayed, Nik's other nature, the unstable one, was never far from the surface. The personality changes were sudden and unmotivated. One of his milder quirks consisted of repeating the same statements over and over again, apparently for emphasis. Other reactions were more dramatic. Once, while on the Camp Verde property, Nik started choking Eva in a fit of rage. Shocked and terrified, she began to scream. This made Nik all the more violent, and he choked her even harder. Fortunately, seconds after she began screaming, they heard the sounds of footsteps running across the roof toward the bedroom side of the house. The ever-present aides were on their way. This seemed to shock Nik back to his senses, and he let her go. Another time, she found a picture of an older woman who she thought might be his beloved grandmother. When she showed it to him, he became violently angry and jerked it away from her. She never saw it again. This was clearly no way to live.

Periodically, over the thirty-one years of their marriage, Eva needed to escape the craziness. The choking incident was frightening, and she had no intention of being victimized by this Jekyll and Hyde character. It happened that her mother was ill, so Eva packed up her eight-month old GMC long-bed pickup truck, and left Camp Verde in early June 1973 for the relatively short trip to Montgomery, Alabama. As it turned out, the trip wasn't so short after all. The truck was a lemon and kept breaking down with engine problems, so the trip ended up taking ten days. Eva hadn't planned on a trip of this length and hadn't brought along enough money for that many nights of accommodations. Her anxiety about her marriage and concern for her mother were now compounded by the aggravation of having to spend several unplanned nights at the cheapest place available, the KOA campgrounds.

In the end, the trip was worth it to her. On August 9, 1973, her mother passed away at the age of ninety, and Eva was grateful to be with her at the end. Her mother was a remarkable woman, and Eva loved her very much. There was no price too high to pay to spend those last days with her.

After her mother's funeral, Eva knew she didn't want to return to Arizona and Nik. She always intended to move to her property on the island of St. Eustatius, someday. With Nik's erratic behavior, "someday" had come a bit sooner than expected. After settling her mother's affairs, she packed her belongings and immediately set out to the island, remaining there for the next eight months. She was in love with the island lifestyle and would have been perfectly happy to live out her retirement there. Her property could be described as rustic, at best. The accommodations consisted of a one-room cabin in an undeveloped area. She tried to find someone to build a real house for her but was unsuccessful. Communication with Nik was rare during this period, and she had no intention of returning to him. She was not about to be an abused wife, and she had no desire to live with a man who was half crazy. There was only one small problem: she was still in love with the half of him that wasn't crazy.

London, 1973

In early 1973, the mystifying Mr. Hughes staged another of his remarkable, miracle recoveries. He left Miami in December 1972 as a barely coherent, drugged, sack of skin and bones with long curling fingernails and toenails. By February 1973, Howard was again ready to take on all comers. The speed of his recovery was probably second only to the Resurrection of Jesus.

The Clifford Irving hoax and the subsequent reemergence of Howard in the telephone interview piqued the interest of millions of people. Among them were Nevada Governor Mike O'Callahan and Nevada Gaming Control Board Chairman Phillip Hannifin. Howard acquired vast holdings of casino properties and gambling licenses. With all of the questions about the authenticity of Howard's signatures and the rumors of his mental incompetence, O'Callahan and Hannifin demanded a face-to-face meeting with Howard to see who was really running the show (Barlett and Steele 488). Howard was the undisputed champion when it came to dodging a meeting or personal appearance, but he apparently felt this one was necessary. He acquiesced. He summoned aide Bill Gay and attorney Chester Davis to London to be present when he met with the Nevada officials. Interestingly, Gay had not seen Howard face-to-face since 1958, and after this conference he would never see him again (Real 72). Davis had been Howard's attorney for twelve years and had never met him in person (129).

The meeting was set for March 18, 1973. Governor O'Callahan and Mr. Hannifin flew to London and joined Howard, Gay, and Davis to sort out exactly what was going on in the Hughes operation in Nevada. They found Howard to be a "commanding personality" who knew exactly what was going on with his gambling properties and left them with no doubt that he was firmly in control of his empire (Barlett and Steele 489). He was emphatic about his intentions. When he wanted to stress a point, his voice rose, and he repeated his statements over and over (489). As with President Somoza and Ambassador Shelton a year before, they found Howard to be a fine, articulate, and charming man (Real 130). They were further encouraged when he told them he wanted to return to Nevada (129). With their questions answered, the matter was closed, and they returned home.

Significantly, this meeting occurred at a time when Nik was in and out of the Veterans Hospital at Prescott, so disappearing for a period of several days without his actual whereabouts being known was a fairly simple accomplishment, particularly with his jet aircraft on twenty-four hour standby.

Lockheed executive Jack Real was a long-time friend of Howard's. In fact, he may have been his only close friend. Howard asked him to join the Hughes organization in May 1971, and they soon reestablished the warm relationship they shared when their aviation interests intersected many years before. Real had the distinction of being virtually the only individual outside of aides and physicians to have regular contact with Howard. He apparently wanted Jack to wield a significant amount of power in the organization, a desire not necessarily shared by his aides who reported to Bill Gay, and communicated with Howard by telephone or notes written on legal pads. Jack Real saw Howard in person.

Real hadn't seen Howard for a number of years until this period. Real reported it was at this point that he became aware of the true extent of Howard's narcotics problem (Real 157). This statement may have been his part in keeping up the image of the mentally incompetent and unprosecutable, derelict character. However, it is equally possible Real was being perfectly honest. Howard had never been properly weaned from narcotics after his near fatal crash in the 1940s, so it is quite likely his drug usage could have increased with a growing addiction.

Whatever the state of Howard's health and drug dependency, it hadn't curbed his desire to fly. On March 21 and again on March 29, Jack Real met with Howard in Suite 901 of the Inn on the Park to set up a program of flying. The release from the burden of the TWA judgment seemed to breathe a new spark of life into him. Flying was the one thing that was meaningful in his life, and his mind became sharper and a bit of humor crept into his personality when he took the controls of any aircraft. With Real's assistance, Howard flew on at least three occasions in England: June 10 and 27, and July 17, 1973 (Real 139-51).

According to Real, Howard's return to the skies was a component of a much larger issue. He considered replacing the Fokker F-27, short range, turboprop aircraft at Hughes Air West Airlines with the British Hawker Siddeley HS-748 aircraft. He wanted to lease an HS-748 and flight test it for the airline and himself. This presented a major problem, since Howard did not have a valid pilot's license. He could neither renew his American Federal Aviation Authority license nor apply for a British license without being photographed, which he refused to do. Tony Blackman, chief flight test engineer for Hawker Siddeley, came up with the solution. The HS-748's flight manual required two pilots to fly but said nothing about both pilots being licensed. Howard was a pilot by anyone's standards, and Tony was a pilot with a valid license. The problem was solved, and Howard was now Blackman's copilot, or vice versa (134).

Sunday, June 10, 1973, was one of those rainless summer days in England, when the beauty of the countryside is particularly apparent. Tony Blackman was at home engaging in the popular British hobby of gardening, when the call came that Howard wanted to fly. Right now. The accommodating Blackman climbed into his personal de Havilland Dove light aircraft and flew down to the Hawker Siddeley Aerodrome at Hatfield to meet Howard, Jack Real, and Hughes's aide Levar Mylar. Howard's leased Daimler automobile was out at the time, so George Francom rented a Rolls Royce from an agency, which sounded elegant but turned out to be decades old and a borderline wreck, for transportation to Hatfield Airport and Howard's long-awaited adventure (139–40).

For the better part of three hours and ten minutes, Howard took the controls for his first experience in the pilot's seat in thirteen years. He flew to the Hawker Siddeley Aerodrome at Bitteswell, about forty miles away, and performed a number of touch-and-go landings and takeoffs. This is not surprising for a man with Howard's experience, but it is shocking for a man who has been repeatedly described as mentally and physically incompetent.

The plan for the second flight was to cross the English Channel to Ostend, Belgium, make sure the authorities knew Howard was on the plane, and return to England. Mother Nature does not always go along with the plans of men, and the weather in England on June 27 was particularly foul, with the visibility down to virtually nothing. Things were further complicated because Howard didn't want to fly in his own plane; he wanted to keep it new. They had to charter the only HS-748 available, which was very inconveniently located in France. The charter craft was late, and the whole operation had to be postponed twelve hours. Blackman wanted to call it off completely because of the weather, but Howard refused. Against his better judgment, Blackman took off to make a scheduled stop at Stansted, England, where visibility was zero. He found the runway with the aid of the airplane's Instrument Landing System (ILS) and autopilot, and to Howard's amazement, the aircraft came out of the fog perfectly positioned on the runway (145–49).

Feeling lucky that they had gotten this far, Blackman made another appeal to common sense and requested they cease tempting fate in the inclement weather. Howard again refused. Blackman demanded a back-up pilot fly in the second seat instead of Howard, and they were off to Belgium. Once there, Blackman performed a touch-and-go landing and declared a hydraulic emergency. The "emergency" was logged by the tower, thus proving that the plane with Howard on it had actually been in Belgium and that Howard had left the U.K. for a period of time, resetting the clock on his allowed stay in England. The return to Stansted was uneventful with the weather less miserable when they landed at dawn. When the whole ordeal was over, Howard admitted it was the worst weather in which he had ever flown.

Satisfied with the performance of the HS-748, Howard next set his sights on a nine-seat business jet, the Hawker Siddeley HS-125. Jack Real arranged for a low hour aircraft, and Tony Blackman was once again engaged to be Howard's co-pilot. The flight took place on July 17, 1973. Real reported that Howard was particularly happy and conversant during the flight. He made a number of touch-and-go landings and takeoffs and generally enjoyed himself thoroughly (150–52). The charming Howard appeared when he had to, or when he was genuinely happy, as he appeared to be then. Blackman, despite some of the unnecessary thrills, was pleased with his experience with Howard. He said he couldn't get over what an average, down-to-earth guy he was (141). Howard, the pilot, was back.

By August 1973, Howard decided he wanted to return to Nevada and begin flying every day. Real dutifully telephoned Howard's attorney Chester Davis to make the arrangements and received a discouraging reply. "Tell Howard that when he left, he had twenty lawsuits against him in the United States. Now he has forty lawsuits. I don't know if he will ever be able to come back" (160–61).

It's true lawsuits seemed to be as integral a part of Howard's life as breathing. For as pleasant as this escape to London seemed to have been, no period of Howard's life would be complete without a certain amount of legal drama. In April and May 1973, word got out about another contribution from Howard to his old pal, Richard Nixon. It seems that the president agreed to allow a Hughes Air West takeover that was legally questionable. The approval was granted on the same day Howard agreed to give the president a $100,000 campaign contribution. Many people remarked on this interesting coincidence!

Additionally, charges of fraud and stock manipulation were brought against Howard by a Las Vegas grand jury, further putting him under scrutiny. The Watergate Scandal heat remained on Nixon as well. As difficult questions continued to be directed at the president, he responded with at least the illusion of a political housecleaning by firing aides, H.R. Halderman and John Erlichman in April. This would turn out to be too little too late.

Still, according to Jack Real, the summer of 1973 was most enjoyable for Howard. In fact, he felt it was the best he experienced in years. The escape from the TWA mess and the ability to take to the skies relaxed him and kindled a desire to resume his once-active life with an optimism that had been missing.

Real felt Howard "had come back to living," which may have been true, but as one Howard was coming back to life, the other was dangerously close to departing it.

The Howard who left Miami in December as a drug-addicted derelict and supposedly made a total recovery to become the articulate Howard by February, was having another health crisis. On August 9, 1973, "Howard II," the derelict, the stand-in, fell in the London hotel, broke his hip, and was carted off to a local hospital in pathetic condition. His muscles and organs were barely functioning. He was attended to by Dr. William Young who reported that "Howard's" skin had a parchment-like quality, he was emaciated, and he had long fingernails and toenails. In case anyone didn't get the picture, he likened Howard to "a malnourished prisoner of war" (Barlett and Steele 492). This is clearly not the type of individual one would have wanted to see at the controls of a jet aircraft only a month before.

The stand-in's condition was not just bad, it was shockingly bad. Whatever rumors the doctors may have heard about the reclusive eccentric, coming face-to-face with a man in this condition, a man with supposedly unlimited means, was much more than the doctors were prepared for. He was dehydrated and suffering from malnutrition. Dr. Wilbur Thain actually checked into a room in the hospital to be near him around the clock. Dr. Robinson ordered a complete battery of physical examinations and tests, which yielded the diagnosis that this man's body was barely functioning. In addition to the physical diagnosis, Dr. Raymond Fowler determined the man was totally mentally incompetent.

The stand-in survived, and on December 20, 1973, he was loaded into an airplane and transported to the Xanadu Princess Hotel in the Bahamas, where he could remain safe from the American authorities, lawyers, and the stack of nasty legal problems that dogged Howard (Drosnin 447). Better yet, he was now officially certified to be physically and mentally incompetent.

It's clear that Jack Real was as loyal to his friend in death as he had been in life. Based on what he wrote in his book, it would be virtually impossible for him not to know about the stand-in and we believe he likely knew of Eva as well. He recalls Howard's "hearty laugh" when he greeted him in Freeport, Bahamas to discuss business (101), yet witnesses clearly describe an emaciated, incoherent Howard who is transported from the island shortly thereafter. Real reports an active and chatty Howard who gleefully pilots borrowed aircraft in England, but during the same period, attending doctors in London describe a Howard that appears near death's door. Could Howard have kept this deception from his best friend? Maybe. Would he? Unlikely.

Notes

Barlett, Donald, L., and James B. Steele. *Howard Hughes: His Life and Madness.* New York: W.W. Norton, and Company, 1979.

Drosnin, Michael. *Citizen Hughes.* New York: Broadway Books, 1985.

Real, Jack. *The Asylum of Howard Hughes.* Bloomington, IN: Xlibris Corporation, 2003.

TEN

NIK, EVA, AND THE RED HOUSE

Alabama, 2002

Mark registered the sign ahead as they sped down Highway 27: Geneva, Alabama.

Eva had gone quiet and Mark was trying to be patient, to give her time. He could tell that, even after all these years, the wounds of Nik's rejection and abuse still pained Eva.

"He was . . . such a complicated man, Mark. Wonderful and sometimes terrible."

Her voice was laced with pain, and when Mark chanced a look at her, he could see why she had gone quiet. It was clear this wasn't her favorite part of the story. No one likes to be rejected, particularly by her spouse.

"In the end, I couldn't stay away. I tried to make things work, so I moved back, to be closer to Nik . . . those were the worst days, because he didn't care. He just kept asking me to stay away. But, what could I do? I did as he asked."

Mark looked Eva's way again and was surprised to see a little smile lighting her face. "What is it?"

"Oh, I was just going to say, in typical Nik fashion, when he did come around, he was all charm again. I never could resist that man's charm. I'll never forget what he said . . . 'Come back, little bird. You have flown away. Let's get back together again.'"

Arizona to Alabama, 1974

By this stage of the marriage, Eva knew this seemingly heartfelt plea for forgiveness didn't necessarily mean everything was going to be cozy from that point on. She was a smart woman, and she had been down this road before. This was a question of some soul searching and the weighing of the many good things in the marriage against the moments of unspeakable coldness and hostility. Would the love overcome the pain? She was not a naïve, young girl who could be swayed by a few emotional words, so she took the time to listen to her intellect as well as her heart. They had been separated most of the time since June 1973, and a little more time wouldn't hurt. Nik had to wait for his answer until February 1974. She took a deep breath and then gave him another chance.

Eva returned to the ranch in Camp Verde, Arizona in April 1974 with a few belongings and a hopeful, if cautious, spirit. She wanted the marriage to work, but she didn't intend to allow him to toss her love aside like an old sweater, only retrieving it when he felt the chill of loneliness. Nik was going to have to be a husband this time, not a master.

Eva had barely unpacked when the first problem arose, but this time she wasn't the victim. The Camp Verde property was an old horse ranch, and the rural postal delivery didn't come to the house. This was fine with Nik, who acquired a bicycle and enjoyed taking a daily one-mile ride to town in the Arizona sun to pick up the mail. One day, a group of men flagged him down, and he stopped to see what they wanted. Unfortunately, they were local robbers, and what they wanted was Nik's money. They knocked him down and struck him with a steel fence post, but he recovered enough to pick up a rock and pitch it through their car window as they made their escape. The result was some bruises and cuts on Nik's back, shoulder, and neck. The assailants didn't get far before the local authorities caught them and filed charges, but the whole unpleasant experience changed Nik's attitude about Arizona. In one of his typical emotion-fueled decisions, he determined they must get out of town right away. In fact, they left so quickly that they were gone before the attackers had a hearing. He was called back to Arizona to testify against them that summer, although Eva was never positive that is where he actually went.

By the end of April 1974, Arizona disappeared from their rearview mirror, and they entered Eva's former homeland, Alabama. Her brother, Thomas, owned a red-framed house in Pike County, just west of Troy, and he was happy to let them live there for a while. Eva was happy to be with family; her brother Everis lived just down the road, and Nik was happy because there was an abandoned home just across the highway and west of their house that the aides could use as an office.

As usual, he wasn't very forthcoming with the information about the aides being present, but the activity at the once-empty structure was hard to miss. When Eva saw that a nondescript black sedan was suddenly parked there all of the time, like the many others she'd seen around Nik for years, she knew what was going on. Nik finally admitted that his aides were using the property as a communications center from which to conduct his business. Eva's brother Everis had his eyes open, too. He was no man's fool, and after trying to follow Nik and the aides into the woods where they met a few times, he thought he had the whole thing figured out. Obviously, they were making moonshine out there and selling it in plastic water bottles! When word of his "business" got back to Nik, he actually laughed out loud. Aside from the general absurdity of the idea, Nik didn't even drink!

After they stayed a few weeks, Eva convinced Nik that they should move to the West Indies to Eva's St. Eustatius property. He seemed agreeable enough about the plan, but suggested Eva travel first, while he cleared up some business. By May, Eva was back on her island. Predictably, Nik told her he would be delayed following her, then further delayed. Finally he said, "I will take care of the place while you are gone." She later learned that Nik had sent an aide or two to the island as something of an advance party, and they reported back to him that the locale was too primitive a location from which to do business, but that was unknown to Eva at the time. All she knew was that she was alone again until September.

Red house located west of Troy, Alabama, on Highway 29.

Nik even went to the trouble to obtain a passport, sort of. He always refused to be photographed, so it wasn't entirely a surprise to Eva that the picture on the passport did not match Nik's handsome face. At least, it was consistent with his retired military ID. That picture didn't match, either. Eva said people never checked their government IDs closely, and Nik was unlikely to be worried about the passport, since he apparently only got it to placate Eva for a while and never planned to use it. By this time, Eva had seen more than her share of strange documents and learned not to ask where they came from.

When Eva returned to Alabama in the fall of 1974, her saga with Nik turned from strange to bizarre. He took a sudden interest in her childhood, speaking often of her parents, grandparents, and siblings. It was a shock to Eva, because he knew things that she hadn't told him. One day, he insisted on going out to find the log cabin that she lived in as a child. He knew how to get to it, and they actually found it. It was uninhabited and in disrepair with a hole in the roof, but otherwise much as she remembered it. He was looking for a church that he said should be nearby. Eva remembered it, but they couldn't find it. They finally stopped and asked a storekeeper who told them there had been an old church in the area that Nik indicated, but it burned down many years before. How did Nik know all of this? Was he investigating her background again? No doubt.

Late in 1974, a long forgotten bit of family business popped up that required Eva's personal attention and necessitated a trip to Florida. She and Nik, always happy to travel, set off for Florida to represent Eva's interests. The resolution was not satisfactory from a financial perspective, but the trip wasn't a total loss. They thoroughly enjoyed the Florida climate and decided that it would be the perfect place to spend that winter, so they quickly returned to Alabama to pack a few belongings with the exciting prospect of a beautiful, beachfront holiday in front of them. Nik was uncharacteristically relaxed. In fact, at home, as they packed their belongings for the trip, he even broke his long-standing rule of privacy and revealed a bit about himself.

He was always painstakingly careful about what he said, what he did, and when he chose to do it. Despite his notoriously odd tendencies, this particular moment of self-revelation stood out among the weirdest of the weird, since it began while he was standing naked in their backyard, while Eva protected him with a pistol. For whatever reason, Nik had decided that he wanted to take a shower with the garden hose. His cohorts, always within shouting distance, were strangely absent. Eva never did learn the reason why he was left unattended that night, but Nik calmly handed her a pistol and asked her to shoot anyone who came near, since the boys apparently had the night off. Separation from the cadre of aides also meant that the notorious "they" couldn't counsel him against speaking of whatever he wished. The newfound sense of freedom moved from his spirit to his mouth with lightning speed, and he began to reveal things about himself that he had never previously hinted to her.

Nik was always comfortable standing and could do it for long periods of time, especially for a man his age. He finished his outdoor shower, and then he and Eva stood close together, while he reminisced about the childhood he'd so closely guarded from her since the day they met. He spoke with ease, perhaps even with relief, of things that he held inside for so long that he did not remember the duration. He spoke of his childhood and running away, until someone came and found him. He spoke of his matriculation in private and military schools. He spoke of his father's desire that he become a doctor and the brief flirtation with the idea before it was aborted by his total lack of interest and the deaths of both his parents. He spoke like a man who had not visited his past for a long time and was now studying it like a picture discovered in some dusty attic drawer. He spoke for a very long time, until Eva began to tire of standing.

She suggested they sit, but her words seemed to jar him from the past to the present. The mood was broken. He became aware of his environment again and slipped back into the semi-paranoid character who was always watching his back. He scanned the area and listened for sounds. They thought they saw a strange shadow move. Story time was over. "They" might be listening. This was the paradox of Nik. He was like a captive who paid his guards to imprison him.

As far as Eva could determine, that was the one and only night that Nik was out of earshot of his aides. They were discreet, but their presence was always obvious. They showed themselves occasionally, but they were heard frequently, either in conversations with Nik or their movements around the property. Nik was careful to always provide a place for them wherever he and Eva lived. In addition to the house across the road from the red house, there were also a couple of old farm buildings and a garage on the north side of the property that Nik and the aides used for meetings. Eva would catch glimpses of their comings and goings and could hear their voices, but she made it a point to never intrude. Nik made it abundantly clear that he did not want her involved in his business, although he made one exception. In October 1974, to further confuse anyone who might be looking for him, Nik had Eva fill out paperwork for the Motor Vehicle Department of Louisiana to obtain Louisiana license plates for their GMC pickup.

Finally, in the late fall of 1974, preparations were complete for the winter vacation in Florida. Once again their possessions were organized into a large pile of cardboard boxes, loaded into a vehicle, and pointed toward the warm, sunny Florida weather. They arrived in the town of Gulf Breeze, where they settled into a residence called Tir-Na-Loc House on Route 1, Navarre Beach. The next four months were among the happiest they spent together. They were both very much in a holiday mood, and even Nik seemed relaxed. One problem occurred during the otherwise perfect vacation in December, when Eva had a severe health issue. She drove herself to the hospital on Eglin Air Force Base for treatment and had to stay for several days. Her daughters and son heard about the problem and came to visit her, but not Nik. He was huddled with his aides who were installed in an apartment close to theirs. Business continued, no matter what.

Eva's health was restored, and she was discharged. She would have appreciated a visit from Nik, but she wasn't upset with him. By now, she understood that this was just the way he was, and it was not a reflection of his love, or lack of it, for her. Instead of pouting, she decided to make a special New Year's Eve celebration just for the two of them. She purchased party hats, special treats, and sparkling grape juice that they used to toast the arrival of 1975 with a rousing duet of Auld Lang Syne at midnight, accompanied by Eva on her treasured little Hammond chord organ she brought from Alabama. Nik enjoyed the evening and said so many times over the coming years. This was all that Eva ever wanted from this marriage: the two of them together and happy.

Howard Hughes in 1974

While Eva and Nik were warming their bones in the Florida sun and the aides were cooling their heels in the shadows, Howard was taking heat from all directions. The Senate Watergate Committee had a few pointed questions for him. His business partner, the CIA, had become aware of his drug abuse (Barlett and Steele 496). IRS agents were trying to shake money from him, and there were six unsolved burglaries of his properties. This would be a healthy dose of trouble for most people, but it was status quo for Howard.

The year started on a deceptively optimistic note. On January 30, 1974, a federal judge dismissed stock manipulation charges that were filed against Howard for his actions with Air West. As it turned out, this was just a battle victory. The war would continue to rage. The judge's opinion notwithstanding, the Securities and Exchange Commission was pretty sure it smelled a financial rat, and they weren't anywhere near finished sniffing around Howard. Rather than approach the problem piecemeal, it chose a broad scope of investigation and subpoenaed all of the financial documents that related to the 1969 takeover of Air West by Howard. They intended to sift through the pile and examine every single piece of paper. Then, a funny thing happened. The pile disappeared.

The nerve center for all of Howard's various interests was an old, nondescript building on Romaine Street in Hollywood. It was the kind of building people wouldn't notice unless they were looking for it, but the SEC wasn't interested in early Hollywood architecture. They were interested in documents stored there that they believed held the clues to the alleged financial misdeeds of Howard in his airline acquisition. The SEC wasn't the only entity following a paper trail. A federal judge ordered Howard to surrender five hundred memos related to Robert Maheu's lawsuit, which were also stored at Romaine (Drosnin 4). To round out a busy schedule of snooping, the United States Senate committee investigating the Watergate break-in, demanded Howard show up in person with his Nixon files stored at the Romaine facility. Without question, Howard's headquarters had suddenly become uncomfortably popular.

The order to produce documents in the Maheu suit was issued on May 31, 1974, the SEC subpoena issued on June 2, and the Watergate inquiry was during this same period. Everyone was converging on the Romaine headquarters at once when, in an amazing coincidence of timing, the Romaine facility was burglarized on June 5, and all of the files were stolen (Hack 367). Howard refused to appear in court for the Maheu suit (Maheu 254). He was trying to keep the SEC and the Senate committee at bay, and now all of the records were gone.

More than one eyebrow was raised at this extraordinarily lucky break for Howard. Was Howard behind it? The odds makers in Howard's own casinos would probably have bet he was, but proving it was another matter. A burglary investigation was conducted, and no one was ever arrested or charged. The burglary remains a mystery, at least, officially.

It is quite likely that copies of the stolen memos existed somewhere, a possibility that was not investigated by the authorities, since Howard seemed to be totally indifferent to the whereabouts of the stolen documents. The uproar eventually subsided, and the whole affair might have been relegated to a minor footnote in the generally bizarre Hughes legend, if it weren't for a detail that set off alarms in still another area of the federal government. Word got to the CIA that memos relating to Project Jennifer, and the *Glomar Explorer* ship that Howard built to recover a sunken Soviet submarine, were also in the archive of stolen documents. When an organization obsessed with secrecy discovers that their secret business is in the hands of parties unknown, it gets very tense. CIA agents now encamped at Romaine Street to head the burglary investigation (Hack 368).

This was a particularly bad time for details of Project Jennifer to get loose, since the operation, which had been in the planning stages since 1968 when the Soviet sub SSBK-129 went down, was about to begin in earnest. The sub was a Golf II ballistic missile vessel of 320 feet in length and it carried a treasure trove of technology with it to the bottom of the Pacific Ocean. Cipher machines and other encryption devices as well as code books and technical manuals were believed to be aboard. If the United States could surreptitiously raise these materials and put them to use, the CIA and Naval Intelligence would be able to know exactly what the Russian submarine service was up to, especially on their visits to Cuba.

When news of the wreck reached the CIA, they smelled blood in the water. The spook machine shifted into high gear and sped to the office of President Nixon, who put his support and resources behind the project in August 1969. One of his resources was Howard. Aside from their secret financial deals, Howard was probably the best choice for the job in Nixon's—and everyone's—minds. It was decided that the *Glomar Explorer* was to be built with the fictitious purpose of an underwater mining vessel searching for deposits of semi-precious industrial metals such as copper, nickel, and cobalt. Howard had mining experience, and was one of the few people who could logically put up the $200 million to $350 million estimated cost of the ship. Most people believed he would do just about anything at this point anyway, and deep-sea mining made about as much sense as anything else.

Howard signed the deal in October 1970 and construction started. The *Glomar* was 618 feet long and had an underwater claw that could scoop up metals—or a submarine—and deposit them directly into the ship's cargo hold without being observed. Naturally it had the latest Hughes satellite navigation system that could keep the ship within ten feet of its desired position—not an easy task on the rolling ocean (Barlett and Steele 546).

The *Glomar Explorer* took to the seas on June 20, 1974, and was on station for the lift on August 8. A Russian vessel watched but did not interfere. The lift was only partially successful, since the sub broke when hoisted and only the forward third of it was recovered. Whether or not the CIA got their money's worth is open to discussion.

There is an interesting postscript to the *Glomar* story. The Hughes organization continued to operate the ship, and in August 1975 it showed up off of Catalina Island on the California coast. For nine days, it stayed in position where the Spanish galleon *Santa Marta* was believed to have sunk in 1582 and the galleon *San Pedro* in 1698. Both ships were believed to have cargos of gold. The Spanish ships were later spotted by treasure hunter Charles Kenworthy who explored the wrecks. Surprisingly, there was no gold in either vessel (http://treasurenet.com/forums/shipwrecks/164798-charles-kenworthy-vs-cia-howard-hughes.html).

Maybe Howard got a bonus on this deal.

Notes

Barlett, Donald, L., and James B. Steele. *Howard Hughes: His Life and Madness*. New York: W.W. Norton, and Company, 1979.

Drosnin, Michael. *Citizen Hughes*. New York: Broadway Books, 1985.

Hack, Richard. *Hughes: The Private Diaries, Memos and Letters*. Beverly Hills, CA: New Millennium Press, 2001.

Maheu, Robert, and Richard Hack. *Next to Hughes*. NY: HarperCollins Publisher, 1992.

ELEVEN

"NIK, THAT'S YOU!"

It may not be easy living a role in one's very own mystery story, but then neither is it dull. Eva stumbled upon enough clues to convince her Nik was not who he claimed to be. In fact, her husband didn't even really try very hard to continue the charade that he was a man named Verner Nicely. He also didn't try very hard to tell her the truth. Once he gave her a very big clue, but even then, apparently for his own amusement, he revealed it as though he was playing a children's game.

As Eva and Mark rolled up Highway 52 near Hartford, Alabama, in the late afternoon, Eva continued the story of how, in the fourth year of their marriage, in February 1975, she and Nik were enjoying an uncharacteristically peaceful and happy period in the sunny Florida Gulf. From their oceanfront apartment, they lived the life of happy retirees. Their relationship seemed quite normal. Perhaps, it was the normalcy that caused Nik to playfully stir up the peaceful waters.

Alabama, 1975

Eva had a few days warning something was up, when Nik suddenly became unusually interested in the mail. He was obviously waiting for something, but he was doing it with a sense of excitement, not concern. Finally, he received the package that he'd been waiting for with such great expectation. It was a copy of *True Magazine*. In a marriage jam-packed with surprises, this was a minor one; at least, it was minor at first.

This was not Nik's typical choice in reading material. He was interested in learning how things worked and had an orientation toward the mechanical, electronic, and scientific. His favorite magazine was *Popular Science*, which he looked forward to with great expectation every month and read from cover to cover. *True Magazine* focused on adventure, with a dash of titillation thrown in whenever the opportunity presented itself. This was not at all the type of material Nik read, so Eva was surprised at his obvious excitement, but the surprises were just beginning.

Nik could act like a teasing little boy at times, and this was one of them. He proudly turned the magazine to a certain page and with a beaming smile held the magazine picture alongside his face so that Eva could compare the picture to him. Eva almost fainted. "Nik, that's you!" she screamed. He didn't say a word and just continued his teasing smile.

He silently handed Eva the magazine to read. The picture that shocked Eva was an old one of Howard Hughes in one of the typical fedora hats he was known to wear. But knowing what she now knew, and allowing for aging, there was no mistaking it was Nik as far as Eva was concerned. Nik and Howard were the same man. Nik was obviously pleased with the article on Hughes, as well as the picture, and allowed Eva to read it. When she finished, he took the magazine away from her, and she never saw it again. Eva was thrilled to death that Nik let her see the magazine (Petrali).

This was his way of revealing his identity to her without saying anything. It was typical Nik. It was also typical of Nik that he would never have allowed her to read the article if it wasn't factual, which further confirmed her suspicions as to the true identity of her husband. When the magazine was taken away, the conversation ended. Nik had sent his message in his own unique and playful manner. The experience was a real turning point in their relationship. From that point on, whenever Eva asked questions about his real identity he wouldn't deny it. He didn't offer much information, but he didn't dodge her questions, either. In her mysterious marriage, this was about as close to a transparent relationship as she could hope for.

With the latest bit of information on Nik's real identity, the constant presence of the aides made more sense. Nik never made any effort to conceal them, and he frequently acknowledged their presence. One time, as if to tease them, he held a pistol up to their apartment window. "Miss Renee has a gun for protection, and she knows how to use it!" he yelled, using her middle name as he often did. Eva and Nik lived on the beach, and Nik directed his words to the apartment above and behind theirs, where the aides stood watch. Eva heard them more often than saw them, but it was clear that they were always close at hand.

One day they were driving along the beach when Nik saw something that caught his interest and told Eva to drive off the road onto the sand. She did, and promptly got stuck. This was long before the days of cellular telephones, and there were no phone booths in the dunes. Nik was unconcerned and, aggravatingly, did nothing. Shortly thereafter, a pickup truck pulled up, hooked up to the car, and pulled them out of the sand. The driver, a rough-looking man, said nothing and made no attempt to collect a fee for his service. Eva attempted to thank him, but he ignored her and drove off. Nik didn't seem at all surprised by this stroke of good luck.

Nik and Eva couldn't have been more different when it came to most things, but they did share one common preference. They both liked unusual vehicles. Prior to them leaving Myer's Ranch in Arizona, Nik found a 1940s vintage "Jimmy" GMC pickup truck that suited their basic transportation needs in a very practical—if somewhat unconventional—manner, so Eva paid for the truck prior to them leaving Arizona. It served its utilitarian purpose, but the opportunity to acquire another, even more unusual, utility vehicle was too much to pass up. Shortly before they left Florida to return to Alabama, they were offered a large, former postal van at a reasonable price. It was a big, square vehicle with the steering wheel on the right side so that the mail delivery driver could put mail in street-side mailboxes without getting out of the seat.

As if the vehicle wasn't conspicuous enough, it was painted bright red. The purchase was timely, though, since their happy winter vacation was over, and it was time to move back north. The boxy vehicle wasn't pretty, but it certainly was useful. So, again, Eva purchased the postal van with her money.

As usual, the move would have been easier if Nik wasn't involved. Instead of getting a good night's sleep the night before they left, he stayed up talking business with his aides all night long. Eva's need for sleep eventually overcame

The red former postal van purchased in Florida with the steering wheel on the right.

the incessant voices, and when she awoke the next morning, she found that Nik was taking a swim in the gulf, apparently having not come to bed at all. This meant they were starting their trip with Nik already exhausted, and he had to drive one of the vehicles.

Since they now had two vehicles, Nik was going to have to drive one of them whether he liked it or not. He had his choice: a standard transmission or a steering wheel on the wrong side. They started out with Eva in the postal van and Nik in the "Jimmy," but the combination of sleep deprivation and an ancient, cranky, manual transmission was giving Nik grief. They decided to swap vehicles before Nik reduced the pickup's gearbox to metal shavings. This was helpful, but Eva continually worried that Nik would fall asleep at the wheel, and Nik continually worried that the aides would fall behind. The result was that they pulled over frequently, and Eva thought they would never get back to Alabama. In the end, Nik had the stamina, Eva had the patience, and the aides had their orders, so they all made it back to the red house that Eva's brother continued to allow them to use. An unpleasant trip was made miserable by another of Nik's inconsiderate actions. It was pouring rain when they arrived at her brother's house, and when they unloaded the vehicles, Nik took her cherished little Hammond chord organ and placed it under the eaves of the house at a point where water was pouring down. Nik knew how much that organ meant to Eva, and this act of mean-spiritedness was another emotional stab in her heart.

Nik's cohorts, as Eva referred to them, became more and more visible to Eva and the community. They set up shop in the same place, the deserted house across the highway, and the comings and goings of the black sedan were an indication of how busy they were. Nik frequently mentioned the admiration and trust that he had in the Mormons, and with their increased visibility, Eva noticed that the aides all seemed to prefer black slacks and white shirts, common dress in the Mormon culture. Whether Nik loosened his tight rules or the aides were just getting bored and sloppy, Eva didn't know, but they now made little effort to conceal themselves as they had in the past. Eva would frequently see two or three of them in the yard. Occasionally, she pointed out to Nik that his cohorts were standing around in the open at night. "Damn fools," he would curse, but he did it while laughing, so apparently he eased up on his long-standing policy of secrecy to some extent. He may have even done it on purpose.

He made it very clear to Eva that he had a fear of her being kidnapped, and he had her watched. Eva never knew if there was some basis for this worry, or if it was just irrational paranoia on Nik's part. Either way, the result was the same. They were watched, now more than ever. One night, they were awakened from sleep by someone walking across the porch and rattling the screen door. Eva picked up the pistol that she kept on the nightstand for protection, but Nik gently pulled her arm back. "They" were just checking the door to make certain that it was locked, he assured her. He frankly told her that "his people" had her under surveillance. By this point in their relationship, that was anything but a surprise. Security was a good thing, of course, but at the same time, she also wondered to what degree her privacy was infringed.

When they weren't roaming the property, the aides were on the telephone with Nik from their observation house. Eva frequently came into the house to find Nik engaged in intense discussion over the phone. She could tell how the conversation was going by the sound of his voice. He used his quiet voice, his normal tenor, when he was issuing instructions, but if he wasn't hearing the response he expected, he shifted into a low, gruff voice that conveyed a sense of authority and aggravation.

Most of Nik's meetings with the aides were conducted out of sight, but frequently within earshot. He and the aides would disappear behind one of the adjacent buildings, sometimes for hours, and Eva could hear occasional bits of conversation. She rarely caught enough to make sense of the discussion, but she got a feel of how things were going by the tone of Nik's voice. The aides seemed to be Nik's connection to the world. He wouldn't allow a television in the house; he thought the programming was worthless, so they didn't have a ready source of news other than the daily radio broadcasts of Paul Harvey.

Sometimes, he would return from a meeting and remark how "they" told him something interesting. "They" also apparently were getting a bit bored, living in rural Alabama. One time, Nik came back and told Eva the aides suggested he give her $100,000 and tell her to leave. Perhaps they felt this would let them return to a more urban lifestyle, a return to Las Vegas. Whatever the motivation, it wasn't a very nice suggestion, and it wasn't very nice of Nik to repeat the hurtful statement to Eva. Ironically, by the end of their lives together, they were both living on Eva's civil service retirement check.

Eva's retirement and Nik's retirement were important elements in their lives, since many of the benefits, including healthcare, were becoming increasingly more important as they aged. In the summer of 1975, Eva decided to update her commissary card, so she could shop in the military grocery store at the nearby Fort Rucker Army Post and take advantage of the low prices. Nik offered to help. He produced a retired military identification card in the name of Verner Nicely that was dated 1963.

"Here," he said. "Use this for my identification." Eva had never seen the card before and the picture on the ID looked nothing like Nik. In fact, since seeing the *True Magazine* article, she was aware that, except for the dyed blond hair and strange, blue eyes, Nik looked exactly like Howard Hughes.

Years later Mark showed the identification card to Verner's son, Gary, and he stated that the picture was not his father. Another mystery.

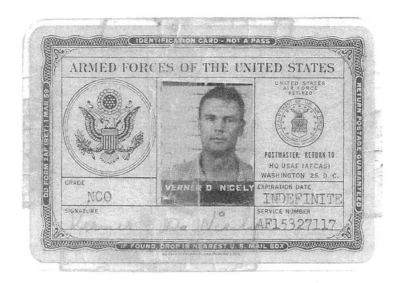

The Verner Nicely ID Nik gave to Eva. The same one Gary Nicely
said was not a picture of his father.

Later that summer, Nik learned the noted oceanographer, Jacques Cousteau, was going to do a one-day presentation at the civic center in Lakeland, Florida. Nik had the highest admiration for the underwater explorer, and he wanted to go to the event in the worst way. Eva was never one to turn down a good road trip, so the adventure was on. Their trusty, red, postal van was selected for the lengthy journey, partially because its size accommodated their camping gear. Nik wanted to avoid motels, which was all right with Eva, since she loved the outdoors, and the summers were comfortable. The only real hitch in the arrangement was the fact that the van's steering wheel was on the right side, which made it difficult to see oncoming traffic. Rather than grumble about the inconvenience, they both laughed it off as part of the adventure.

The trip was great fun, and Nik was looking forward to the event, until they got to the civic center parking lot. Suddenly, he got cold feet about going into the auditorium, but he insisted Eva go in and hear Cousteau's address, while he waited outside in the van. She was to tell him all about it later. Eva knew enough not to argue, besides, she had driven a long way and wanted to attend the event. When she went in and found her seat, she discovered the program was being televised, and her seat was situated so that it was in one of the frequent camera shots. Like it or not, she was going to be part of the background scenery for the show. This became all the more amusing later that night, when they stopped to have dinner with some of Eva's relatives in Tallahassee, Florida. Nik continued to remain under cover, so he stayed in the van, but Eva joined her family in the restaurant. Their waitress watched the Cousteau program on television earlier in the day and recognized Eva from her numerous, prominent appearances in the background. They all had a laugh about the "star" in the family.

Eva read a bit about Howard Hughes and gently probed Nik for information to piece together the puzzle of her husband. Nik had numerous burn scars that still caused him pain. He always wore boat deck shoes or boots that were too big for him, since it was too painful for him to wear the correct size. His scalp was scarred from burns, and he always wore oversized gloves to protect his burned hands. The evidence left on his body made it clear that he went through a very traumatic event, yet he refused to discuss it with Eva. He refused to allow her to put lotion on the painful scars on his hands and head. Instead, he suffered in relative silence, relying on his floppy shoes and gloves for relief. He bought the gloves by the dozen, since they served two purposes for him. He needed to protect his hands from the sun, but he was also fanatical about cleanliness and would not touch a doorknob, even their own, with his bare hands. He was phobic about germs, so he discarded gloves frequently when he felt they were germ infested and replaced them with a new pair. He admonished Eva to be careful about what she touched and where she stepped, and she actually followed his advice. Until the day she died, she would not think of stepping in a spot of oil in a parking lot after Nik convinced her they were teeming with germs.

In her heart, Eva really wanted some resolution to her mystery marriage. In the fall of 1975, she asked him again, "Are we ever going to be married under your real name?" "Someday," he replied. Always someday.

One thing Nik clearly didn't want to do was put anything in his own handwriting. Eva filled out all of his personal correspondence to outside parties and signed his name for him. She had practiced his signature since 1970 and was now quite good at it. Nik even showed the signature to his aides, who apparently handled forging his signature on business documents, and they agreed; Eva made a great forger. Eva didn't view this as an inconvenience. As far as she was concerned, she was simply helping her husband who couldn't write or spell very well. Besides, compared to all of the other weird things he did, this was just a drop in the bucket.

Nik with gloves and hat.

Bahamas, 1975

Things were also going peacefully, as far as one could tell, for Howard II, the derelict. He was in the Xanadu Princess Hotel in Freeport, Grand Bahamas, tended by another group of aides. According to what was made available to the public, he had been bedridden since he broke his hip two years earlier. Dr. Chaffin reported he attempted to examine "Howard" on a nearly daily basis, but the aides continually cancelled appointments. On the rare occasions when he did get into the room, he was not allowed to actually see or touch the patient. The aides only allowed him to observe the very sick man from behind a screen (Real 225).

This would clearly be a challenging way to practice medicine, but the doctor had to accept these conditions or stay away. Even from behind the barrier, the doctor saw enough to determine the patient was not doing well. After a visit in December 1975, Dr. Chaffin noted the man was going downhill. He was pale and stopped eating regularly, resulting in a loss of weight (224–25). Given the man's critical condition, why would his keepers hold the doctor at arm's length? One can only speculate. Perhaps, they were just as bored as the aides in Alabama and wanted to get the whole thing over with.

Whatever their motivation for acting as they did, the aides had good reason to keep quiet about it. Key Hughes personnel had employment contracts that included a very strict nondisclosure clause to prevent information leaks and post-employment books. A man as secretive as Howard wasn't going to allow a rogue former employee to embarrass him, or anyone to reveal information he so carefully guarded. The agreement stated: "Employee agrees that he will not at any time during, or subsequent to termination of his employment by Summa, whether such termination is qualified or non-qualified, disclose any confidential records or information, nor publish nor write any material which will in any way embarrass or be harmful to Summa or any of its affiliated companies or individuals. Or submit or make available any such confidential records or information to any person whosoever which might result in its general dissemination to the public, unless such public dissemination has specifically been authorized in writing by Summa (Barlett and Steele 572)."

In addition to the threat of legal action, the aides had long-term contracts, which made a high degree of circumspection worth their while. All of this was in addition to the fact that Howard allowed these people to be close to him and his organization, because he was absolutely convinced they could be trusted. Based on the lack of inside information from the aides that exists to this day, he appears to have been a very good judge of character.

By the third anniversary of the Summa Corporation, written communication from Howard virtually ceased. Howard read messages, apparently at random, and responded to those he selected by having an aide write a summary of his thoughts. This kept the business running but left no verbatim record of his instructions (555). The obvious advantage was he could dictate orders from anywhere by telephone. He could actually be in the Bahamas or in Alabama. The arrangement worked fine for Howard, but it made his staff nervous. Without an actual memo in Howard's handwriting, who was to say the numerous business and legal activities proceeding worldwide were really at Howard's direction? In an organization where the boss has a longstanding record of playing fast and loose with government rules and regulations, who would really be held responsible if he was found in violation again? Without the instructions written in Howard's hand, how could it be proven the orders came from him? To insulate themselves from possible legal woes, the aides began to write memoranda of their conversations with Howard. In certain instances where the orders really had serious implications, two aides would sign the memo (555).

Was it really worthwhile for the aides to go to all of this trouble and face the potential risk? Apparently the answer was "Yes." Howard frequently assured his aides they would be cared for in a handwritten will he prepared earlier. Being mentioned in the will of a man with the assets of Howard Hughes would certainly be a great motivating factor for most people. The combination of loyalty and dollar signs was apparently enough to ensure compliance with his instructions, no matter how troubling. That left only one question. Where was the will? When asked, Howard replied, "You don't expect me to actually tell you, do you?"

And the mystery rolled on.

Notes

Barlett, Donald, L., and James B. Steele. *Howard Hughes: His Life and Madness.* New York: W.W. Norton, and Company, 1979.

Real, Jack. *The Asylum of Howard Hughes.* Bloomington, IN: Xlibris Corporation, 2003.

Perry, Dana. Interview with the authors. August 1, 2014.

Petrali, Joe. 1975. "O.K., Howard." *True.* February, 16–22, 94–96.

TWELVE

ONE LESS HOWARD

Howard II on the move, 1976

If one were to believe the stories and rumors about Howard Hughes—and most people did—he was a shell of a man living on borrowed time. The few people who saw him when he was transported from country to country gave consistent descriptions of a dying man. There was nothing to imply any recovery was in progress or even possible. The demise of the drugged man, whom the aides referred to as Howard Hughes, was imminent.

"Howard II" was holed up in the Xanadu Princess Hotel in Freeport, Bahamas, for twenty-five months. In keeping with the long-standing policy of shuttling the sick man around, it was determined it was time to leave the island and take up residence in Mexico. At 2:08 a.m. on February 10, 1976, the wheels of a private jet left the ground with the apparently sedated stand-in strapped to a seat in the rear of the aircraft. Dressed in an overcoat and wrapped in a blanket, he was on his way to Acapulco, although he didn't realize it. Witnesses described him as looking terrible, like a zombie (Real 221). Other than being conscious, he had few characteristics of a living human being. He certainly was incapable of having any role in the decision-making process as to his own welfare. The continual sedation made him compliant to the wishes of his keepers. This is far from the treatment a man of his stature would expect from his subordinates, but it was what one would expect for an ex-derelict or body double.

The change of location did nothing to improve the man's health. He was in a steady physical decline, and a different hotel room was not the cure. If anything, a hospital might have been helpful, but no hospitals were ever on his travel schedule. The only plan for the man's welfare seems to have been to keep him moving and away from any close scrutiny or medical examination until he died. The plan was slowly working. After several months in Mexico, he was less than ninety pounds of colorless skin stretched over a six-foot-plus frame (221). He was basically a cadaver with a pulse.

During this period, some startling conversations took place. The first occurred shortly after the arrival in Mexico, when Howard contacted Jack Real and told him he wanted to buy more hotels and start flying again (222). Presumably, he meant he wanted to fly in a manner other than the recent drug-induced stupor of the Freeport to Acapulco trip. This was quite ambitious for a cadaver.

The second conversation occurred on April 1, 1976, when Howard and aide George Francom spoke by telephone. Howard sounded depressed, as he thought back on his life. "George, I suppose I should have been more like other men; I was not nearly as interested in people as I should have been, but I'm not a robot, as some have called me. I was merely consumed by my interest in science" (Magnesen 174). This was an insightful comment coming from a drug-addled zombie. That is, of course, unless the man on the other end of the telephone was in Alabama, not Acapulco.

The aides did a very good job of keeping doctors at arm's length, literally, from the ailing man. They "examined" him through a screen, or from across the room, or over the telephone, but they rarely got a good look at the patient and virtually never touched him to record vital signs. In Acapulco, a Mexican doctor got close enough to the dying man to form an opinion of his condition. The doctor was disgusted and appalled at the condition of the living skeleton. He reported later, ". . . it was apparent the people around the patient were just waiting for him to die. He died of an illness called neglect" (43). Once again, this is a strange way for an aide to treat his employer, especially if he happens to be one of the richest men in the world. On the other hand, it makes sense if the man is actually a nobody, and his death will trigger a long-term compensation package for the aide and allow him to free himself to go elsewhere to lead his life.

After years of avoiding, or denying Howard II the most basic forms of personal hygiene, the Mormon aides decided the man should make his exit from this life in a more dignified form. Whether it was their own initiative, guilt, or orders from someone who didn't want his name associated with such a shabby individual, the time came to clean the man up. One of the aides gave the unconscious man his third haircut in ten years. Another aide soaked the man's fingernails and toenails, so they could be trimmed to a reasonable length (Drosnin 457). When the man died, there was no avoiding the fact the authorities would need to be involved in some way to issue a death certificate. "Death by neglect" (Hack 3) was not what anyone wanted it to read.

On April 5, 1976, four days after his telephone conversation with George Francom, Howard II was loaded onto an aircraft for the last time. The destination was Houston, Texas, but the chief passenger would not breathe the air of the United States again. Somewhere en route, the man they called Howard Hughes passed from this dimension into the next. What arrived in Houston was the corpse of an elderly, white male, six feet four inches tall, and ninety-two pounds (13). Whoever he had been, he was no more.

The man who was so carefully hidden in life now became the object of much scrutiny in death. Upon arriving in Houston, the crew declared an in-flight death had occurred. Customs officer Mary Denton was one of the officials involved in the documentation of the event. She commented Hughes appeared to be "like an old, emaciated man. Well, really, I couldn't even tell that it was a man from the side view" (13).

A medical doctor from the Houston Methodist Hospital saw the deceased. His description of the body was consistent with Denton's. "I found an elderly white male, with gray hair, somewhat thinned, and a gray beard. The body appeared remarkably emaciated and dehydrated." The customs official added, "No one, including his doctors or his aides, seemed unduly upset or distraught" (13). The description of the body sounds more appropriate for a derelict found in an alley than one of the wealthiest men in the world.

Since the aircraft crew identified their deceased passenger as Howard Hughes, the authorities began the search for the next of kin. They didn't have to search far. Howard's eighty-five-year-old aunt, Annette Gano Lummis, still lived in Houston. She was a woman who normally shunned the public eye, but she stepped up to deal with the situation. She asked her son, William, to see to all of the arrangements and left the matter in his hands, making one stipulation: she did not want an autopsy (14). Perhaps she felt this was undue desecration of the body, or perhaps she was encouraged to prohibit the postmortem by the aides who desired to keep the man as isolated in death as they kept him in life.

Whatever the reason, it was not a decision warmly embraced by the Houston medical examiner, Dr. Joseph Jachimczyk (14). Given the condition of the body and the questions regarding the man's care, it was his responsibility to conduct a thorough investigation. William was surprised to see the condition of his "cousin" as well. "This is Howard Hughes?" he asked, in bewilderment.

In addition to Dr. Jachimczyk's professional responsibility to determine the cause and circumstances of death, there was also the very real question of proving exactly who the man was. The aides stated the deceased was Howard Hughes and it's likely no one doubted it. However, given the high public profile of Hughes and his web of legal entanglements, Dr. Jachimczyk was clearly aware of his obligation to provide positive proof of the identity of the deceased. He wasn't about to take anyone's word for it if there was an alternative. By now the FBI had arrived. Having chased the elusive Hughes for years, they also wanted some proof their quarry was finally in their hands, albeit dead. Like everything else in the Hughes saga, this wasn't easy.

The first issue in the process of positive identification was the family. For some reason, Aunt Annette was opposed to photographing and fingerprinting the body (15). The reluctance for a photographic record may be explained by the condition of the deceased. By now, William had reported the condition of his "cousin's" body to her, and she would certainly be sensitive to seeing that pathetic image on the front page of every newspaper in the country. The resistance to fingerprinting, however, is curious. Did she know something was fishy? Did the aides encourage her to reject any positive identification?

Maybe she just wanted everything put to rest as quickly and quietly as possible. We don't know, but the reluctance to allow fingerprinting remains interesting.

This was not good news for Dr. Jachimczyk. He found himself placed in the position of honoring the wishes of the family of the deceased or conducting the most thorough investigation possible. In the end, he decided to follow Solomon's wisdom and split the problem down the middle. He did not allow photographs of the body, but he insisted on fingerprint identification. This proved to be the more difficult of the two options, since the body was in such a state of dehydration that the first attempt at fingerprinting didn't produce a recognizable image. Dr. Jachimczyk then called in fingerprint expert Horace Tucker for some assistance. Tucker directed water be injected under the skin of the fingers to counteract the shriveling that occurred. The next attempt at printing yielded an image, which was sent to Washington, DC (17–8). Nothing more was said about the prints.

For all of the mystery and confusion that still surrounds Howard Hughes, years later, the fingerprints of the stand-in rise to the top. Dr. Jachimczyk seemed to wash his hands of the uncertainty immediately after the second set of prints appeared to be usable, most likely with a big sigh of relief. It seems unusual with all the problems of obtaining a usable set of prints, that the FBI could evaluate and compare them in a relatively short period of time, a few hours, so the burial could be accomplished forty-eight hours after the passing. That was certainly quick action on everyone's part. The government isn't known to work that fast.

Where would any original set of prints come from to ensure a comparison with those taken from the body? Were they Howard's from earlier in his life? Were they a set from the stand-in that Howard somehow planted so they compared positively? Maybe they did not exist at all. After all, Howard seemed to be able to do just about anything he wanted to accomplish, especially when it muddied up any clear water that might exist.

Whether the second set of prints matched or not, the attempt at due diligence provided the FBI with a convenient way for the government to close out a very mysterious case. Most likely, the body was buried prior to anyone even looking at the second set of prints. Then, whether they matched or not became a moot point. To the intrigued public and the grieving family, the body was Howard Hughes. To the government, the mystery still existed.

The body was released to the family for final arrangements, and the funeral for Howard Hughes was as small as the man's life had been large. On April 7, 1976, only twenty-five people gathered at Glenwood Cemetery, just west of downtown Houston, to send the tycoon back to his maker. There was no chapel service, just a perfunctory, seventeen-minute gathering at the graveside attended by Aunt Annette and Cousin William Lummis, as well as a few other family members who hadn't seen the deceased in decades (Magnesen 45).

Ex-wife Jean Peters did not attend, but she commented in an interview, "I'm saddened."

Curiously, no aides attended. They paid no more attention to this man in death than they had in life. Clearly, they had little emotional attachment to the man in the casket, whoever he was (45). For all of his accomplishments in many fields, only the CIA sent a representative to acknowledge his service. Chief of Counter Intelligence James Angleton stated, "Howard Hughes, where this country's interests were concerned, no man knew his target better. We were fortunate to have him. He was a great patriot" (Drosnin 458).

With that, the saga of Howard Hughes ended. Supposedly.

Meanwhile in Alabama

"Play dead and see who shows up at your funeral. That's how you really know who your friends are," Nik laughed, as he and Eva listened to reports of the burial on the radio. "If they only knew," Eva responded, and they both smiled with amusement. This may have been the only time Nik would have appreciated a television set, as they sat in the living room of the red house in Troy, Alabama. It struck Eva the whole event seemed rushed, as though they wanted to get it over before anyone caught on.

When the news reports ended, Nik made the comparison of the Hughes funeral to that of President John F. Kennedy. "What a shame it was that the nation took a day off for the funeral of John F. Kennedy. I suppose you even took the day off.".

"Yes, I did," she admitted.

Nik scowled in disgust. He had sufficient contempt for Joseph Kennedy to cover the entire clan, Jack, Bobby, and Ted included. Howard's hatred for Joseph Kennedy was well known in Washington, but it originated in Hollywood (Drosnin 255). Kennedy arrived in Hollywood about the same time as Howard, intent on showing "that bunch of pants pressers" how to make movies. He successfully used his notable financial skills to reorganize existing film companies, and created the RKO film corporation, a studio that Howard would later own. Howard and Kennedy were a lot alike. They were both ruthless businessmen and they both had an eye for the ladies. This last characteristic may have been the root of Howard's lifelong hatred of Kennedy. It was also rumored that Kennedy was dallying with Howard's girlfriend at the time, Billy Dove. Howard was never one to share anything, least of all a woman (Hack 268).

The funeral proved to be a real turning point in the lives of Eva and Nik. Their marriage had swung from unusual to bizarre, since they'd taken the vows, but the funeral triggered something in Nik that launched a cycle of increasingly weird behavior. All of his bad qualities were suddenly unfettered and became worse. Always private, he now became obsessed with isolation. Prior to the funeral, Eva could entice Nik to take her out for dinner or shopping. All of that ended abruptly. Instead, Nik preferred to stay on their property or spend his time alone, hiding in the woods, naked. For some reason, Nik felt compelled to shed his clothes and commune with nature at a very basic level. "Compelled" may not be the best word to describe it. He was obsessed with running in the Alabama woods alone and naked. He became a total recluse; in fact, Eva described him as "the greatest recluse of all recluses."

Nik's compulsion to reject clothing did not apply to gloves and boots. To the contrary, his previous habit of wearing gloves frequently now became the obsession to wear them constantly. He maintained this practice for the rest of his life. The gloves provided protection for his burned hands, and the boots for his feet, as he ran naked through the woods. However, he never removed the gloves in the house. He would not risk leaving a fingerprint on anything or contacting a germ.

With Nik running around alone, naked in the woods, Eva was left to fill in the time as best she could. She went into town alone to eat and shop, and there was an apartment there where she could stay for a day or two at a time to write her poetry. She was aware of her isolation, which led her to the realization that the ever-present aides were less present. In fact, they slowly disappeared. If Nik needed to make contact with someone, he sent off a postcard. Thereafter, someone would be in touch with him. Eva's life had become uncharacteristically quiet.

With Howard Hughes out of the picture, officially at least, the other players in his empire began jockeying for position and plugging any potential leaks in the carefully constructed legend of Howard's last days. Shortly after the funeral, Jack Real had a discussion with Bill Gay in which Gay stated, "We decided not to give you a contract, but we're going to give you a real sweetheart gift. You're going to get $25,000, providing you leave right now, never write a thing and never mention Howard Hughes again. He's gone from your memory. Sign your name right here. You leave Summa this week, and you get the $25,000" (Real 253). Apparently "Howard" wasn't the only thing Gay wanted buried quickly. Jack Real knew too much of the real story. He didn't sign. His book was published in 2003, two years after Nik's death. It appears to be an attempt to make some sense of a story that makes no sense, while not betraying the cloud of fog his friend so carefully crafted.

Then there was the mystery of the will. LaVane Forsythe was in possession of the will Howard gave to him and instructed him to deliver, and the burial was his release from this obligation. He prepared to deliver it for execution. As it turned out, that would be no less complicated a legal matter than anything else in Howard's life. Approximately two weeks after the funeral, on April 27, 1976, an information specialist for the Mormon Church found the mysterious Mormon Will on his desk. The find launched a story stranger than fiction that would drag on for years.

Meanwhile, as the corporate players plotted and the lawyers litigated, a naked old man ran happily through the Alabama woods.

Notes

Drosnin, Michael. *Citizen Hughes*. New York: Broadway Books, 1985.

Hack, Richard. *Hughes: The Private Diaries, Memos and Letters*. Beverly Hills, CA: New Millennium Press, 2001.

Magnesen, Gary. *The Investigation*. Fort Lee, NJ: Barricade Books, 2005.

Real, Jack. *The Asylum of Howard Hughes*. Bloomington, IN: Xlibris Corporation, 2003.

THIRTEEN

WHERE THERE'S A WILL

Alabama, 2002

It was evening now, as they headed up Highway 52 near Slocomb. The afternoon had flashed by them. Mark reflected on how uncomfortable he'd felt at the start of this story, because it sounded like a delusion. But after several hours of detailed explanation, he just couldn't believe Eva was unbalanced. Actually, he didn't really know what to believe. If he was honest with himself, Eva had convinced him, and her story no longer sounded impossible. At this point, if Eva was Howard's wife, and Howard was dead, there was one big question to be answered.

"Whatever happened to the money?" Mark asked.

"I asked him, 'What happened to your estate?'" Eva responded, "And he said, 'I was screwed out of it by my relatives.'"

Dispute of the Mormon Will, 1976

For a man of Howard's vast financial and legal resources, one would think he would have paid a bit more attention to a document like his will. Wherever he may have been at the time, it's likely there was an attorney within walking distance who could have drawn a simple will for him for a fee of twenty-five dollars. Maybe that was the problem. Howard rejected the simple.

It was known Howard inquired with attorneys about the legality of a holographic, handwritten will, and LaVane Forsythe was supposedly in possession of a handwritten will given to him by Howard. A handwritten will turned up at the headquarters of the Mormon Church in Salt Lake City, Utah. After an examination, a document examiner stated it was possible the handwriting was that of Howard Hughes. So far, so good. Unfortunately, approximately three dozen other wills were submitted to various courts around the country. Roughly $2.5 billion was up for grabs, and there was no shortage of potential grabbers. The problem for the courts was no one really knew which will, if any, was real, and expressed the true last wishes of the tycoon.

Of all of the documents, the will delivered to the Church of Jesus Christ of Latter-day Saints headquarters, which became known as the Mormon Will, came with the best story. The three-page document took the prize for the most unique bequest by allocating one-sixteenth of the Hughes fortune to one Melvin Dummar, the owner of a small gas station in Willard, Utah. Shock rippled through the Hughes family and the Summa Corporation. Who was Melvin Dummar? When contacted manning the gas pumps in Willard, Dummar also expressed shock at the generosity of the millionaire, but he knew the reason for the gift. He told the story of picking up an old man in the desert in 1967, saving his life, in fact, and taking him to a Vegas Strip hotel. The man said he was Howard Hughes, a claim that Dummar was never certain he believed. Apparently, he actually was Hughes, Dummar deduced. Maybe, but for almost $156 million, the family decided it was worth arguing about. If this and the other wills were declared fakes, the entire $2.5 billion would go to the next of kin.

The Untidy and Misspelled Mormon Will

Photocopy of envelope containing the Mormon Will.
Photo: Brigham Young University Special Collections

Last Will and Testament.

I, Howard R. Hughes being of
sound and disposing mind and
memory, not acting under undue
fraud or the undue influence
of any person whomsoever,
and being a resident of Las
Nevada, declare that this
is to be my last Will
and revolk all other wills
previously made by me.

After my death my estate
is to be devided as follow

first one forth of all my assets to go to Hughes Med-
ical Institute of Miami.

second: one eight of assets
to be devided among
the University of Texas.
Rice Institute of Technology
of Houston.
the University of Nevada
and the University of Calif.
Howard R. Hug

page one.

Photocopy of the Mormon Will – Page One.
(Photo: Brigham Young University Special Collections.)

Last Will and Testament

*I Howard R. Hughes being of
sound and disposing mind and
memory, not acting under duress,
fraud or the undue influence
of any other person whomsoever,
and being a resident of Las Vegas
Nevada, declare that this
is to be my last Will
and to revolk all other Wills
previously made by me.*

*After my death my estate
is to be devided as follows –
first: one forth of all my assets to go to the Hughes Medical Institute of Miami –*

*second: one eight of my assets
to be devided among
the University of Texas –
Rice Institute of Technology
of Houston –
the University of Nevada –
and the University of Calif.*

Howard R. Hughes

third: one sixteenth to Church
of Jesus Christ of Latter day
Saints — David O. Mackey Pre

Forth: one sixteenth. to estat-
lish a home for Orphan
Cildren —

Fifth: one sixteenth of assets
to go to Boy Scouts
of America —

sixth: one sixteenth; to be
divided among Jean Peters of
Los Angeles and Ella Rice
of Houston —

seventh; one sixteenth of assets
to William R. Lommis of
Houston, Texas —

eighth; one sixteenth to go
to Mrjelvin Du Mar of
Gabbs Nevada —

Howard R. Hughes

— page two —

Photocopy of the Mormon Will – Page Two.
(Photo: Brigham Young University Special Collections.)

*third: one sixteenth to Church
of Jesus Christ of Latterday
Saints – David O MaKay – Pre*

*Forth: one sixteenth to estab-
lish a home for Orphan
Cildren –*

*Fifth: one sixteenth of assets
to go to Boy Scouts
of America –*

*sixth: one sixteenth: to be
devided among Jean Peters of
Los Angeles and Ella Rice
Of Houston –*

*seventh: one sixteenth of assets
to William R. Lommis of
Houston, Texas –*

*Eighth: one sixteenth to go
to Melvin Du Mar of
Gabbs Nevada –*

Howard R. Hughes

–page two–

devided among my
personal aids at the time
of my death —.

tenth: one sixteenth to be
used as school scholarship
fund for entire Country —

The spruce goose is to be given
to the City of Long Beach, Cal.

The remainder of my
estate is to be devided among
the key men of the company
I own at the time of my
death.

I appoint Noah Dietric
as the executer of this will

signed the 19 day of
March 1968

Howard R. Hughs

— page three —

Photocopy of Mormon Will – Page Three] .
(Photo: Brigham Young University Special Collections.)

Ninth: one sixteenth to be
devided among my
personal aids at the time
of my death –

tenth: one sixteenth to be
used as a school scholarship
fund for entire Country –

The spruce goose is to be given
To the city of Long Beach, Calif –

the remainder of My
estate is to be devided among
the key men of the company's
I own at the time of my death.

I appoint Noah Dietrich
As the executer if this Will –

Signed the 19 day of
March 1968

Howard R. Hughes

–page three–

For a while it looked like Melvin Dummar may have been one of the few to actually strike gold in the Nevada desert. However, while the rags-to-riches story of rescue and reward was consuming gallons of newspaper ink and capturing the hearts of an enthusiastic readership, the Hughes family, aides, and the Summa Corporation joined forces to erase the happy ending from this fairy tale. Too much was at stake to accept this story without some research and a court fight, and their rejection of the document was not subtle. Howard's personal aides were designated hostile witnesses by the proponents of the will for their distinct lack of cooperation on the witness stand. The aides had a story, and they were sticking to it: Howard never left the Desert Inn. Period! Admitting anything else would have opened the door for too many other questions.

By all accounts, Melvin Dummar was an average guy, that is, he went to work, had a passion for music, and generally wanted to live a normal life like pretty much everyone else. Raised Mormon, although not practicing at the time of the trial, he was not argumentative or boastful, and those who met him considered him a very nice guy. A man like Dummar wouldn't have much chance against the Machiavellian Summa Corporation, but the Mormon Will came with an unusual twist. Former Hughes executive of over three decades, Noah Dietrich, was named in the will as the executor. Many considered Dietrich to be the day-to-day mastermind of the Hughes fortune, but one thing was certain; he wasn't a pushover. Dietrich was charged with defending the legitimacy of the will, and that included the legitimacy of Dummar's claim. Like it or not, the shy Dummar was about to be pushed into the spotlight of a world-class legal drama.

Dietrich started building his team by hiring attorney Harold Rhoden as lead counsel. Rhoden was small of stature, but a vocal, aggressive opponent in the courtroom. He had been a prisoner of war in World War II, so he may have reached the point in life where not much scared him. Summa certainly didn't. Rhoden brought in two other attorneys: Marvin Michelson, who went on to fame—or infamy—for creating the concept of "palimony", financial compensation after the breakup of unmarried couples; and George Parnham, a young attorney who was on his way to building a practice in criminal defense. Rhoden then needed one more player on the team. The opposition was pretty good at burying things, so he looked for someone with some guts to prowl around and see what he could dig up. He found his man.

Jim Spiller, then a twenty-eight-year-old private investigator, was in his office in Dallas when he got an unusual call. It was Rhoden who, with characteristic abrasiveness, began the conversation by saying that he didn't think much of Texans, but that Spiller had been recommended by several people so he was willing to set his prejudice aside, at least for a while. He told Spiller what he had in mind, and mentioned that there was a definite possibility that some physical rough stuff might come with the job. Spiller said he was fully capable of taking care of himself, so with that the deal was made. Spiller hung up thinking it had been a prank. Then an envelope stuffed with money and an airplane ticket to Las Vegas showed up. Spiller figured he had nothing to lose by going to Las Vegas and looking into the situation. He ended up on the job for almost two years (Jim Spiller interview with the authors).

The split between Dietrich and Hughes had been acrimonious, which some thought was proof that the will was a forgery. Spiller doesn't agree. "There was a split with Hughes alright," he told us, "but Hughes still respected him. He knew who made him his money." Rhoden challenged the accusation in court with a memo handwritten by Hughes to Robert Maheu in 1968, which indicated that Hughes was willing to use Dietrich "in the future" (Rhoden 242).

One of the first of many mysteries in the Mormon Will was the question of how it got to The Church of Jesus Christ of Latter-day Saints headquarters in Salt Lake City and who brought it there. Dummar, at first, claimed he had no knowledge of the document prior to being notified that he was a beneficiary, but when the FBI found the fingerprint of his left thumb on the envelope, he had some explaining to do. After some aggressive questioning by his attorney, Dummar changed his story. He said the will had been delivered to him at his gas station by a mystery man who dropped it off while Dummar was waiting on a customer. Panicked and unsure of what to do, he delivered the will to the LDS headquarters himself and then went back to his gas station to see what would happen (Magnesen 72).

The mystery deliveryman turned out to be Howard's long time bag man

LaVane Forsythe, who had been on his payroll since the late '40s. One of his specialties was dropping off little envelopes of Howard's money to various important people in an effort to get them to see things Howard's way. He was also a beefy physical figure, which came in handy if further encouragement was necessary, a fact that gave him something of a bad reputation. Surprisingly, Spiller had mixed feelings about him. "He was a bag man and a bouncer, but he wasn't immoral. He wasn't a bad guy at heart. It was just a job." Whatever the state of Forsythe's character, he didn't obfuscate when it eventually came time to answer questions.

Spiller, however, had to start at the beginning of the trail. The word was that Forsythe had the will stashed in the shower in his home. Beginning there, Spiller followed the trail. First stop was a bank where Forsythe had cashed in some $100 bills. This would not have been memorable if it weren't for the fact that the bills were very old and issued at a time when the seals on hundred dollar bills were printed in red ink. The bank cashier at first thought they were counterfeit. From there, Forsythe's itinerary showed a flight to Ogden, Utah, a rental car reservation, and a drive to Willard, Utah. Here Spiller got a break when he learned that a local farmer may have seen Forsythe. Thrilled with his luck, Spiller drove to the farmer's property, where he was greeted by a series of large signs that read, "Trespassers Will Be Shot on Sight." Spiller had an awkward moment. But he knew he wasn't going to get the job done parked out in the road, so he took a deep breath and leaned on the car horn as he drove onto the property. He wanted to make sure everyone knew he wasn't trying to sneak up on them. It worked. The farmer came out to see what the racket was. "I'll never forget his face," Spiller recalled laughing. "I saw it for the first time down the barrel of the rifle he had pointed at me." Once the uncomfortable introduction was complete, the farmer vividly recalled seeing Forsythe. In the rural community, a big man like Forsythe, dressed in a suit in a brand new, black car was unusual. The farmer remembered that he had a conversation with the man. The man asked him how to get to Dummar's gas station (Jim Spiller interview with the authors).

Forsythe didn't come forward with his story with great enthusiasm, but he came forward nevertheless. He said he had a secret code word with

Howard so if an aide contacted him with instructions and used the code word, he would know the message was really from Howard. He said that someone using that code word called him and told him to go to Las Vegas and straighten things out because Dummar had "screwed everything up by lying" about ever having the will. Forsythe reluctantly did as instructed.

He stated that it all started when he met with Howard in July or early August 1972 at the Bayshore Inn in Vancouver, British Columbia at Howard's beckoning. At that time, Howard asked him to take charge of a large brown envelope, which he was to open upon Howard's death. Howard told him that someone else had previously had the envelope, but no longer wanted responsibility for it. Curiously, a few weeks prior to this meeting, probate court records show that someone called a judge in Salt Lake City and told him that he had the will of Howard Hughes and it was addressed to a president of the LDS church who was now deceased and he wanted to know what to do with it. The judge told him to submit the will to the court when Hughes died. Nothing more came of that (Magnesen 75). It's speculated, but not proven, that former Hughes associate, John Meier, may have been the original holder of the will.

Forsythe said he accepted the envelope, held it for about four years, and upon hearing the news of Howard's death, set out on April 26 or 27, 1976, to deliver the will as promised. He was totally bewildered as to why some kid in a gas station was the recipient, but he followed his instructions. After a brief conversation with Dummar, Forsythe said he left the will on a stack of Dummar's paperwork while he was with a customer and departed. Forsythe was given a lie detector test and asked if Hughes had given him the envelope, if he had received instruction to deliver it to Dummar, and if he had, in fact, made the delivery. He said he had, and the test results indicated that he was telling the truth (76).

Sometime later, Spiller was in Ogden, Utah, where Dummar and his personal attorney were located, when he became aware that a local dentist, Dr. Jonathan Ford, who was married to a cousin of Hughes aide Kay Glenn, had information about Howard's comings and goings. Spiller took a handwritten affidavit from him in which Ford stated that he was in Las Vegas at dinner with Glenn and other family members when Glenn got a call. When he hung up, he apologized to the group, saying he had to leave because, "The old man ran off again." Spiller had Ford sign the document and told him he would be back the next day with a typed copy for him to sign. Spiller had a feeling that someone would get to Ford before he got a signature on the typed document, so he overnighted the original to Las Vegas. That was fortunate, since his hotel room was broken into and searched that night (Jim Spiller interview with the authors). Dr. Ford later testified at the trial, "Hughes would take off in the desert without the aides having knowledge of his whereabouts. Mr. Hughes had gone out in the past to the desert and something happened out there in 1967, and he was picked up and brought back to Las Vegas by someone passing in a car" (Magnesen 105).

Naturally, the Hughes family and aides denied Howard ever left the hotel. "They were trying to say that Hughes never left . . . that he just stayed in his hotel room," Spiller told us with a laugh (Jim Spiller interview with the authors).

As in most trials, the burden of determining who was telling the truth fell on the jury. For Melvin Dummar, it was his own action that created skepticism in that group. By now the Summa investigators knew almost as much about Dummar as he knew about himself. While probing into all of his activities, they discovered he had checked out an interesting book from his local library. It was Clifford Irving's, *The Hoax*, the account of how Irving had written his fake autobiography of Howard Hughes. The lawyers for the family floated the idea that Dummar and his wife simply copied the handwriting samples in the book to create a fake will naming Melvin as a beneficiary. In response, Dummar stated that he had simply looked at the handwriting in the book to see if it matched the handwriting on the will, since he was obviously very curious. Then a cadre of document examiners and handwriting experts from both sides were called to testify for and against the validity of the will, each adamant that the will was either authentic or a forgery, depending on which side was paying them.

The case went to the jury, which had some doubts about whether Dummar's 1967 adventure really took place, and the consensus was that the will was a fake. The fairy tale would not have a happy ending for Dummar, and the Hughes family would be out millions of dollars in legal fees for the seven-month trial. In the end, it was ruled that none of the wills were valid, and the Summa Corporation, seven casinos, and thousands of acres of land in the Las Vegas valley would be inherited by William Lummis, son of Howard's Aunt Annette, along with twenty-one other relatives (108–9).

There was one other thing. The family received the inheritance only after the back taxes Howard owed were deducted (109). The IRS finally had its happy ending.

The jury has spoken and the matter is closed, but many feel that the verdict was wrong. Jim Spiller is one of them. He is adamant that Dummar could not have created such a complex hoax, and he also vouched for his character. "He is as nice a guy as you'd ever want to meet."

Aside from personalities, there is also the troublesome little matter of evidence. "There was so much circumstantial evidence that was in favor of the will being true," he told us. "It was overwhelming, the circumstantial evidence. As an investigator, hard evidence is great, but when you have tons of circumstantial evidence, to me, it's harder for people to make that up" (Jim Spiller interview with the authors).

Spiller is quite correct; there is a massive amount of circumstantial evidence that supports the will, and we have barely touched it. But, right or wrong, Melvin Dummar didn't get the money.

The Mormon Will came with a plethora of questions and an army of lawyers on each side with contradictory answers. You can look at the evidence and make up your own mind as to the truth. However, from our perspective in the story of Eva and Nik, there is still one question that remains unanswered: What did Nik mean when he told Eva that his family had "screwed him out of the money?" If one takes the position that the Mormon Will was genuine and reflected the wishes of the real Howard Hughes—and we do— the answer must be in that will. Who named in that will might possibly have been charged with funneling money to Nik after the official death of Howard?

The educational institutions that were bequeathed money can likely be eliminated immediately. They would not participate in such a scheme, but more importantly to Nik, too many people would have to know the truth. The LDS Church can be eliminated because they seemed as bewildered by the will as everyone else. The Boy Scouts? Not likely. Hughes employees and aides would be a possibility, except that none of them are referenced by name. Someone specific would need to be in charge of distributing the money. Jean Peters and Ella Rice could be possibilities as could William Lummis, although Peters and Rice had been out of Howard's life for years or decades, and Lummis had never even met him. There's one other possibility: Dr. Wilber Thain, who *isn't* named in the will.

Our speculation about Dr. Thain stems from a legal memorandum filed in 1980 by the Hughes estate. Although the court had ruled against the Mormon Will and given Howard's money to his family, the arguing continued for decades. The family charged that Howard's inner circle had seized control of his operations in the last ten years of his life and used them for their own enrichment. This period coincides with the time we believe Howard became Nik and gave up all but cursory involvement in his empire.

It's no secret that the real Howard had a drug problem. Starting around 1961, according to the memo, Dr. Norman Crane began writing prescriptions for the buffet of drugs that Howard grazed at daily. As the years passed, this responsibility weighed heavily on Dr. Crane, resulting in an obvious excessive use of alcohol. He stated that the man for whom he was providing drugs did not need them. In April 1974, Dr. Crane flatly refused to provide any more drug prescriptions. Crane escaped his patient, but not his responsibility in the matter. He was later indicted and convicted for distributing codeine to Howard.

Dr. Crane's departure left the aides with a problem. They needed a doctor to write narcotics prescriptions in a sufficient quantity to keep him stuporous and in no condition to cause trouble. Hughes aide Bill Gay had a solution. He had a brother-in-law, Dr. Wilber Thain, who might fill the pharmaceutical vacancy. Thain saw the opportunity of a lifetime and he took it.

According to the 1980 memo, Dr. Thain agreed to write the prescriptions for as long as necessary, presumably until the malnourished patient died. The deal came with a few demands on Dr. Thain's part. Aside from taking care of his own financial needs, Dr. Thain also negotiated lifetime contracts for certain employees. Bill Gay and other aides suddenly saw salary increases of up to 400 percent in the '70s. The memo states that Dr. Thain did this by threatening to withhold drugs from the patient. All of Thain's demands were approved by the Summa Corporation (Schumacher 82–7). If the patient was really Howard Hughes and had legitimate medical needs, Summa would not have had to submit to extortion to have the prescriptions written.

Back to the money. In addition to his other perquisites, Dr. Thain was offered an executive contract at the Hughes Medical Institute in Miami, which is a beneficiary in the Mormon Will. Was Thain providing drugs to both "Howard II" and Nik? (We know that Nik received some drugs in the mail, as is discussed in a later chapter). Did part of Thain's deal at the Hughes Medical Institute include the obligation to divert some funds to Nik? Given the nefarious way this entire situation was handled, we believe it's a valid theory. We can't prove it, but it fits.

Money had never been a big factor in Nik and Eva's marriage. Yes, Nik could be very generous, and in the early stages of their relationship, before she had all of the facts, he occasionally purchased things that seemed way above what she thought he could afford. As nice as that was, she wasn't a particularly material person, and at Nik's age, his interests and curiosities were satisfied with technical publications and little gadgets. The fact that Nik was "screwed out" of his money, as he put it, really had no effect on their lifestyle. They continued on as they had before.

There was the question, though: If Nik was really Howard, and Howard was supposedly dead, now what?

The departure of the once-ubiquitous aides allowed the peace and tranquility of the rural Alabama countryside to slowly seep into Eva and Nik's marriage. She had long ago resigned herself to the fact that this marriage would never be "normal," whatever the standard for that might be. Nik was unique, and he wasn't going to change. There were only two choices for her, she could stay put and live with him, or she could leave. She had left before and came to the conclusion she loved him enough to put up with him, but that didn't make life easy. Still, with the aides gone, they finally had some privacy, and even if Nik liked to spend his days communing nude with nature, he was with her at night. She was no longer brushed aside with a terse, "I have business to attend to."

After the funeral of Howard Hughes, there was a subtle change in the dichotomy of Nik's personality. While he became much more reclusive to the outside world, at the same time, he became slightly more open to Eva. He revealed more of himself to her than he ever had before. These revelations created a closeness between them. They also filled in missing pieces of the portrait of the man who was her husband. Slowly, through the fog of Nik's previous secrecy, the image revealed was that of Howard Hughes.

Notes

Magnesen, Gary. *The Investigation*. Fort Lee, NJ: Barricade Books, 2005.

Rhoden, Harold. *High Stakes*. New York: Crown Publishers, Inc., 1980.

Schumacher, Geoff. *Howard Hughes: Power, Paranoia, and Palace Intrigue.* Las Vegas, NV: Stephens Press, LLC, 2008.

Spiller, Jim. Interview with the authors. June 12, 2014.

FOURTEEN

THE MANY, MANY MOVES

1976–1982

Some people just can't sit still. The average family seeks the security of a place they can call home, but Eva and Nik were far from average. Something inside of them compelled them to keep moving. They didn't go far, and they didn't go fast. They just didn't stop moving for a long, long time.

The next leg in what already became something of a marital road trip began late in 1976, when Eva and Nik moved from the red house to Goshen, Alabama. There they settled into a house on top of a hill, overlooking the countryside they both enjoyed so much. This house had the added benefit of wonderful neighbors, Mary and Paul Bozeman, who lived across the street.

The Bozemans were special to Eva for many reasons, but there was one big one: Eva was lonely. That's a fair statement, but also something of a dichotomy, since Eva was also a very private person. To the few people who knew her and her obviously eccentric husband, it was clear that neither approved of too many questions, and certainly not of outright snooping. Privacy was one thing, but isolation was quite something else. Living with Nik was certainly no walk in the park, and having him as her only source of conversation and companionship apparently wore thin sometimes. Mary provided Eva with some much-needed female companionship, and even the curmudgeonly Nik stepped out of his normal isolation to greet the couple with actual enthusiasm, a true rarity.

The Bozemans were a young couple just starting their life together when Nik and Eva came into their lives. Paul was twenty-six years old and a native of Goshen, Alabama. Mary, twenty-three, grew up in the nearby town of Henderson. Together they farmed peanuts, with Paul taking occasional truck driving jobs on the side and Mary pitching in to help tend to their livestock in addition to her responsibilities as a mother. They were a typical family of the rural South, friendly without being intrusive, and quick to lend a helping hand—expecting, and wanting, nothing in return. They were pretty much the definition of good neighbors.

The Bozemans became acquainted with the Nicelys late in 1976 when Nik and Eva drove up to their newly rented house on a hill in Goshen. Mary recalls that they made something of an entrance in "that potato chip van"— the red postal van they had purchased in Florida. Aside from the size, color, and the fact that the steering wheel was on the wrong side, the real attention-getter was Eva's difficulty negotiating the hill up to the house. In fact, she didn't negotiate it. The van rolled backward and got thoroughly stuck. It was pretty apparent to the Bozemans that their new neighbors, an elderly man and his not-so-young wife, had a problem that they weren't going to be able to resolve on their own. Well, what are neighbors for if not to come over and get your potato chip van out of a ditch? The Bozemans were off to the rescue.

They say first impressions are important, and that's probably true. They can certainly be lasting. Paul quickly evaluated Nik and saw he was a very tall man. Paul was five feet eleven and he had to look up quite a bit to see Nik eye-to-eye. It was also clear Nik wasn't in the best of health and had some coordination issues, so Paul was happy to help him out. Mary also had a lasting first impression: Nik's feet. He was wearing sandals, and his long black, reptilian toenails curled over the edge of the soles. Nik's toenails suddenly had her undivided attention and she continued to look at them until she realized she was staring. She broke off her gaze, but it was a bit late. Eva had noticed the look of shock on Mary's face. Eva had an awkward moment. Nothing further was said at that moment and the vehicle was extricated from the ditch, but later Eva confided in Mary that Nik had been a prisoner of war in the Pacific during WWII and had bamboo shoots driven under his toenails, which was why they remained disfigured. Apparently that was the best story Eva could think of on short notice. The toenails were never discussed again (Mary Bozeman interview with the authors).

Nik and Eva's house in Goshen near the Bozemans.

After only a few months, they were off again, this time to Grady, Alabama. Their life, reduced to a pile of boxes, didn't get unpacked there either. After only a few months, they were off again, this time to a white house on rural route Ramer, Alabama. This place seemed to suit them, and they stayed for nearly five years.

Although the locations changed, Nik didn't. He was still an eccentric collection of idiosyncrasies and a real handful to deal with. One of their minor episodes involved a topic that was something of a sore subject with Nik. Eva learned there was going to be a movie on television about the billionaire Howard Hughes and wanted to see it. Nik predictably went into a huff and refused to watch it or discuss it, other than to state firmly, "The books and movies about Howard Hughes are nothing but lies." Since television was still banned in the Nicely home, Eva watched the show at a neighbor's house. She was not at all surprised when the man depicted in the movie had exactly the same mannerisms as Nik.

The white house in rural route Ramer with their van. Compare Nik's actual height to the van height, which is six feet four inches high.

It wasn't too long before Eva needed another vacation from the craziness of Nik. Her daughter, Denise, rented an apartment for her in Florida, so Eva took off for several months of peace and quiet. It wasn't that she didn't love him; she did. It was just that he had a way of making his craziness her craziness, and she had to leave and regroup occasionally so the condition didn't become permanent. When she returned, refreshed, to Alabama, she discovered Nik hadn't done a very good job of caring for himself. At this time, the aides were not available to help, as they had returned to a more normal existence. He hadn't been eating properly and was in poor physical condition. Eva was concerned and set to work caring for him, but it was a few months before his strength was totally restored.

Nik remained reclusive. Since the announced death of Howard Hughes, he had virtually gone into hiding. Eva was used to this, but it still was aggravating. Only a couple of times since 1976 had he accompanied her anywhere, even to the store. In the late 1970s, country singer Marty Robbins was playing a concert at a nearby military base, and Eva wanted to go in the worst way. She was a huge fan of Robbins, and she did her best to entice Nik to go with her. He was familiar with Robbins and remembered his songs of the Old West from his youth. Eva could tell he wanted to go, but in the end, he remained in hiding, and Eva went alone. Her disappointment was offset by the graciousness of the singer, who socialized with the military personnel and retirees after his concert. Eva had a long conversation with him and was as thrilled as a schoolgirl. It always stood out as a special memory.

After staying in one place for about five years, by 1982, it was time to pick up the boxes and move again. This time the choice of the location was going to be unilateral. Nik refused to go out in public and left the house hunting exclusively to Eva. She found a place not far away, on Goshen Rural Route, about seven miles northwest of Goshen, so the boxes were again placed in vehicles and hauled to their new home.

They really didn't get a chance to unpack. Their landlord was a sociable type who wanted to be on the property and spend a lot of time visiting with them. Naturally, this was the last thing in the world Nik wanted, so the tenancy ended predictably with Nik and the landlord having a colossal argument. The owner couldn't get Nik off the property fast enough, and Nik was happy to oblige.

This left Eva once again in the position of having to find a new place to live, only this time there wasn't a great deal of time to shop around. However, she had purchased twenty acres of beautifully wooded land just east of their current location several years earlier, and it was available and convenient. There was one small problem: there was no structure on the property, so they had to live in a tent. Under the circumstances, that seemed like the only choice, but this wasn't the way Eva had envisioned her golden years.

Nik with a smile, showing the rounded lines around his mouth
as in pictures of Hughes.

Notes

Bozeman, Mary. Interview with the authors. April 24, 2014.

FIFTEEN

THE RANCH

Nik opens up, 1982

Even for a couple of nature lovers like Eva and Nik, the prospect of living in a tent, on a more-or-less permanent basis, was not attractive. A nosy landlord and Nik's lack of diplomacy suddenly made Eva homeless. As an unfortunate situation teetered toward miserable, Eva finally caught a break. Glancing through a newspaper, she saw an ad for a travel trailer for sale. While not luxurious, it was several rungs up the ladder from a tent, so she made the deal. They now had twenty beautiful acres and a real roof, of sorts, over their heads.

The travel trailer located on the twenty acre wooded ranch.

The property was beautiful. It extended far back from the road, through a thick wood and into a pretty little meadow that rolled onto a high bluff. It was a little paradise for the two lovers of the outdoors, especially for the one who wanted to disappear. The odds of anyone randomly stumbling upon their little trailer in the woods were pretty low. The twenty acres made a first-class hiding place. Eva's luck with the classified ads continued, and she quickly found a twelve-foot by twenty-four-foot storage structure, so now even their massive collection of boxes had a secure home. This was important, since Nik would never let Eva fully unpack. In all of their years together, he always wanted to be able to make a fast exit if necessary, and he didn't want to be slowed down by having to gather his belongings.

Nik petting Koni, his favorite dog. Note Nik's chin and line on his left cheek.

Moving the boxes was made easier by the fact that Eva purchased a brand new 1982 Chevrolet van a few months earlier in the fall of 1981. What wouldn't fit in the van was tossed in a U-Haul trailer and towed. With less than ten miles between the properties, driving to the new home wasn't much of a trip, but the moving and lifting was something less than enjoyable. Fortunately, they'd had a lot of practice, so they were good at it.

Howard Hughes in 1947 after the Senate Hearings. Note lines on left cheek and chin.
(Photo: UNLV Libraries, Special Collections)

It was a very special moment for Eva when the last load was finished. She had been dreaming of having her very own piece of land. The St. Eustatius property didn't really count because it was foreign, but the soil she now held lovingly in her hands was in the good old USA; she owned a piece of America! She was speechless as she scooped up the soil. Although Nik was less emotionally moved by the quasi-ceremonial moment, he was no less happy to be in such a serene environment. He was every bit as committed to trees, animals, and nature as Eva, and the experience of planting and nurturing on their own property brought them together and filled them both with joy. The animal life seemed pleased with their new neighbors as well. Eva quickly gained the trust of the birds by feeding them and talking gently to them. A frisky mockingbird was a daily visitor, and Eva had a special little wren that stopped by every morning, so she could feed him his breakfast of pecan bits. The arrangement was clearly working out well for everyone.

Once settled in their small but adequate trailer, the couple set out on a program of planting trees and flowers that bordered on the obsessive. They always cultivated plants wherever they were, but it had always been on someone else's land that they might leave at any moment. Now they had permanence. Eva knew she would be around to pick the flowers she planted, if she chose to do so, and Nik knew he would be able to watch his trees mature for as long as he lived. The trees were especially important to Nik, so it wasn't surprising he devised a strange ritual for the planting and caring of them. He began with a display of energy that belied his age, as he grabbed his shovel and set to work as though his very life depended on it. The holes he dug to plant his trees were tremendous, much larger than necessary. He apparently equated all of this extra effort with quality. He wanted to be the perfect tree planter, so he would grow special trees. He dug and shoveled and patted the trees gently into place with his gloved hands. He was deadly serious about his mission and overjoyed with his work. Watching him made Eva smile.

Nik finished off the planting ritual by placing a strong staff next to each little tree. Atop the staff, he would place an overturned paper bag or tin can. He called them his voodoos. The idea was the rustling of the bags and cans would frighten the deer away and keep them from eating the young trees. As his obsessive planting continued, he soon had an army of voodoos surrounding their trailer and adjacent outdoor living area. Nik was pleased with the results of his efforts and confided to Eva that at night his voodoo army could easily be mistaken for people and frighten off potential intruders. Eva went out to take a look for herself one night and found sure enough that he was right. She didn't have to get too far away before the voodoos, gently swaying in the breeze, began to look a bit eerie. The spectacle was certainly not inviting to trespassers.

Nik wasn't too far into his planting marathon when he was sidelined by a problem he couldn't conquer on his own. He started to have pain in two of his teeth. His natural inclination was to ignore the problem, but after a few days, it was clear the pain wasn't going to go away spontaneously. Now, he had to make a decision about which was worse, the pain in his teeth or the pain of going out in public and possibly being seen by someone he didn't want to see him. He stalled and considered this for as long as he could, but the tooth pain eventually won. He had to see a dentist. Nik never went to a dentist in all of their time together, except when he was in the VA Hospital, so Eva set out to find someone local.

She settled on a Dr. Blumentritt at the Dixie Dental located high on a hill off the Troy 231 bypass. Nik resigned himself to the fact he wasn't going to find a dentist in the middle of the woods, so this location seemed to be

The "voodoos" Nik set-up at the ranch.

about as rural as he could hope for. By this time, the pain became so severe his normal stubbornness diminished to an unhappy grumble, so he climbed into the van with Eva to get it over with. The dentist dealt with the two bad teeth, and the rest of the trip was uneventful. If Nik wished he hadn't stalled and lived with the pain so long, he never confided it to Eva. They were both happy to be done with it.

Shortly after they settled into the twenty acres, Nik began to refer to the property as "the ranch." When he did this, there was a subtle, but visible change in his nature. The word "ranch" had a very positive association for him. It reminded him of something enjoyable in his youth. As they sat there on their ranch at night, he began to do something he rarely did before. He began to reminisce about his life. He talked about his youth, his parents, his grandparents, and about growing up in Texas. This last subject was always of interest to Eva, since his government paperwork stated he was raised in Ohio. Nik never mentioned Ohio, not once.

The conversations were casual and relaxed. He was still guarded and not entirely forthcoming on many issues, but sitting outside, surrounded by their beloved plants and trees, he felt comfortable revealing himself to her to a degree he had never done before. Naturally, Eva was pleased her husband finally had come to the point he could be open with her. However, by this time she also had the opportunity to do a bit of research and compile a fairly lengthy list of questions she was dying to have answered. As they sat quietly in the evening air, Eva would ask questions, and Nik, more often than not, would give her an answer, or part of one.

Since he acknowledged his identity as Verner Nicely was a ruse, Eva was curious as to what happened to the real Verner. She asked him, "Whatever happened to Verner? Did he die in the war? Then you took his identity?"

Nik replied, "Yes, something like that. Not quite accurate, but pretty close." At this point, Eva assumed Nik had used Verner's identity for much longer than he actually had. As she asked more questions and he gave her more bits of information, she eventually understood that the switch occurred in the '60s.

Nik was a master at laying down a fog of confusion about himself. Twice in their marriage, he registered their cars in states where they didn't live, once in Louisiana, and another time in Oregon. His reason was to "throw people off" his trail. Even in the stories he told during these quiet moments at the ranch, he mixed the lives of Verner and Howard, although Eva didn't know that at the time.

He told her he was in the Philippine Islands in the late '40s and early '50s and caught a tropical disease. He mentioned several colonels and generals of the period that Eva remembered from her time there with her first husband. She told him she arrived there in 1949, and Nik said he had been in and out of there at that time.

All these years later, it was difficult to determine if he was reciting the cover story he memorized of Verner's life, or if he was there as Howard in one of his secret government projects. Nik also said he was in the Panama Canal Zone earlier in the 1960s, before Eva arrived. This also sounded more like Verner, but the fact he had a special relationship in the Canal Zone is without question, so it's difficult to verify whose life he was recalling all these years later.

He also came up with a story to explain his blond hair—even though he told Eva it used to be black—claiming the maiden name of one of his grandmothers was Bjorn and he had Scandinavian ancestry. This doesn't match either Howard or Verner, so it's likely it was a component of his compulsive need to "throw people off." Much of this mystery is likely never to be solved.

From the first day they met, there was no question Nik knew his way around airplanes. He had no reason to hide his knowledge, since he was posing as an aircraft maintenance supervisor. Over the years, he dropped bits of information about being a pilot in his youth, but he never said anything substantial about the subject until they moved to the ranch. He was aware Eva now knew his real identity, so he answered questions he had earlier rejected. At the same time, he occasionally tossed in bits of disinformation, like the Scandinavian ancestry story, apparently just to stay in practice. Identity deception was so ingrained in him he couldn't stop, even though he knew Eva was aware he wasn't being truthful. Earlier in life, Eva had read about Howard Hughes and was anxious to hear stories about aviation, and Nik frequently accommodated.

Their conversations covered a lot of ground and were filled with surprises for Eva. One day, Charles Lindbergh came up in the conversation, and Nik mentioned he'd known Charles many years before, apparently through their mutual aviation interests. Another aviation legend, Chuck Yeager, the first man to break the sound barrier in an airplane, also came up in conversation. Nik said the two were acquainted and told Eva about what exceptional eyesight Yeager had. There was a bit of envy in his voice when he said it, given his own vision problems. Yeager flew into Troy, Alabama, once, and Eva asked Nik if he wanted to go and see him. Nik just shook his head, because he wouldn't go out in public.

Occasionally, he would add detail to something he had mentioned earlier in their marriage, as in the story he hinted at when they were at the Grand Canyon several years previously. He said that when he was young, he flew through the Grand Canyon for a considerable distance with a passenger in his airplane. The memory of the experience made him smile, as he described his daring aviation feat. One story produced a smile and a frown. He told Eva about flying around the world in 1938, receiving a ticker-tape parade in New York, and meeting President Roosevelt. He was smiling up to the point that Eva asked a question about an old newspaper picture of Hughes and Roosevelt she'd seen.

"Even though you did not like President Roosevelt, you shook his hand after you flew around the world, didn't you?"

The frown arrived. "Well, that is different. I had to do it for the publicity," he responded sharply with a slightly grumpy edge in his voice. Eva had heard his feelings about Roosevelt and his economic policies many times before, so she dropped the subject while she was ahead. If Nik got angry, he would stop talking. However, if he wanted to talk, but not about the current subject, he had a unique ability to filibuster. He could talk around a subject for as long as necessary without actually saying anything. Eva told him many times he would have made a great senator with his ability to fill up time talking for hours without saying anything of value. She made the comment lovingly, and it was received that way. He was probably proud of it.

One of the sore spots in the life of Howard Hughes was the way he was treated by the U.S. Senate after World War II. Mentioning the subject brought color into Nik's face, and he would never initiate a conversation about the experience, but occasionally, he answered a question or two about the source of the controversy, the Hercules aircraft, dubbed "The Spruce Goose" by the media.

"Why were you so anxious to fly it? Eva asked. "Taking off in it was a very dangerous feat."

"Because they said it couldn't be done. I wanted to prove that a plane constructed of wood could fly." He told her this had been his pet project, and having built the largest aircraft at that time, he intended to show it would work. Eva had been studying on this particular subject, so she probed him with a few more questions. He answered without hesitation. He knew exactly where the plane had been stored in Southern California and exactly where it was moved. He gave her a mini-lesson on how it was built, right down to explaining the workers had to wear "booties" when they worked on the plane. He always called her socks "booties", so she knew he was referring to a cloth covering for their shoes. Nik would talk in great detail about some subjects and skim over others, depending on his mood or whether he felt it was something Eva should know. He was still careful about certain things he felt were for her not to know.

As the years went on, Nik was much more open in talking about his youth. His birth certificate, at least the birth certificate issued to Verner Nicely, indicated he was born in Ohio in 1921. He was clearly much older than that date would have made him, and he never once in thirty-one years of marriage mentioned Ohio. Instead, he went on and on about his youth in Texas and in a series of boarding schools that he didn't like and tried to get away from. He told stories about raising horses, roping, and learning things, both good and bad, from the cowboys. The stories of the cowboys and the ranch made him smile. The stories of the boarding schools made him frown, but he finally reached the point where he felt comfortable talking about most things in his youth.

Most things, however, did not include his father and mother. He stated proudly his father was in the oil tool business, but he couldn't find a great deal else to brag about with either parent, other than to mention his father helped him build a motorized bicycle. He said his mother had a fiery temper, and no one got along with her very well. This included his father. Nik said his parents' marriage was a stormy one, and no one, including him, was very happy. Eva got the feeling he hadn't spent as much time with his parents as most children do, but he spent quite a bit of time with his grandparents. He refused to be specific about which grandparents he was speaking of; sometimes he talked of ranches and cowboys other times about lavish parties with civic dignitaries. What he never spoke of was Ohio, a bakery, or brothers and sisters. He was always an orphaned only child from Irving, Texas.

Although he indicated little affection for his parents, he obviously loved his grandparents and loved talking about them. Eva learned the ranch in Irving, Texas, belonged to his maternal grandparents; one grandmother, he never specified which, was a socialite, and his grandfather was a civic leader. Visits to at least one set of grandparents involved train trips, which he loved.

As a teenager, Nik said he had an assortment of odd jobs, some of which may have been when he was with his grandparents. He worked with a veterinarian, who was apparently connected to one of the grandparents, and had the opportunity to have contact with animals in a passing circus. The veterinarian was an alcoholic, and Nik was appalled by his drunkenness. He told Eva it was one of the reasons he always hated alcohol. He got a construction job one summer, but his employer found out he was too young, and they kicked him off the job. Another time, he got a job toting buckets of water to workmen up a spiral ladder on a high tower. He was unafraid of heights, which made him one of the few candidates for the job. One job he enjoyed occurred late in his teen years when he was briefly employed by a California power company to read meters. With this job, he was allowed to live in a crow's nest tower for free, and he became friends with the firemen in a local station. Then, he reminded her again, he earned his wealth by taking it away from his relatives in court.

The times were pleasant on the ranch. Nik would talk, and Eva would listen, as they sat outside surrounded by their beloved plants and trees. They were happy!

Verner Nicely did not attend a college or university. Nik told Eva many times he attended a technical university. Howard attended the Rice Institute, a technical school, and biographers also stated he attended Cal Tech, although there is no documentary evidence to support the latter assertion.

Despite the fact that Nik didn't identify which grandparents he spoke of so lovingly, the stories fit well into what is known about Howard's life. Nik told Eva his grandmother was something of a socialite and enjoyed many parties at her home with local dignitaries, such as the mayor. Nik laughed when he told Eva he would mortify his grandmother in front of her guests by demonstrating things he picked up from his cowboy friends, such as the latest spitting technique.

Howard's fraternal grandparents lived in Keokuk, Iowa, where Howard's grandfather held several civic jobs. His grandmother was from Virginia, maintained her upbringing as a "Southern belle" and loved to entertain. Nik said his grandmother took him on many train trips to the south and he was comfortable traveling on trains, but he didn't like Southern fried chicken. Nik wouldn't eat chicken in any form. Nik said his grandfather died by falling off a ranch wagon and breaking his neck. Howard's maternal grandfather, the ranch owner, died in 1913. When Eva asked Nik where the ranch went, he told her it was inherited by the relatives of his maternal grandparents.

Although Nik never spoke of brothers or sisters, he frequently spoke of a friend he had as a youth in Texas. This boy was about his age and his only close friend. Nik told about how their families were close, and he laughed as he reminisced about how he and the boy had swam in rain-filled gravel pits and gone off to camp together. The boy's father died when he was a child, and he lived with his widowed mother. Nik and his friend were together whenever possible, Nik said, and he spoke of the boy frequently and with great respect and affection. In typical Nik fashion, he never revealed the boy's name. He often said he wanted to go and visit his childhood friend, but he never did. While they were living in the trailer on the ranch in 1987, Nik suddenly became sullen one day. Eva didn't know what was wrong, so she assumed she'd done something to anger him. Finally Nik told her that he just received word that his childhood friend had died. Many people would turn to their spouse for consolation at such a time, but not Nik. Anger seemed to be his outlet for grief.

Howard Hughes also had a best friend when he was growing up. His name was Dudley Sharp and he was the same age as Howard. Dudley was the son of Walter Sharp, a business associate of Howard Sr., but Walter died in 1912 at the age of forty-two, leaving Dudley's mother a widow. Howard and Dudley spent a great deal of time together, even going off to camp in Pennsylvania together in the summer of 1916. Dudley Sharp died in 1987.

Although most children have grandparents and best friends, the similarities between Nik and Howard also reveal some unusual matches. Both Nik and Howard learned to play the saxophone as children, and neither was accomplished. Nik spoke proudly of building a motorized bicycle with his father, but then he had an accident. Howard built a motorized bicycle with the help of his father. This was unusual for that period of time, and both Nik and Howard learned to fly an airplane as teenagers.

Perhaps the most telling similarity between Nik and Howard is in an answer Nik provided to a question Eva asked late one night. She wanted to know how he got his wealth. Nik replied quite firmly he had not been given his wealth. He earned it through his own initiative by going through the courts and taking it away from his relatives. What could be more Howard-like than that?

SIXTEEN

HIDING IN THE TREES

1982–2001

After a long, emotional, surprising, and somewhat bewildering day, Mark and Eva were close to arriving back at her apartment. Mark had dismissed the idea she was delusional a couple of hours earlier, because she was absolutely convincing in her story and unshakable in the details. This didn't necessarily mean he believed her. That was far too great a leap of faith to take based on one conversation. The fact remained this was a very convincing conversation, and the only way Mark was going to get to the bottom of it, one way or another, was to do some research. Perhaps, all of this was just a series of strange coincidences. On the other hand, perhaps she was right.

Mark encouraged Eva to continue her story, and she did so with an apparent sense of relief, but he also sensed a bit of apprehension. Nik had coached her well when it came to keeping their secrets, and it was hard for her to release them now, even though she wanted so badly to share the story. Nik's paranoia wore off on her a bit. She told Mark how Nik established the habit of never speaking first when he answered the telephone. He would pick up the receiver, hold it to his ear, and wait. If he recognized the voice, he would speak. If not, he hung up. When he recognized the voice of one of his aides on the telephone, he would launch into his commanding voice. Eva got special treatment. When he recognized her voice, he would gently say, "That's my little bird."

Nik's communication with his outside business associates diminished, but it did not cease. The daily, hushed conversations in the shadows were long gone, but Nik still needed occasional contact. The rituals of meeting behind barns or parked cars were replaced by new ones. When Nik needed to contact someone, he would drop a postcard in the mail. Within a few days, the phone would ring, and he would conduct whatever business he needed to do. Several times, the communication was much more spectacular.

Sometimes Nik walked through the woods at a specified time, and a helicopter would fly low over the ranch and land in a clearing on the west side of the trees. These personal meetings were infrequent but not the sort of thing that happens to average people. Eva followed Nik outside on one of these occasions, and as the helicopter flew over, she waved at the occupants. They seemed amused by being spotted by her, so they waved and flew a slow circle around the property before landing a few hundred yards away in the clearing. Eva got her camera and took a picture. If Nik was upset by her "poking her nose into his business" as he always put it, he said nothing. He was already through the woods, so maybe he didn't even know.

Eva took this picture of a helicopter she said landed at the ranch.

A more sinister incident occurred one afternoon while Eva was shopping in Troy. From the way Nik told it to her later, their relationship was saved by his dogs. Nik loved nature, especially dogs. He was accompanied by them wherever he went. He worshipped them, and they worshipped him, although he would not let them touch his bare skin. He always petted them through his thick work gloves. If a dog came in contact with his skin, he would almost have a breakdown and run to take one of his frequent, outdoor showers with the hose.

One afternoon, Nik and the dogs were out for a walk when a big car drove down their lane. The car pulled up alongside him and stopped abruptly, as an occupant told him this was his "last chance to leave." Nik was totally caught off guard by this and apparently did nothing, so another man grabbed him and pulled him into the backseat.

As the car started to move, the dogs started howling and running alongside the car, and the racket brought Nik out of his shock. He demanded they stop the car. The driver did so but told him once again this was his last chance to leave. Nik told them he couldn't possibly leave and quickly climbed out of the car. Having delivered their message, the men drove off abruptly.

When Nik told Eva the story later, she wasn't sure if she should believe it or not. Did it really happen, or did he make up the story to convince her he loved her so much that he forever forfeited his wealth? Nik was reluctant to show his love for Eva, and staying was the best demonstration of love she could expect. After some thought, she concluded it probably did happen, since it fit in so well with all of the other odd things that surrounded him.

Even though he passed up his "last chance," and they were supposedly free from Nik's former entanglements, he would still frequently disappear. Dressed (when he bothered to dress) in what had now become his ranch uniform—knee-high rubber boots, thick rubber gloves, and a metal hard hat—he would walk into the woods with his dogs and not return for the longest time. Eva would worry, of course, and when he returned, she would demand to know where he'd been. He never gave her convincing answers. "I fell from a tree and was unconscious," was a typical response. Eva never really knew if that was the truth or if it was another way of saying "mind your own business." He was certainly not a man who enjoyed being watched. This was particularly evident on the day when the local sheriff stopped by to see how they were doing. It was summer, so Nik was communing with nature in his favorite manner, stark naked. The sheriff had an awkward moment.

"Hello," he finally managed. "You don't wear many clothes, do you?" After a very brief conversation the sheriff hastily departed, figuring if he hadn't seen everything in life yet, he must be getting close.

The isolation of the ranch from the surrounding community was one of the characteristics of the property that gave Nik the most comfort. He had no intention of compromising that in any way by welcoming intruders onto the property; this included mail delivery. He also wanted to make it harder for people to track him by not having an address. All of this security came at a cost to Eva, since it was up to her to drive into Troy each day to pick up the mail. It wasn't that she minded going out; in fact, she enjoyed going into town. She just wasn't certain that all of this security was still necessary. Her attitude changed quickly when she had a number of small incidents in her local travels that led her to believe she was still being followed.

On three separate occasions, she had a flat tire, an engine breakdown, and the van overheated. In each case, there was someone there to help her as soon as she pulled over, as though they were watching her. The men were nice and helpful, but it bothered Eva that they knew who she was and where she lived. She had never seen the men before. Nik was upset by these incidents, and he was always cautioning her about going out alone and possibly being kidnapped. He told her that "they" might harm her to get certain information. This was an interesting predicament for Eva to be in, since he didn't want her to go out alone, but he would never go with her. She didn't bother to ask who "they" were or what they wanted. She knew better than that by now. Occasionally, Nik's demanding peculiarities and her own insecurities about what was going on around her got the better of her, and she would run off to an apartment in Troy. There she could relax in peace and write poetry. On these occasions, she was so fed up with everything she ignored her fears about being followed and kidnapped. Being alone for a while was worth the risk, so she locked the door and took her chances.

When they moved onto the ranch property, it was their intention to build a house as soon as possible. Living in a travel trailer was a bit spartan, even for nature lovers, so they viewed it as short-term accommodations. Weeks turned into months, and it became clear that building a house was a daunting proposition for two people their age. They decided the compromise would be to acquire a larger trailer, something closer to a mobile home or pre-manufactured house. Eva shopped around and found another, much larger, trailer that they parked on the property. She later found a second large trailer to hold their personal items, particularly Nik's. He still refused to unpack his belongings, but he shifted his clothes out of the boxes and stored them in plastic barrels. Apparently moving from a cardboard box to a plastic barrel was his idea of putting down roots.

Despite the availability of more spacious accommodations, Nik wasn't anxious to move even a few yards. He still slept in the travel trailer and would join Eva for breakfast in the larger trailer after his morning walk. This became his pattern, although he started showing up for breakfast later and later. One day he didn't show up at all. Eva called down to the travel trailer and got no response, so she walked down to get him, only to fall on a loose concrete block on the steps.

She was furious and yelled at him, who was still in bed. "Why is this block loose? Did you rearrange the concrete blocks?"

He denied doing it, but she knew the block was secure before. This was probably one of his new security devices. Either that or he was trying to kill her. Her life had become so strange she no longer knew what to believe.

When Eva would get extremely mad, she would threaten to expose him. "I'm going to tell the public who you really are!"

"Go ahead. They won't believe you," he would respond with a smile. The topic came up several times when they weren't angry at one another, but Nik always seemed amused by the prospect of Eva going public about his real identity. He was probably right, she thought, but on the other hand, she'd saved a great deal of documentation on their relationship.

In spite of all the strangeness and nonsense he brought into her life, Eva really did love Nik, and knowing who he was and all of the beautiful women who surrounded him in his earlier life made her proud to be his wife. She even made up a little song about it that she sang to him with a loving smile:

From this great big world,
You have chosen me.
They will never believe me.
They will never believe me.
And when I tell them how wonderful you are,
They will never believe me.
They will never believe me.

At this point, Nik would chime in with a smile, "No, they will never believe you." It was really moot, because she would never reveal who he was to the world while he was alive.

Living in a trailer, even a larger trailer, got pretty old. Nik was perfectly happy with his rustic lifestyle, but Eva really wanted to live in a house again. If she waited for Nik to make up his mind to move, it would take forever, so she acted on her own. In the early 1990s, she went house shopping and ended up actually buying two houses. They were both very nice and located in the city of Troy, one on Murphy Street and one on Ray Avenue. Eva was delighted by the prospect of living in a solid structure, not one propped up on blocks, but Nik didn't share her enthusiasm. In fact, he absolutely refused to have anything to do with either of them.

"I do not like the houses, and I am not going to move into either of them. The houses are going to fall down, and the roofs are going to leak," he argued.

Eva knew his real concern, of course. He simply didn't want to be seen, and he was not about to move into the city. In the end, he won. They lived on the ranch, and Eva rented out the houses.

Despite the substandard accommodations, life on their twenty acres was peaceful. Nik, particular about everything, made slight adjustments in his wardrobe and lifestyle. He decided the Sperry Top-Sider boat shoe was the superior form of footwear, so leather soled shoes never again touched his feet. In fact, he gave away all of his dress clothes—suits, shoes, shirts, ties—everything he purchased in Panama. His "courting clothes" were gone forever. When not completely naked, he preferred a simple wardrobe of sport shirts and khaki pants. He couldn't stand to have a shirt tucked into his pants, and he thought it was sloppy to have long shirt tails dangling down, so

The house Eva purchased on Murphy Street in Troy. Nik claimed that the roof was unsafe as an excuse not to move in.

Eva stepped in with scissors, needle, and thread and modified all of his shirts so they had straight bottoms that could hang neatly outside his pants. Eva laundered and ironed all of his clothes, and then Nik neatly folded them and placed them in plastic barrels in the woods behind the metal storage house. This apparently satisfied his need to feel he was ready to move at a moment's notice, while offering more weather protection than the cardboard boxes, which accompanied him for years. Eva didn't say much about the barrels. In comparison to everything else he did, they didn't seem all that unusual.

Nik's phobia of germs continued to rage. He had heavy-duty gloves for outdoors and light cotton gloves for indoors. He made certain all of their cookware was heavy-grade stainless steel. This was fine with Eva, since it was quality cookware, but she asked him why he was so specific on the matter. He explained it was his belief that stainless steel didn't retain germs. Eva didn't pursue this conversation any further.

Life was simple, and they both loved their gardening and tree planting.

Eva enjoyed writing poetry and short stories, and Nik was absorbed in continuing to learn. He read *U.S. News and World Report, Reader's Digest,* and his all-time favorite, *Popular Science.* If there was a project described in the magazine, Nik would try it. He loved to fix things, not necessarily to avoid buying something new, but just to prove he could fix them. Frequently, if he didn't have the right tool to do the job, he would invent and make a tool to do it. If that didn't work, he had a multitude of catalogs from which to pick and choose new tools for his new collection. Money, wherever it came from, was never an issue. All of this gave him great satisfaction, and Eva found it all fascinating. She'd never met a man so intent on making old things work and making new things to try out.

Nik's obsession with tools may have been a factor in his willingness to slightly open up to the world. By the 1980s, Eva was in no physical condition to pick up heavy boxes of whatever had caught Nik's mechanical fancy and haul them back to the ranch. He simply had to accept the fact that he needed to allow delivery people onto the property. He may have also taken some comfort in the fact that Howard was now long out of the news and Nik was forty years older than the pictures of Howard that people remembered. Depending on his whim, he was clean shaven, had a bushy grey beard, or something in between. The full beard covered the distinctive facial lines and features that had made him so identifiable in years past. With slightly reduced trepidation and paranoia, he allowed deliveries to the ranch and this brought a great blessing into both their lives: the red-haired UPS lady.

Dana Perry was in her early forties in 1987 when she picked up the UPS route that included the Nicely residence. The sound of her truck coming up the long drive was enough to send Nik scurrying into the woods to hide for the first six or seven months she made her deliveries. She learned that it was because Nik's everyday outdoor wardrobe consisted of an oil riggers hat, rubber boots, and sometimes a kind of thong with a hunting knife slipped into it. Once when she drove up, Nik was pouring water into a tub with the hose and didn't hear her. He was stark naked. She pretended to be busy with her new delivery computer until he noticed her and ran for the woods. Eventually the sound of her truck would send him running for the house where he would put on some clothes and come out to greet her. Clothes may be something of an overstatement. He would only put on a shirt—a very large, military khaki fatigue shirt that hung to his knees like a dress. Pants weren't necessary.

While Nik was lurking in the woods, Dana and Eva struck up a friendship pretty quickly, since they shared a hobby. "I wrote her a poem once and she really, really liked it," Dana told us. "She told me she was in the poet's society and had been published and she really encouraged me to write some more stuff. I wrote three or four more poems and she always bragged on them." If her delivery schedule allowed it, she would stay a while and talk to Eva, and eventually to Nik.

It was obvious to Dana that both Eva and Nik had physical problems. One day Eva mentioned that she was unhappy because her hair needed washing and she was having trouble raising her arms high enough to do it. Dana offered to help her and ended up helping Eva wash her hair many times, much to Eva's delight and gratitude. If Dana had time, she would call Eva from town and ask her if she needed anything. Usually it was something small, like a bar of soap or a food item. One day Eva told her, "I haven't had any ice cream for the longest time," so Dana told her she would stop at the store and pick up a pint of chocolate ice cream for her. Eva was concerned about the heat and the time it would take to get to the ranch. "That's okay," Dana told her, "if it melts you can drink it." Ice cream became a regular delivery.

"I think me and the mail lady were their lifeline," Dana told us. "They were reclusive. Nobody went to see them. She [the postal delivery woman] would take Eva down to the Walmart in Troy when they had to have stuff. When I would come by M&F Grocery up on Troy Highway, I would call her and say, 'Miss Eva, do you need anything from the store?' and she would say, 'Well, if you could, maybe you could bring me . . .' whatever, a bar of soap or something. I would buy it and take it to her. She loved Hershey's chocolate bars and I would take her one every time I saw her. Once I brought her a whole case and she hid them. She said Nik would eat them all if he found them."

Nik and Eva were prodigious consumers, a fact that generally had Dana delivering items to the house at least three times a week. As if it wasn't odd enough that they bought all of these things, it was apparent that they didn't even open the boxes when they arrived. Dana saw that the house was "full of everything" when she went in to help Eva. Boxes were everywhere and the new items she brought went unopened. While Nik ordered tools and gadgets, Eva liked ornaments. One of her favorite items was a collection of commemorative coins. Dana recalled that the stack of commemorative coin sets was so heavy that Eva couldn't lift it.

Probably Eva's most unusual purchase was a steel shipping container that had been used on an ocean-going cargo ship. She was deathly afraid of snakes, which were abundant in the area, and someone put the idea in her head that she could sleep absolutely snake-free in this vault-like box. Dana tried to talk her out of it, as did the woman who delivered the mail, but Eva was not deterred. Not only did she buy the container and convert it to a bedroom, but she said she paid $17,000 for it! Dana and the mail carrier felt she had been taken advantage of. As for Nik, he refused to go into the thing.

Since there weren't many people in the area, the few who were there got to know one another. The woman who delivered the mail was also delivering boxes of stuff to the house all the time, and on occasion she and Dana talked about all of the things they bought and never opened. The purchases, particularly the shipping container, indicated that the couple must have a lot more money than they appeared to have. The mail carrier told Dana that Nik got an envelope every month, presumably a statement, from a bank in New York City. Since neither of them had ever been in New York, it's just another mystery.

Since Nik liked Dana, it was Nik's nature to want to give her gifts. He didn't give her flowers; that would have been most inappropriate for a married man. Instead, he gave her tools. He even went so far as to give her a brush cutter, a heavy duty, self-propelled mower used to cut underbrush. (Dana and her husband, David, affectionately named the machine "Miss Eva.") "My husband and I went down and got it. My husband was a real talker and mechanically minded. Nik took him on a tour and he started pulling out things and showing them to him and he ended up giving him several things. Brand new things in boxes. They never opened them. He talked to my husband like he hadn't talked to anyone in years" (Dana Perry interview with the authors).

In a sense, Dana's observation was correct. Nik had been defensive and kept his thoughts to himself ever since he'd met Eva. Now he began to open up a bit. For Eva, one of the best parts of these final years together was listening to his stories. Eva felt free to ask any question about his real identity, and Nik was usually forthcoming; at least, he was more open than he had been in the past. He still avoided mentioning names of his business associates, telling her it was dangerous to know too much about those dealings, but on other parts of what had become the Hughes legend, he was willing to share information. Sometimes, he actually was amused by doing this.

Nik with Koni. Note the roundness of his head.

Eva asked a lot of questions about his life in the 1930s, when he was very much in the public eye. The way he told it, Nik was apparently not all that happy in high society. He told her that he would get invited to the opera by friends and feel obligated to attend. He would grudgingly put on his tuxedo and join them at the appointed time and place, but Nik soon discovered he wasn't the only one in the group who had disdain for high society. After the performance started, a number of the men would sneak out to the lobby to smoke and swap stories. Nik quickly joined them and had a pretty good time, until intermission, when everyone had to slip back into their seats next to their wives and dates for the conclusion of the performance.

Nik made it clear he hadn't been any more comfortable in groups as a young man than he was as an old one. He told Eva he would pass through Hollywood parties just long enough to be seen by everyone and then try to make his escape. He laughed as he told her that he would sometimes sneak out through the kitchen door, asking the chef if he could get a plate of the evening's meal to take with him. The chefs were no doubt dumbfounded, but they did it. Once, in New York, he was invited to a party at the Rockefeller's. He was particularly uncomfortable that night, so he asked Mr. Rockefeller, "Would it be possible to take our meals in the kitchen? I am not comfortable with the other guests." Rockefeller, surprisingly, thought this was an excellent idea, so the two of them ate in the kitchen and had a very entertaining conversation.

Howard Hughes during Senate Hearings in 1947. Note his rounded head.
(Photo: UNLV Libraries, Special Collections)

Not every story was a pleasant one that made him laugh. He mentioned the time he got into a fight, and his eye actually popped out to a degree, and his nose was severely damaged. He wasn't too proud to admit it would have been a lot worse if his aides hadn't arrived in time.

Another sore subject was Hollywood. Nik hated Hollywood with a passion that was chilling. Most of the time he would avoid the subject altogether, but occasionally he would comment through gritted teeth. He told Eva most movie stars really weren't very good people. He had a serious dislike for Jack Benny, but he had to admit Jimmy Stewart and Bob Hope were good guys who he'd known, enjoyed, and admired. For the rest of them, he had contempt.

He told her, "I should take you out there to Hollywood and let you see for yourself just what fakes and phonies they are. Maybe you wouldn't be so crazy about them."

Other than these few comments, movies were off limits, even his own. It was obvious something in that business had wounded him deeply.

He also admitted some failures in his life. Eva had been very impressed by his knowledge of the mining business when they were touring Arizona and asked him how he did with the mines he purchased when he was younger. He admitted this was not one of his successes; in fact, he stated quite plainly the mines turned out to be useless, and buying them was not a good idea. He repeated his earlier comment, telling her to forget about the mining business. Yes, the mountains were beautiful, but the business was tough, and she wouldn't be happy in that environment. She didn't need the mountains. She was perfectly happy sitting with her husband, their plants, and their animals in the cool Alabama evening breeze.

Things changed in 1993. Eva had overcome a number of health issues in the preceding years, but now a doctor's report sent a chill through her. She had breast cancer. The very word stirs fear in most people, and Eva was no exception. It is an all too common disease. Virtually everyone has a friend who survived cancer, and virtually everyone had a friend who didn't. She asked herself, which will I be? When the shock subsided, Eva decided to fight the illness with all of the courage and strength she could muster. Her doctor recommended immediate surgery, so she broke the news to Nik and prepared herself for the ordeal. Nik was not as robust as he once had been, so he was somewhat limited in what he could do physically to help her, but she knew he loved her, and that meant a lot. His loving encouragement was a strong support against a merciless emotional onslaught. Eva underwent a successful surgery and undertook a series of radiation treatments that extended into the next year. It was tough, but she was tougher. She fought her way back to health. She drove herself to all of her treatments in Montgomery, since Nik's coordination diminished to the point where he was now unable to drive. He probably wouldn't have been much comfort to her behind the wheel anyway, since he was constantly fretting about leaving the ranch.

About the same time she dealt with her cancer, she noticed a discoloration on the rim of Nik's left ear. She kept asking him when he was going to go to the doctor and get it checked, but he stalled. He agreed to go to the Veterans Administration Hospital "when he finished his business."

"What are you doing?"

"A lot of things," he answered vaguely. He didn't even have enough enthusiasm left in him to put up a decent fight. He had been a recluse for so long he no longer had the slightest interest in going anywhere or doing anything. Eva was afraid he wanted to die.

The burn scars on his hands, feet, and the left side of his head were always noticeable, but Eva now saw a bump on the burned area of his head, and it was getting larger. The area was tender; in fact, just washing his ear would cause it to bleed. Regardless of the obvious critical problem, Nik made it clear to Eva that he had no intention of going to a doctor. He hadn't been under a doctor's care for years and he wasn't going to begin now. Not surprisingly, the condition grew much worse. The cancer slowly, but noticeably, spread from his left ear to the surrounding area, and, ultimately, throughout his body. If Nik had any fear for his life, he didn't convey it to Eva. She felt a great sadness as she realized that he wasn't going to fight this. He was prepared for the end.

The acquisition of a second trailer was motivated by the cancer that decreased Nik's mobility. He no longer had the strength to walk across the property to the many places where he had his possessions stashed, and the small travel trailer hadn't the volume for the things he wanted close at hand. They needed to rearrange things for his convenience and that required more space. In 1998, Eva purchased a third trailer, which she used as an office for her poetry writing. Nik continued to live in the trailer furthest down the hill, the one that Eva cooked in, and he maintained his habit of keeping his clean clothes in plastic barrels.

By this time, he knew he was in no condition to make a fast getaway. He eventually grudgingly consented to some minimal medical treatment, but that may have been in response to increasing pain. He never complained of the pain of cancer to Eva, or if he did, she didn't convey that to us. However, since he clearly understood that there would be no recovery, and he seemed willing to accept his nearing demise, the logical reason for allowing brief contact with medical personnel was likely that the pain was getting the better of him.

To the degree possible, Nik retained his enigmatic demeanor. He had contact with a select few people who had earned his trust and a few more people had entered his life through necessity, but he had no intention of opening up to strangers. People from the South love to ask where a person is from, as a way of socializing. This was not a local custom Nik appreciated, so he had his ways of avoiding personal questions. Occasionally, a visiting nurse would ask questions of him, not so much to actually learn anything, but more to engage him in conversation and check his mental alertness. He was aware enough to know someone was probing into his life and was adamant nobody should ever do that, then or ever. He was mentally alert and shifted smoothly into his filibuster mode and talked circles around the nurse. He once again displayed his considerable verbal skills without ever really saying anything. As sad as the whole spectacle was, it still made Eva smile a bit to see how he could control a situation.

Two trailers Eva acquired for the ranch in the early 1990s.

Faced with clear indications of his mortality, Nik became very concerned with Eva's future welfare. He told her of a trust fund he'd set up for her, and he thought it might be a good idea for her to have a little business to bring in some steady cash. He created, on paper, a business called "Koni's Ranch," named after their favorite dog. His plan for this business was never clear to Eva, other than to create income, and his health slipped to the point he couldn't follow through on whatever it was he had in mind. The trust fund eventually ran into trouble as well.

One day, Nik had to inform her that his investments were uniformly miserable. He was hit with major losses. The only thing he could offer her was his $10,000 life insurance policy. She told him not to worry. She didn't care what he did or didn't leave her. All she wanted was his love and respect for the time they had together.

His declining health forced him to reluctantly interact with more people, primarily health care providers. He was still authoritative and emotional, so much so, that he started gesturing with his hands a great deal in conversations. Eva cautioned him about this, since the mannerisms were those of his former life, and she was afraid if anyone was still looking for him, someone might notice. She was totally loyal to him and would not divulge anything about him during his lifetime.

Not until 1999 did Nik allow himself to be checked into the Veteran's Hospital in Montgomery, Alabama. He had developed a disabling hernia that caused him so much pain he couldn't stand it anymore. Fortunately, Dewayne Henderson, one of the few new people that Nik trusted, was kind enough to take Nik to the facility. Dewayne had come into their lives as Dana Perry had, by making deliveries. Grocery shopping had become too much for Eva, but the local market was happy to send Dewayne to deliver whatever Eva ordered over the phone. As Dewayne continued to make deliveries, Nik warmed to him and they eventually began to have conversations. Nik didn't disclose anything of his past in these conversations, but they were friendly encounters that Nik apparently appreciated.

It was at the VA Hospital where Nik became uncharacteristically talkative. He was using Verner's benefits that indicated he was an Air Force veteran, and at some point someone apparently asked him something about old aircraft. Once Nik got started talking about his aviation passion, he was hard to stop. He was an encyclopedia of information on aviation history and his knowledge went right down to the depths of minutia. There were other Air Force veterans in the hospital who recognized that he was a storehouse of information, and everyone, patients and visitors alike, enjoyed his stories and plied him with questions. Behind his false identification and scruffy beard, he was comfortable, and he delighted to expound on his favorite subject. At some point, a visiting Air Force colonel and instructor from Maxwell Air Force Base in Alabama was pulled into Nik's aviation orbit and was so impressed with his knowledge that he brought a number of his students to the hospital to visit and ask questions. Nik was enormously enthusiastic about the session and extremely honored that so many airmen would come just to hear him speak.

In many ways, the hospital experience perked him up. When he wasn't talking about airplanes, he flirted with the nurses. Actually, it was more than flirting; he loved them with such a passion that it was even noted in his medical files. They used terms like "mother complex," which could have been true. On the other hand, maybe he just liked women.

Although Nik's attitude was frequently on the upswing, his physical condition declined. Several times, the VA Hospital thought he was close to death and sent him home to the ranch to die, but Eva had no intention of letting him go without a fight. She cared for him and built him back up. He would do all right for a few months, and then it would be back to the hospital, and the cycle would repeat.

Eva's love and care were not unappreciated by Nik. He would frequently grab her around the waist, hug her, and tell her, "Oh, Miss Renee, I love you." He knew he put her through a lot, but he wanted there to be no doubt about his genuine, heartfelt love for her.

An obvious question that arises in Nik's dealings with the Veteran's Administration is if Howard Hughes was using Verner Nicely's identification to get medical treatment, wouldn't someone at the VA notice the discrepancies between the man they were treating and the very extensive medical records of Verner? The answer is, apparently not.

In September 2009, Mark asked Eva to have the Veteran's Administration release Nik's records from the Montgomery, Alabama, facility. The facts they reveal support the theory of an identity swap. On March 21, September 27, and November 24, 2000, Nik's height was measured at six feet tall (seventy-two inches). If the patient was actually Howard, he would have, at the age of 94, lost about three or four inches of height. This would be normal, since most people become shorter with age. If the patient was Verner, it would indicate that, at the age of 79, he had grown one inch since his Air Force induction physical. That is simply impossible. And then there is the issue of Nik's surreal blue eyes. They didn't match Verner or Howard, or apparently any other living human.

The discrepancies continue. The patient stated he never smoked or drank and showed no physical evidence of the effects of smoking or drinking. Howard did not smoke or drink, but Verner had enjoyed alcohol. The interviews with the patient also reveal a family and personal history that matches Howard, not Verner. According to the VA file, the patient reported his parents died when he was young and much of his youth was spent with his grandparents. He stated he had no siblings, no children, and a favorite leisure activity was flying airplanes when he was younger. This is an identical match with Howard, not even close to Verner's story.

The remaining question is whether the VA simply accepted the identification that was provided by Nik as factual, or if they were encouraged to overlook a few details at the request of some helpful government agency like the CIA. We don't know. All we can state as fact is that Verner Nicely, known as Nik, showed up on the doorstep of the Alabama VA Hospital in 1999 and was not the Verner Nicely who earned the benefits in the Air Force.

By 2000, it was pretty clear that neither Nik nor Eva were in any condition to care for themselves on the remote ranch anymore. Nik's cancer was at a stage where living in a remote location was no longer possible. Even for a man who obsessively guarded his privacy, the writing was clearly on the wall. He was going to have to hide closer to town. The Ranch was only four or five miles from the Bozeman's and one day Mary Bozeman was present one day after Nik returned from a doctor's visit with Eva. He was unsteady on his feet, and his cancer had left open wounds on his head that bled through the bandages. It was time for them to leave.

The departure was fairly rapid, and all non-essential items were locked up in the multiple trailers on the property. They took their clothes and household items as well as boxes of whatever personal items they felt they couldn't part with. Nik left the bulk of his box collection locked in the trailer, but took a few boxes of odds and ends that he felt he needed. An assisted living facility seemed like the answer, so they moved to Brundage, Alabama, to a place where they hoped to be comfortable. But, as it turned out, the stay there was short. The ever-volatile Nik couldn't stand the interaction with so many people, so after only two months, they took their boxes and headed to the Fieldcrest Apartments in Dothan, Alabama. This suited the aging couple better. Sadly, neither of them would ever live at their beloved ranch again.

Nik's health was failing fast, but his habits were unshakable. He continued to wear his gloves in the apartment. Even so, it was clear that the end was near, but Eva was not ready to give up on Nik. The doctors at the Veterans Administration Hospital wanted to send him to a nursing home for his final days, but Eva adamantly refused. With the aid of hospice workers, she kept him in their apartment where she could shower him with love and attention. She was not willing to see him turned into just another patient. He was her husband, and she would take care of him for as long as God allowed them to be together.

The day arrived on November 20, 2001. Cancer claimed Nik in their little apartment in Dothan. He died a pauper. How ironic that the richest man in America fought for his wealth all of his life, and in the end he found he didn't need it. He realized the greatest treasure he ever had was his wife, Eva Renee McLelland.

THE FRONT OF THIS DOCUMENT IS PINK - BACK OF THIS DOCUMENT IS BLUE AND HAS AN ARTIFICIAL WATERMARK - HOLD AT AN ANGLE TO VIEW

THIS IS A TRUE AND EXACT COPY OF THE RECORD ON FILE WITH THE
HOUSTON COUNTY HEALTH DEPARTMENT.

SIGNATURE OF REGISTRAR

NOVEMBER 30, 2001
DATE OF ISSUE

ALABAMA

CERTIFICATE OF DEATH

State File Number **101**

1. DECEASED-NAME First Middle Last	2. DATE OF DEATH	3. COUNTY OF DEATH	
Verner Dale NICELY	November 20, 2001	Houston	

4. CITY, TOWN, OR LOCATION OF DEATH AND ZIP CODE	5. INSIDE CITY LIMITS	6. PLACE OF DEATH
Dothan 36301	Yes	44 Fieldcrest Lane Apt. # 2606

7. IF HOSPITAL	8. OF HISPANIC ORIGIN	White	9. RACE	10. SEX
	No		White	Male

11. AGE 80 YRS	12. UNDER 1 YEAR MOS DAYS	UNDER 1 DAY HOURS MINS	13. DATE OF BIRTH July 7, 1921	14. DECEASED'S SOCIAL SECURITY NUMBER 274-12-8132

15. EDUCATION College 4	16. MARITAL STATUS Married	17. SURVIVING SPOUSE Renee Campbell	18. Was Decedent ever in Armed Forces Yes

19. STATE OF BIRTH Texas	20. RESIDENCE-STATE Alabama	21. COUNTY Houston	22. CITY, TOWN Dothan 36301

23. INSIDE CITY LIMITS Yes	24. STREET AND NUMBER 44 Fieldcrest Lane #2606	25. INFORMANT-Name and Address Renee Nicely 44 Fieldcrest Ln. #2606 Dothan, AL 36301

26. USUAL OCCUPATION U. S. Air Force	27. KIND OF BUSINESS OR INDUSTRY Military

28. FATHER-NAME First Middle Last Verner Nicely	29. MAIDEN NAME OF MOTHER First Middle Last Hazel C. Roush

30. DISPOSITION OF BODY Cremation	31. DATE OF DISPOSITION Nov. 21, 2001	32. CEMETERY OR CREMATORY Southern Cremation Ser	33. LOCATION Dothan, Alabama

34. FUNERAL HOME BYRD FUNERAL HOME 3409 W. MAIN STREET, DOTHAN AL 36305	35. FUNERAL DIRECTOR Max B. Jackson	36. DATE SIGNED BY FUNERAL DIRECTOR Nov. 26, 2001

37. Certifying Physician _Medical Examiner _Coroner

Signature:

39. TIME AND DATE OF DEATH 10:20 AM November 20, 2001	40. DATE AND TIME PRONOUNCED DEAD	41. NAME AND TITLE OF PERSON WHO COMPLETED CAUSE OF DEATH Ted Faulk, M.D.	38. DATE SIGNED Nov. 28, 2001

42. ADDRESS OF PERSON WHO COMPLETED CAUSE OF DEATH 1812 E. Main Street Dothan AL 36301	43. CORONER LICENSE NUMBER 6629

44. REGISTRAR Gloria R. Thorne	For State or County use only	45. DATE FILED Nov. 30, 2001

MEDICAL CERTIFICATION

46. PART I. Enter the diseases, injuries, or complications that caused the death.

IMMEDIATE CAUSE a.	DUE TO (OR AS A CONSEQUENCE OF):	APPROXIMATE INTERVAL BETWEEN ONSET AND DEATH
b.	DUE TO (OR AS A CONSEQUENCE OF):	
c.	DUE TO (OR AS A CONSEQUENCE OF):	

This is a legal record and must be filed within five (5) days after death.

CDC - ADPH-F-HS 2/Rev. 11-93

Nik's Death Certificate dated November 20, 2001. Eva ensured his birth place was listed
as Texas, not Ohio, since Nik only talked about being from Texas.

Notes

Perry, Dana. Interview with the authors. August 1, 2014.

SEVENTEEN

NIK ... FRIEND OF CONGRESS?

The publication of the first edition of this book in May 2010 drew a fair amount of attention. Numerous newspapers did stories on the book, and there was a seemingly endless series of radio interviews. NPR did a segment, but most of the radio exposure was on shows that specialized in unusual stories. *Boxes* certainly fit into that category. Everyone loves a mystery, especially when the mystery involves billions of dollars, the movie industry, the CIA, and a man who reportedly has six-inch fingernails. There's something here for everyone.

The first major event surrounding the release of the book wasn't related to any of the above topics, but rather to the significant contributions Howard Hughes made to the aircraft industry. Aviation enthusiasts view him, quite correctly, as a pioneer in aircraft design as well as a daring test pilot. However, it's virtually impossible to study any one part of Howard's unique set of accomplishments without being drawn into the mystique of the man's bizarre personal life. The Nebraska Strategic Air and Space Museum, recognizing the story of Nik and Eva, added a new and fascinating layer to the Hughes aviation legend. In September of 2010, they organized an exhibit centered on the book, in their large facility in Ashland, Nebraska, to honor the man and display artifacts of the reclusive couple.

The first artifact was a game changer.

After Nik's death in November 2001, Eva carried on as best she could. She was always a very strong woman and that hadn't changed. She had loved Nik deeply, but his long decline had given her time to adjust to the inevitable. Hearing her tell her story, one got the feeling there might even have been a degree of liberation in finally getting off of the emotional rollercoaster that had been her marriage, and a release from the burden of dealing with a very sick man. One burden remained, however: Nik's ever-present boxes, all packed and ready to move at a moment's notice.

As the end drew near, Nik had begun to selectively destroy the things that he would no longer be able to protect and that he didn't want others to see. He picked through the paperwork alone, as always, coveting his privacy to the end. He destroyed those documents he felt were most sensitive. He locked the ones that remained in a storage building on the ranch, which Eva was not allowed to enter. Although the reduction in paper was significant, the number of boxes was still substantial. Whatever secret world he had once lived in had been replaced with a new passion: purchasing things. Anything mechanical fascinated him, so he spent his final years buying things he didn't need and having them delivered to the ranch in Alabama. The new things kept coming and they came in boxes. More and more boxes.

When it came to hanging on to things, Eva was no slouch herself. She clearly had attachments to certain things that most people would discard. If a receipt or ticket stub reminded her of a happy occasion, she kept it. She loved to write poetry and she kept it. If an item had a memory or potential future use, she kept it. She kept it all and had acquired quite a few folders and boxes of her own. The combined accumulation of her and Nik's stuff wasn't an issue on the ranch, where there was an abundance of space, but when Nik's health forced them into an apartment, and Eva's own health issues took priority after Nik's death, the boxes became a problem.

Mark had become totally engrossed in researching the legend of Howard Hughes and comparing it to Eva's story. He had also become very close to Eva, stayed in touch with her, and he went to her assistance whenever needed. In 2003, Eva developed the very firm notion that she wanted to move to Jacksonville, Florida. Her friend, Mary Bozeman, tried to dissuade her from the move, but Eva was determined. So, with the aid of a suspicious new friend, Eva was off to Jacksonville.

The Cathedral Terrace apartments on Ocean Street near downtown Jacksonville became Eva's new home. In addition to the pleasant Florida weather, the Cathedral Terrace offered another big advantage. Age was catching up to her. Sometimes she needed a little help, and the Cathedral Terrace was an independent living facility that offered her a decent amount of freedom while providing staff to help her when needed. It also offered her the opportunity to socialize when she felt like it, something she had been denied during her long marriage to Nik. The arrangement worked well for five years, but age continued to take its toll.

In the summer of 2008, Mark picked up his ringing phone one morning and heard the concerned voice of Eva. She told him that her mobility had become a serious issue, so she had temporarily moved to Beauclerc Manor, just off San Jose Boulevard, a few months ago. The problem was that it had become clear this was no longer a temporary move. She was not going to recover sufficiently to be able to return to her former home. This presented two big problems for her. Firstly, she was still paying the rent at Cathedral Terrace, and the double outlay of money was becoming a financial drain. Secondly, if she stopped paying the rent at Cathedral Terrace she would obviously need to remove her possessions. Stopping the rent checks was easy. Moving the piles of boxes was not. Mark got on a plane and went to Jacksonville.

Mark learned that Eva and Nik's possessions, once so carefully guarded, had become spread over several locations. During the hasty move from their beloved ranch in 2000, they had taken what the assisted living facility in Bundage could accommodate, but still left many of Nik's boxes in the trailers at the ranch.

When Mark arrived in Jacksonville, the belongings Eva still had at the ranch were of no concern; the issue at hand was clearing her apartment. It was a significant task. Anyone who has ever lived anywhere for a long period of time and then moved knows the daunting feeling of facing years of accumulated, and generally fairly useless, belongings. In Mark's case, he was facing decades of boxes—someone else's boxes—and he had no idea what was important and what wasn't. All he knew for certain was that they couldn't stay where they were. There was nothing else for him to do but dive in, sort, organize, and try to find a new place for the collection. Since none of the items were Mark's, they carried no memories and they had little meaning. It was all just stuff. Poking through the clutter, Mark discovered a little blue jewelry box, the size that would hold a ring. He took a quick look inside and noticed an attractive pin. He snapped the box shut, put it with the jewelry, and got on with the task at hand. The boxes were sorted into three piles: the boxes Eva needed in her new home, the boxes that contained material that needed to be stored, and boxes that contained items appearing to have no value and needing to be discarded. Mark disposed of the trash and delivered the important items to Eva. It was at this point that Eva asked Mark to take everything that remained, including everything at the ranch. Mark agreed and took the boxes that Eva didn't need.

Back to 2010

The Nebraska Strategic Air and Space Museum devoted a separate room to the Boxes exhibit and created some beautiful artwork to highlight the exhibition. As the authors, we were invited to speak at the opening of the event. First and foremost, however, the event needed content and that meant Mark had to go back to Nik's boxes and search for items that best exemplified Eva's contention that Nik was, in fact, Howard Hughes. This time, the examination of the items was slow and deliberate. Each piece had to be evaluated in the broad context of oil, aviation, movies, casinos, and a dozen other threads that wove the fabric of a very, very complex and full life. The search began. In fact, it began very well, with a closer look inside the small, blue jewelry box.

The pin in the box was not just ornamental jewelry. It was a lapel pin of high quality, but it was the inscription that was startling. It read "U.S. Congressional Advisory Board." Advisory board? What advice could Eva or Nik possibly give Congress? Eva McLelland had been a secretary.

Verner Nicely was an aviation mechanic. Neither had been anywhere near Washington, D.C. There was no possible link between either of them and the pin. However, a link to Howard Hughes was big, bold, and obvious.

Howard's dealings with the military and CIA are well documented. From designing, building, test flying—and even crashing—experimental aircraft for the government in the pre-and post-WWII era, to pioneering satellite communications and spy technology, Howard worked hand-in-hand with the government. If the pin had actually been given to him, the first guess was that it was somehow related to work done during World War II, the Korean Conflict, or the early days of the Cold War, when he was still accessible to certain people, if not the general public. It was a decent theory, but it had a major flaw. Research revealed that the pin was not issued until the 1980s. Howard supposedly died in 1976. So, the pin was either presented to two obscure people who had nothing to do with Congress, or it was issued to Howard Hughes by someone who knew he wasn't really dead. So . . . who could that someone be?

Research on the pin reveals that the U.S. Congressional Advisory Board was established by the American Security Council Foundation on August 28, 1981, during the administration of President Ronald Reagan. The vice president was George H.W. Bush, who coincidentally (or not) happened to be CIA Director at the time of Howard's supposed death, which was preceded by a period when satellites were just coming into their own as prime spy technology. We know who was building the satellites. Howard's companies (http://www.ascfusa.org/).

A phone call to a staff member at the American Security Council provided some interesting insight. The source stated that the pins were given to members of congress and the retired military personnel, diplomats and scholars who provided them with expert advice. He stated that occasionally an exception would be made to provide a pin for someone like Dr. Henry Kissinger. We find it very hard to believe that an exception would be made to provide a pin to Nik Nicely; however, Howard Hughes would most certainly qualify.

Further research into the U.S. Congressional Advisory Board reveals another prominent board member with a personal connection to Howard

Hughes. Remember Paul Laxalt? Paul Laxalt was a senator from Nevada and a former Nevada governor from 1967 to 1971. It was during Laxalt's gubernatorial term that the FBI and U.S. Justice Department cast a suspicious eye on Nevada's prime revenue generating engine, the casinos. It was no secret that the mob was skimming the top layer off of the gambling pot of gold, but the question of who should put the lid on it became contentious. There were those who took a very firm states' rights approach to the matter and wanted to self-regulate without any interference from Uncle Sam. Governor Laxalt felt a certain degree of cooperation with federal authorities was beneficial to solving the problem as well as having the public relations benefit of showing the country that Nevada was serious about cleaning up crime. Conveniently, Howard arrived in Las Vegas just in time to not only build his gaming empire, but to be the poster boy White Knight of legitimate business.

Gambling had long been considered everything from a questionable activity to an outright sin by a large portion of the population. The accusations of mob influence certainly did nothing to enhance its already tarnished reputation. When Howard set foot on the Las Vegas Strip with the intent to go on a casino shopping spree, he represented not only a change to the image of Nevada gaming, but a fundamental change to its operation. The days of the small-time casino owner who may or may not have a shady reputation were quickly being replaced by a business model that treated gaming like any other industry, and Howard was unquestionably a captain of industry. Whatever people may have thought of him personally, he represented business with a capital B. With his lawyers and professional management team that included former FBI/CIA man Robert Maheu, he was the antithesis of the mobbed-up thugs who slipped out of casino back doors with paper bags full of money. Howard symbolized big business, and big business brought financial accountability. With a little luck, it might even bring respectability.

It wasn't all about image. Howard's involvement with Nevada gaming came at the leading edge of a trend for corporate ownership of casinos. The obvious tie-in was with hotel chains, but it went much further. Any large corporation might now consider gaming as a means of diversification, no matter what the core business was. Large corporations brought solidarity, proper oversight and, most of all, clean money. Corporate funds invested in the Nevada gaming industry brought growth, and growth created jobs. The arrival of Howard Hughes was just what Governor Laxalt needed at the moment he needed it.

Like pretty much everyone else, Governor Laxalt needed to make a few accommodations for Howard in order to do business with him, such as turning a blind eye to the fact that both Howard and Bob Maheu seemed to have an uncomfortably close relationship with mobster Johnny Roselli, who represented the Chicago mob in Las Vegas and Los Angeles (Higham 202). But the most important accommodation, at least from Howard's perspective, was for Laxalt to waive the requirement for a personal appearance before Nevada's gaming regulation authorities. Howard had made it abundantly clear on numerous occasions that he had no intention of appearing before anyone at any time, ever, so Nevada could accept one of his representatives, or he would take his money and go somewhere else. Just in case his threats and the blessing of the governor weren't enough to push the licenses through, there is some evidence that the winds of change in the Nevada gambling industry blew a few dollars from Howard's pockets into those of at least one Nevada Gaming Commission member (Magnesen 31). It was a typical Howard Hughes business solution: Any problem that could be solved with money wasn't really a problem.

Las Vegas didn't turn out to be an enormous success for Howard, but Howard turned out to be an enormous success for Las Vegas. His high-profile acquisitions in the town ushered in a wave of other corporate investments, and the city entered a period of unprecedented growth. The small gambling oasis in the desert became a full-scale adult playground, and with that came jobs, families, and an entire infrastructure to support them. Las Vegas became a real city.

While Howard's investment in Las Vegas was corporate, Governor Laxalt's investment in Howard was personal. By making it as easy as possible for Howard to set up shop in Las Vegas, Laxalt, to some degree, put his personal and political credibility on the line. When word reached the governor that Nevada's premiere gambling mogul may not be playing with a full deck, it couldn't have been welcome news. As previously mentioned, Governor Laxalt made personal telephone calls to Howard to assess the billionaire's mental status. What was said in the conversations is unknown. What is known is that the governor took no steps against Howard. One would have to assume that if the governor felt in any way that Howard was a liability to Las Vegas, or to his personal reputation, he would have taken action to protect both. In this case, when Governor Laxalt said nothing, he actually said quite a lot.

Las Vegas wasn't the only point of mutual interest between Howard and Governor Laxalt. As Las Vegas boomed and the entire state of Nevada benefited from it, the governor set out to build infrastructure to enhance the quality of life for the citizens. With Laxalt's vision and Howard's money, the state was soon building its first community colleges and medical school. Laxalt and Howard were allies.

There was one other area of shared interest between the two men, and it was an important one. Paul Laxalt moved on to Washington, D.C. as a Nevada senator, and in that role the boundary of his responsibilities extended across the entire nation, not just Nevada. He was known to believe that a strong military was the best way to ensure peace. Howard not only agreed with this position, but he had made it his policy to put his money where his mouth was on the subject. Once again they were allies. Laxalt had the political connections to establish the plans, and Howard had the money and technical resources to execute them. What conversations they had and what actions they took are unknown, but Laxalt paid a brief tribute to Howard in his book *Nevada's Paul Laxalt—A Memoir*. He writes, "Unfortunately, his [Howard Hughes's] contributions to our national security through Hughes Tool Company have largely been overlooked" (Laxalt 142).

And that takes us back to the pin.

Paul Laxalt's political career and Howard's objectives intertwined over a number of years. By his own words, Laxalt clearly felt that Howard was not appropriately recognized for the work he did for the United States government. Laxalt was on a committee that awarded pins of recognition, which had the words *U.S. Congressional Advisor Board* engraved on them. The pins were struck after Howard was supposedly dead. A man hiding in Alabama named Nik Nicely, whose wife says he was Howard Hughes, got one of the pins.

Isn't that an interesting coincidence?

U. S. Congressional Advisory Board Pin found in Eva's possessions

Notes

Higham, Charles. *Howard Hughes: The Secret Life*. New York: St. Martin's Griffin, 2004.

Laxalt, Paul. *Nevada's Paul Laxalt—A Memoir*. Reno: Jack Bacon and Company, 2000.

Magnesen, Gary. *The Investigation*. Fort Lee, NJ: Barricade Books, 2005.

EIGHTEEN

FRIENDS IN GOSHEN

It was Eva that connected Mark with Mary Bozeman when he was doing the initial research for the first edition of this book. Eva not only placed her trust in Mary, but also the keys to the ranch. On a mission to retrieve something for Eva, Mark stopped by the Bozeman place to get the keys, and they had a brief conversation. Mary also gave him a picture of Nik that she had saved. In December 2010, when Mark was giving a *Boxes* book lecture locally, Mary reconnected with him to give him some additional information that she and Paul remembered, along with some more pictures.

When the Bozemans were sent a copy of *Boxes* to read, it didn't take them very long to make the connection between Howard and Nik. In fact, Mary didn't even have to open the book. It only took one look at the picture of Howard on the cover for Mary to exclaim, "Paul, that smile is Nik!" Paul agreed. The smile, with its distinctive facial lines, was Nik. The picture was of a much younger man, but the flashing smile and the shape of the head was all Nik. Mary stated that she wished she had written down the things Nik said, since they were fascinating at the time and likely would mean more now that she had read the book. Still, she remembered a great deal about the couple.

Nik was a tall man, she recalled, who wore his straight-bottomed shirts out over loose-fitting pants that were almost like pajama bottoms. He always wore light colors. Physically (in addition to the unique toenails) he had some distinctive features, most notably, his eyes. They were a strange blue and didn't look natural. "I never could figure out what it was [about them]," Mary told us. He also had vision problems and relied on magnifying glasses for close work, like reading, and he kept several of them at hand around the house. His hearing was also bad, and she remembers him turning his head toward the person speaking to hear more clearly. Then there were his hands. There apparently was something wrong with them, perhaps scarring or disfigurement, because he always tried to keep them out of sight. When the Bozemans would visit unexpectedly and catch Nik without his gloves, he would often slip his hands under his thighs when he sat so they were covered. He was careful and consistent about this, so Mary never really could determine what the issue with them was.

Not surprisingly, Mary was closer to Eva than Nik. Neither was the type to be running in and out of each other's house all day, but Mary and Eva shared the common interests of running a household and speaking of things of interest to women, such as cooking, one of Eva's passions. Mary recognized Eva as a woman of intellect and culture who appreciated classical music and poetry, and they spent many hours discussing the arts. Eva shared her poetry with Mary and was always extremely interested to see her response. In fact, she was insistently interested. "If you read one of her poems, you'd better comment on it. What you saw or thought it meant." Eva spoke with authority on many subjects, and she was highly opinionated and a stickler for facts. Underneath this sturdy façade, however, was a strange undercurrent of uneasiness, even fear. It didn't take Mary long to realize that Eva was dealing with a severe case of paranoia. In fact, Eva laid it out pretty clearly. She told Mary she knew too much, was afraid of being spied on, and was afraid of people coming after her. She didn't offer any more details other than, "You'll find out after I'm dead."

Eva may have been paranoid and afraid, but she was no shrinking violet either. Mary found this out one day when Eva asked her to accompany her to her bank. It seemed like a routine visit to a safety deposit box until Eva reached into it and pulled out a .38 caliber revolver. That got Mary's attention. "Miss Eva, they're not going to like it if we walk around here with this thing" she warned. Mary quickly slipped the pistol under her jacket and they left without causing a stir. Years later Mary visited her in her home in

Dothan and noticed that Eva still had the pistol. "Is it loaded?" Mary asked. "It wouldn't do much good if it wasn't" was Eva's response.

Eva didn't reveal a great deal about Nik to Mary, but sometimes the things she said only pointed out the obvious. Nik, she told Mary, had trouble sleeping and frequently roamed aimlessly from room to room at night. Mary and Paul suspected as much. They weren't snooping on their neighbors, but for some reason Nik had installed different colored light bulbs in each room of the house, so as he wandered from room to room they were treated to a continuous display of colors as he illuminated one room at a time. It was pretty hard not to notice.

Occasionally, Eva would let something personal slip. She confided in Mary that Nik had no capacity for love. In his mind, sex was love. He had a voracious appetite for the physical act, but the emotional intimacy was lacking. The comparison to Howard is obvious, since he was well-known for his promiscuous lifestyle, which rarely involved staying with one woman long. He appeared to lack the capacity for emotional love.

Picture of Nik in 1990 that Eva gave to Mary Bozeman.

When the Bozemans spoke with Nik and Eva, it became clear they got a bit of the truth with a bit of fiction thrown in. It was often difficult to sort out which was which. Early on, Eva told Mary she had no children, but one day while visiting her, Mary saw some pictures of young people. She asked who they were and Eva admitted they were her kids. She didn't say a great deal about them, other than they had let her down at some point. It's another curious aspect of Eva's personality that she would deny having children yet continue to display their pictures in her home. Conversations with Nik also were full of surprises. One day Mary and Paul were visiting, and Nik told them the story of his youth and growing up on his grandfather's ranch. He told them his grandfather was killed in a ranch accident and he had been sent away to school. Coincidentally (or not), this is exactly what happened to Howard. Having finished that chapter of his life, Nik went on to mention he had then joined the Merchant Marine. (He didn't say whether this was before or after he was a prisoner of war.) The Merchant Marine story got a rise out of Eva. "He told you more than he told me!"

It would be stretching it to say the two families were close, but just as Mary had a certain level of personal interaction with Eva, Paul Bozeman found areas of common interest with Nik. A simple conversation about a Dodge truck with a diesel engine launched Nik into a discussion about engines and then a full-on lecture on motors and all things mechanical. "Goodness," Paul said to Mary later, "how could a person know all that?"

It wasn't just motors that Nik would expound on. Paul found his range of knowledge to be quite astounding and wondered if he had a photographic memory. He could see that Nik's curiosity about mechanics was fed by numerous subscriptions to magazines that dealt with machinery and engineering. Nik commented on the articles with the authority of one who had not only knowledge, but personal experience with the subjects. It was clear Nik was exceptionally intelligent with a strong aptitude for mechanics.

A visit to the Nicely residence was usually more than just a visit; it was an experience. Nik was exceptionally charming and likable, and he treated Eva lovingly, calling her his Vargas Girl, a reference to the artist Alberto Vargas who painted beautiful women in the style of pin-up posters. He was obviously very pleased to have a beautiful wife. But one didn't need to look too far beyond the loving relationship, or façade of a loving relationship, to see that the Nicelys were anything but Ozzie and Harriet. First, there were the boxes everywhere. Nik made it clear that the boxes were not to be unpacked or snooped into by anyone, including Eva. He made notes about various things, and Mary noticed his spelling was "atrocious", which seemed very odd for such an obviously intelligent man. The Nicely acreage, however, was a little wonderland of its own. Nik, in either an early stab at recycling or an attempt to keep himself from touching dirt, used the old issues of his mechanical magazines to create a sidewalk to the garden. At the end of the paper trail one would encounter his famous "voodoos". He told Paul and Mary that the bizarre little army of wooden stakes and tin cans was designed to scare people off of the property. They acknowledged that it would probably do the trick. Empty tin cans, possibly "recruits" for an expanded army, were kept nearby. The Bozemans noted that the cans were stacked in an order so obsessively precise that the image of it has remained with them all these years.

As Nik's health failed and it became clear that living on the ranch was not going to be feasible for long, Nik and Eva undertook the process of moving things around. Organizing would probably be too strong a word, but they did clear some things away. In addition to disposing of things, Nik was careful to move many of his boxes into a special trailer. Occasionally it was just too much work for the couple. Having not heard from Nik and Eva for a while, the Bozemans got a surprise call one day asking for some help moving a trailer. Paul and Mary Bozeman, with their young son, Heath, got a pickup truck with a trailer hitch and went to help. Nik and Eva were very grateful and tried to pay them, but Paul and Mary declined. They were just doing what neighbors were supposed to do, and they didn't want compensation. Eva was insistent, however, and finally gave Heath a check. "You wouldn't deprive him of that, would you?" she asked. She got her way. Later, when leaving the ranch was becoming imminent, Nik wanted Paul to take all of his tools. Paul wasn't comfortable with that, but finally took a couple of things at Nik's insistence.

Like much of her life with Nik, Eva's departure from the ranch came with high drama. Nik was spending more and more time in the hospital, which left Eva alone in a very secluded area. Apparently, some of the local folks were concerned for her welfare. This all boiled over one night when Eva felt that someone was on her property. She told Mary and Paul that she heard people laughing and the sound of something, maybe stones, hitting her trailer. Whether out of fear or aggravation, Eva went outside with her pistol and fired a couple of shots into the air. The result was a visit from the sheriff who ended up dragging her out of her trailer in the middle of the night in her nightgown. Over her strenuous objections, he insisted she could no longer live on the property alone. Paul and Mary came to the rescue again, setting her up temporarily in a motel. They really didn't want to leave her there, but she insisted that she was fine and stayed there briefly until she could find an apartment in town.

The friendship with the Bozemans didn't end when Nik rejoined Eva and they moved to the Fieldcrest Apartments in Dothan, Alabama. Paul and Mary were in Dothan one day and decided to pay Nik and Eva a surprise visit. Nik was ecstatic. "Eva, the Bozemans are here," he shouted as he happily opened the door for them. The big welcome was heartfelt, but also curious. Nik was careful not to shake hands with Paul and, in fact, kept his hands hidden. He pulled some chairs in a circle and the four friends had a great conversation. Nik, with his hands concealed under his thighs, spoke about their new home as well as reminiscing about his childhood on a ranch. Finally, as though he had been storing it up, he engaged Paul in an excited conversation about motors. He was especially interested in turbochargers on that visit, right down to giving Paul the exact temperature of the gases before and after the intercooler unit. Age had attacked his body, but had not subdued his excitement about the things he loved. Nik and Eva were genuinely happy and grateful that their friends had visited them. Their friendship had endured, and it meant a lot to them.

After Nik's death, the Bozemans stayed in touch with Eva periodically. Mary remained a dependable friend that Eva could count on for conversation and the occasional errand. Eva apparently had no illusions about ever returning to the ranch, so she continued to tell the Bozemans she would really like them to take any or all of the things that remained on the property. After a great deal of prodding, Paul and Mary went out to take a look. The remnants of Nik's voodoos, along with some tools and junk, were still there, but it was the room in Nik's old green trailer, formerly a forbidden zone that was locked and off limits to all but him, that held a couple of surprises. When they walked in, they were confronted by high stacks of boxes—not just the ones Nik had been toting around for years—but rows and stacks of boxes of brand new tools, appliances, and gadgets. They were all unopened. One could assume these were the items the friendly UPS lady had been delivering for years, but wherever they came from, they went directly into storage in the trailer without even being unpacked. Mary never got a full appreciation of what was there, since when she tried to make her way down the narrow path between the stacks she got a second surprise. She came face-to-face with a large, unfriendly looking snake perched on a box. She decided to come back later.

Newly widowed, Eva returned to the poetry that had been her comfort and refuge for her entire adult life. It was a creative method of self-expression and, perhaps, even a way to articulate the thoughts that Nik could never understand. Eva loved the solitary time she spent writing, and she saved her work. In 2003, she decided to take some of her accumulated works and have them published in a book she called *Restless Winds*. She was proud of her book and happy to sign copies for friends and anyone interested. This is how the Mystery Lady entered the picture. We call her the Mystery Lady because her full, or real, identity is unknown. She appeared at Eva's residence one day, telling her that she had read her book and she was a fan. Naturally, Eva was flattered and invited her in. The visits became frequent and the Mystery Lady became a friend and confidant. At some point, the Mystery Lady began insistently suggesting that Eva move to Jacksonville, Florida, because, in her opinion, everything would be better for her there. She must have been convincing. Eva decided to go.

Mary Bozeman didn't like the Mystery Lady. Worse, she didn't trust her. Eva's few other friends had the same reaction to her. There was something wrong, and it all revolved around this woman. Eva was strong-willed. Obstinate and downright stubborn would also apply. Mary and the others implored Eva not to go, but she had made up her mind and there was nothing that could be done to change it. Then things got worse.

Having convinced Eva to leave her home and friends, the Mystery Lady then appointed herself to supervise the move. This involved packing Eva's belongings, and what remained of Nik's, and arranging transport. Once Eva was in Florida, the Mystery Woman stayed around for a while, and then disappeared. What also disappeared was Nik's stuff, including the unique oil riggers hat that he wore on the ranch. All gone, and the Mystery Lady was never to be seen again.

Paul and Mary Bozeman, 2015

Unfortunately, that wasn't all that was gone. When the Bozemans returned to the ranch to clear out Nik's trailer, they discovered that they were a little late. Someone had broken in the door and cleared it out first. If it was a simple burglary, the removal of the tools, appliances, and gadgets made perfect sense. That's the kind of thing burglars steal. The curious thing was that the sink and drainpipe had also been removed. (Mary Bozeman interview with the authors) This was an old, thoroughly beat up trailer. The plumbing wasn't worth much when it was new, so why go to the trouble of removing it when it was stained, rotting, and worthless? Maybe it wasn't the sink and pipe they were after, but what may have been in them. Was someone concerned that there may be hair or something in the sink from which DNA could be extracted? Maybe. Or maybe this story has so many twists and turns that we've become overly suspicious of everything. Whichever the case, we'll likely never know for sure.

The green house on the hill near the Bozemans, where Nik and Eva once lived, is now occupied by Jimmie and Tom Hall. It was the Hall family that owned the house and rented it to Nik and Eva in 1976. With the publication of the first edition of *Boxes*, and the continued research in the area, Tom was also drawn into the mystery. After some conversations with Mark, Tom began a little research on his own. First, he made a trip to the ranch to investigate the trailers. Eva mentioned there was a concrete block used as step in front of the door to the small travel trailer, which, at one time, appeared to have been moved. It occurred to Mark that perhaps Nik had hidden something there, so Tom dug and looked under the rock. Unfortunately, nothing was found.

Undaunted, Tom continued his search of the premises and made a curious discovery: a complete set of the *Thomas Register* from 1996. These are a massive set of reference books that list specialists in all areas of industry. If a manufacturer—an aircraft manufacturer, for example—needed a specialist in metallurgy, the *Thomas Register* would be a path to find experts in this specific field. This is a ponderous set of books and not the type of thing that is found anywhere except in large manufacturing and research and development operations. In fact, it was the type of thing that one wouldn't even know existed unless they were in the manufacturing business. This is not at all light reading, particularly if you need a magnifying glass to see. You only buy these books if you need them.

The story of Howard/Nik and Eva can become addictive, and Hall was soon hooked like the rest of us. The fact that Howard Hughes made a telephone call—a recorded telephone call—in 1972 to refute the Clifford

Irving biography hoax also got Tom's attention. He theorized that if he could get a copy of the recording and play it for a few of the people who had spoken to Nik, he could see if they recognized the voice. After some research, he located a copy and went off to see the Bozemans. Their reaction was immediate and positive. The voice sounded exactly like Nik's, but it was more than that. People who heard him speak agree that he had a specific way of speaking, particularly if he was excited or upset. At these times, he used a unique speech pattern and the pitch and volume of his voice changed in a very recognizable manner. Mary stated that Nik had a "purposeful voice that reached up" when he got excited. His voice was exactly like the extremely excited Howard Hughes on the recording (Tom Hall interview with the authors).

Would the Bozemans absolutely swear that Nik was Howard Hughes? Maybe. Maybe not. However, they do confirm that he looked like him, talked exactly like him, and acted like him. You can't get much closer than that.

Notes

Bozeman, Mary. Interview with the authors. April 24, 2014.

Hall, Tom. Interview with the authors. August 1, 2014.

NINETEEN

HOWARD'S CHILDREN—CINDY

The world of Howard Hughes is sometimes unfathomable. Between the things he did do, the things he didn't do but was accused of, and the things he did but covered up, his life is a bewildering series of conflicting stories. He was a master of secrecy, intrigue, and diversion, which is apparent from the abundance of books and articles on the man, many of which are contradictory. Biographers pick up pieces of his trail and follow them, hoping they're not a carefully crafted dead end. Sometimes you end up in a place you never expected to be. That's where we are now. Although we are going to depart from the story of Nik and Eva for a moment, everything that follows is the result of the first edition of this book and important to the Howard Hughes legend.

When the first edition of this book was published, co-author Douglas Wellman was an assistant dean at the University of Southern California, which was noted in the biographical information on the back cover. As such, he was pretty easy to find, and emails and phone calls came to his office with regularity. Almost all were positive, one was violently angry, and a few were weird. All were enjoyable in their own way—even the angry one— because people have very interesting ideas about this fascinating man. One email, however, stood out. It was from a woman named Cindy Hughes who claimed to be the daughter of Howard Hughes. Unlike several others who made this claim to Doug, she said she could prove Howard was her father and asked him to contact a certain private investigator in Texas who could verify her claim. There was nothing to lose but the time for a phone call, so Doug picked up the phone.

It's undisputed that Howard was a world-class philanderer. Maybe he would be called a sex addict today, but maybe he was just a handsome, powerful, filthy rich playboy who attracted women and capitalized on it. Whichever the case, he made a triumphant pilgrimage through the bedrooms of Hollywood—and anywhere else he happened to be—that lasted for decades. In a pre-birth control pill world, the odds were that this kind of prodigious fornication was bound to produce a few unplanned offspring. Society frowned on illegitimate births in those days, and it wasn't uncommon for the woman to "take a little vacation" until the happy event had taken place. Howard had the financial means to take care of the expectant mother and subsequent child in any way necessary—if he wanted to. Although speculation about Howard's progeny has been rampant, he has remained, for the official record, childless. Until now.

Since Cindy offered the option of verifying her story before we even heard it, that sounded like a reasonable place to start. The name of the private investigator was Jim Spiller, who was introduced in Chapter Thirteen. This was our first contact with him, and he established his credibility quickly and surprisingly by revealing that he worked with attorneys Harold Rhoden and George Parnham for Hughes executive Noah Dietrich on the infamous Mormon Will legal case in 1976. He verified he had worked on Cindy's behalf and firmly believed she was Howard's daughter.

After the initial conversation with Spiller, one thing was clear: a call to Cindy was more than warranted. She was grateful to be taken seriously and went on to tell a tale of decades of frustration trying to prove her parentage. She'd been lied to, double crossed, and had files and documents stolen. At one point she almost gave up, but in the end she just couldn't quit. This was as personal a mission as could be. It was a quest to establish the facts of her very existence.

Our question to her was quite simple: What makes you think you are the daughter of Howard Hughes? A number of people have made the claim that they are the children of Howard, but they lack any verifiable link between their mothers and the notoriously libertine tycoon. Cindy's story was quite different. Not only could she place her mother in direct contact with Howard, but there was even a link to the extended Hughes family. In addition to her mother's statements, both verbal and written, Cindy had amassed a file of supporting documentation from years of relentless research. The biggest clue that she was on the right trail was the enormous amount of opposition she received from parties that had an interest in keeping Howard officially childless. People generally don't fight without a reason. We will get to that in a moment, but first we will tell the story as related to Cindy by her mother, Barbara.

Barbara Kelly was a fairly typical teenage girl growing up in the slower, simpler time of 1950s Houston. Before the Internet and video games, young people took pleasure in the basic things of life, some of which now seem to be forgotten. For Barbara, a ride in the car with her sister, Alice, to deliver lunch to her brother-in-law was a pleasant way to break up the day. Alice Kelly married a man named W.D. Rice, who was the nephew of Ella Rice, the first wife of Howard Hughes. W.D. Rice worked at a company called McEvoy Valves, and Barbara frequently accompanied Alice on the lunch run. One of these trips turned out to be life changing, when W.D. introduced Barbara to a tall, handsome man named Howard. According to W.D., Howard also worked at McEvoy Valves, which later proved to be a lie, but wherever the man came from, there was an immediate mutual attraction.

Although Howard was in his fifties and Barbara was only sixteen, the multi-decade age difference didn't bother the couple. Howard would pick up Barbara at her sister's house in one of his two brand new 1957 Chevrolets, one red and white and the other yellow and white, and present her with a fresh gardenia. He was a dashing, charming man and Barbara was thoroughly smitten. Howard acknowledged their special relationship by giving her a ring. It was a man's ring, but a ring nevertheless, as far as she was concerned. He was always impeccably dressed, Barbara stated, and had excellent taste in clothes. He generally wore a sweater over a white shirt and white deck shoes, but occasionally he wore suits that appeared to be tailored and expensive.

There were a few hints that Howard might not be exactly who he claimed. The expensive clothes were one, since he appeared to dress beyond the means of a machinist, and he also had long, manicured fingernails that seemed impractical, if not impossible, for a machinist to maintain. Occasionally, when she was lonely for him, Barbara would pass by McEvoy Valves, just to catch a glimpse of his car. Neither of the flashy Chevys were ever there.

Their evenings together would usually start at a nice restaurant in Houston where they would have dinner before driving to one of their favorite parking spots. The isolated area adjacent to the railroad tracks near Barbara's sister's house on Magnolia Street was a favorite necking spot, as was a nearby park. Howard was always prepared for romance, keeping blankets and several boxes of tissues in the trunk of his cars. They listened to the radio, hoping their favorite song, "In the Misty Moonlight," would play during their romantic interludes. Howard was an excellent lover, Barbara said, and she fell deeply in love with him. To the end of her life, she believed he loved her as well. If circumstances had allowed, she believed he would have married her.

When Howard eventually told Barbara who he really was, it didn't mean much to her. She was a very naïve young girl who knew almost nothing of the world. However, although the billionaire-mogul Howard Hughes meant little to her, the personal lover Howard Hughes meant the world to her. It was the personal man she wanted to know. As one would expect, Howard wasn't very forthcoming with details of his life, but he did discuss one passion with her: aviation. "He told me he had an airplane and a helicopter and he was going to take me to see them, but he never did," Barbara said with a bit of irritation in her voice. Apparently, even after all these years, she was still a little unhappy about the oversight. She got tired of waiting for him and decided to go looking for them herself. He'd told her the airplane and helicopter were located in the Hughes Tool hangar at Houston William P. Hobby Airport. At that time, Barbara's family lived across the street from the airport, so the Hughes Tool hangar was a brief walk from their residence. One day she decided to go to the hangar and see the aircraft for herself. She identified herself to a man who was working there and told him she'd come to see Howard's airplane. The man graciously led her to the aircraft, opened the door, and helped her into the cockpit. She knew nothing of airplanes, but vividly remembered the cabin and upholstery were finished in a beautiful red color.

There was another family connection to the Hughes organization. Barbara's mother's uncle, Charles Matney, worked for Hughes Tool and had a good personal relationship with Howard. Barbara accompanied her parents to Hughes Tool to visit Matney on several occasions, and on two of those occasions Howard was there. He was dressed in expensive-looking suits both times, and he and Barbara spoke but kept things on a slightly formal level. Barbara and Cindy don't believe that Barbara's parents had met Howard at this point, since he always picked her up at her sister Alice's house. Barbara doesn't remember her father talking to Howard, even though they were in the same room. It's likely her parents didn't know about the relationship at that point and wouldn't know until it became obvious that something had been going on.

After a time, the parked car couplings had consequences. Barbara became pregnant. She doesn't remember what Howard said when she told him—she was in a very emotional state—but he seemed to take it in stride. He continued to visit her at her sister's house through the pregnancy and for several months after Cindy's birth. Her Aunt Alice told Cindy that Howard would visit, pick her up in his arms, and tell her how beautiful she was and that he loved her. When Cindy was five months old, Howard finally showed up at Barbara's parents' house and, in typical Howard fashion, totally unexpectedly. Barbara was dressing Cindy to go outdoors when he arrived, smartly dressed in a suit. He was met by Barbara's mother who wanted to know if he had come to take mother and child with him. "Not at this time," was his response. After a short visit, he was gone for good (Barbara Kelly written statement).

Unlike most men who abandon their families, Howard took a slightly different approach. He seems to have arranged for surrogates to pick up some of the slack in the father department. "Soon after Howard left us, Uncle Rice introduced two men to my mother," Cindy told us. "They used different names, but by looking at their pictures it was easy to see they were related. They were both Mormons and would bring gifts to me. The elder man called himself Oliver Williams and the younger Emmitt Sanders. I was very sick as a young child, and Emmitt would play his guitar and sing me to sleep. My family had never met Mormons before." Uncle Rice told Barbara that the men also worked at McEvoy Valves, which was how he knew them.

A couple of years passed and another guardian appeared. Not surprisingly, W.D. Rice was involved again. This time he introduced Barbara to a man named Cecil Edwards, who he said worked as a security guard. After a short courtship, they were married and it seemed that things would finally go a little more smoothly, but life had a couple more surprises in store for Barbara and Cindy. The first came shortly after the wedding, when Cecil, W.D. Rice, and the doctor who had delivered Cindy convinced Barbara that a move to California would be good for Cindy's delicate health. By a remarkable stroke of good luck, Cecil had been given a job there at Hughes Aircraft! The family packed up and moved to a trailer park near the Hughes facility and things seemed to be going well. Cindy was able to play in the warm sun and even made a friend, a kindly white-haired man who doted on her and always had some much appreciated bubble gum for her. Unfortunately, he also had some bad news. One day he made it known to Barbara that Cecil had another wife in the area and that Barbara was in a bigamous marriage. Crushed and angry, Barbara packed up Cindy and they quickly returned to Texas. She would never remarry.

Cindy eventually began to wonder who her real father was and where she could find him. It was Aunt Alice who spilled the beans to her about Howard, and contrary to what one would expect, the news was not well received. It was 1982 and Howard Hughes had been reported dead. Cindy, more than anything, wanted a living father that she could find and talk to. She rejected the idea that Howard was her father and set out to prove Aunt Alice wrong. The more she researched, the more the facts turned against her. She contacted current and former employees of McEvoy Valves and discovered that no one named Oliver Williams or Emmitt Sanders was ever employed there. There was, however, one man in the records named Howard. Cindy spoke to the woman who was in charge of payroll and asked her to describe him. She was told he was short, obese, and bald. Cindy described her mother's Howard, and the woman assured her she knew all of the employees and no one of that description had worked there in the period around Cindy's birth. At this point, Cindy began to consider that Howard Hughes might, indeed, be her father. Her search shifted to biographies of Hughes. It didn't take long to find similarities in the stories that she had heard before . . . from her mother.

In 1984, actress Terry Moore published an autobiography entitled *The Beauty and the Billionaire*, which was the story of her live-in romance with Howard Hughes in the 1940s. Moore claimed they were actually secretly married at sea in 1949, but the records had been lost or destroyed. Moore's marital status, or lack thereof, was of no interest to Cindy, but her recollection of life with Howard was very interesting. Her descriptions of Howard and his courtship characteristics matched what her mother had told her, right down to the his habit of presenting his mate with a fresh gardenia. There was another curious coincidence: pictures of the young Terry Moore and young Barbara Kelly bore a very strong resemblance. In Hollywood they call that typecasting.

At this point, Cindy decided she wasn't going to be able to research this on her own, so she opened the Houston telephone book to the section on private investigators, picked one out, and made an appointment. She brought her documentation to the meeting, and the investigator was sufficiently impressed to take the case with the assurance that he could help her substantiate her claim. He also interviewed Barbara and told Cindy she should "prepare herself and her mother for court." All he asked was that she speak to no one and allow him to handle everything. This is where things started to go wrong. Cindy was impatient.

Cindy was aware that a large, powerful Houston law firm had been charged with finding any potentially overlooked Hughes heirs, so she found the name of the attorney in charge of the matter, called him on the telephone, and announced that she was Howard's daughter. Cindy describes his voice as becoming "shaken" and he told her he couldn't speak to her because "he was working for the other side." This took Cindy by surprise since it was her understanding he was supposed to be working for the heirs. She gave him her investigator's name and phone number in the hope that he could vouch for her and clarify the matter. Instead, things fell completely apart. Her investigator stopped taking her phone calls. He agreed to a face-to-face meeting, but when Cindy arrived for the appointment, his office door was locked. Worse, he didn't return her records. After numerous fruitless attempts to recover her materials, she finally went to the Texas Board of Private Investigators for relief. A lengthy investigation was conducted, but the private investigator denied ever having the records and they were never recovered. This would not be the last time her efforts would be subverted by someone she trusted.

Time passed and Cindy continued to plow through the books, articles, and rumors about the mysterious Mr. Hughes. It was in the book *High Stakes* where Cindy got her next lead and a bit of encouragement. Author Harold "Hal" Rhoden was an attorney on the Mormon Will case and the book was his personal account of the research, preparation, and trial. Rhoden had changed some of the names in his account to save him the potential legal problems that come with being overly blunt, but on page 202, there was the name of a private investigator, Jim Spiller, that was not only genuine, but listed in her telephone book. Cindy called and made an appointment (Cindy Hughes interview with the authors).

When Cindy showed up in Spiller's office with her remaining documents, he was surprised but not shocked. In fact, Cindy had come up—sort of—in the Mormon Will investigations years earlier. "I heard there was a girl in Houston, a daughter, but I didn't have a name. It wasn't my job to investigate that [on the Mormon Will case], so I didn't follow up," he told us. He remembers thinking at the time that no one was investigating her because, "They were afraid she was the real deal." Since Spiller already knew she was out there somewhere, Cindy didn't have to worry about being taken seriously. He looked at the documents, and one in particular stood out. It was a picture of her son, Billy, who was a dead ringer for Howard. Cindy left the file of documents for him to examine and offered to pay him for his time. Spiller knew she had very little money, so he declined to charge her and worked for her pro bono. "She has spunk," he told us, "I like spunk." After an investigation and interviews, which included Cindy's mother, Spiller compiled sufficient evidence to take the next step. Cindy now needed a lawyer. He told her he knew people who would be interested, and he set up a meeting (Jim Spiller interview with the authors).

Ginger Rogers—She dumped him when she caught him cheating. It was the only time anyone saw Howard Hughes cry. UPI

A young Howard Hughes and Cindy's son, Billy Ramey.

With Jim Spiller's help and encouragement, Cindy thought she was finally on her way to some kind of personal justice. She told Spiller, and everyone else she confided in, that she wasn't after money, she just wanted to be acknowledged as Howard's daughter and be accepted as part of the family. Spiller put it best: "She just wants to be loved." Since the family would not acknowledge her willingly, she would have to prove her parentage in court.

Spiller took Cindy, her documents, and the material he had accumulated in his investigation to an attorney he had worked with on an earlier case. Cindy remembers two specific comments that the attorney made, "Jim, you've really got something here" and, "These people are dangerous." Apparently, the attorney was more focused on comment two than comment one. He did nothing. Later, when DNA testing finally became within the financial reach of the average person, Spiller and Cindy went back to the attorney to try to get access to Hughes's DNA. Again he showed interest, but again he did nothing. Finally, in frustration, Cindy's son, Billy, got the attorney on the phone and asked him flat out if he'd been scared off of the case. He acknowledged that he had been. Spiller summed up his feelings on the matter, "He's a coward." Cindy went on to engage another attorney, but their requests for DNA and documents were ignored. The issue went cold.

Years passed and Cindy, although discouraged, continued her research. Two books came to her attention that lifted her spirits and motivated her to press on in her quest for recognition. The first was the first edition of this book, *Boxes*. After reading it, she contacted us and provided documentation of her claim. We agreed the evidence pointed to her being the daughter of Howard and started a file on her, although we really didn't know what we were going to do with it at the time. The second book was *Family Secret* by Warren Robert Hull with Michael B. Druxman. The book was fascinating on many levels, but most importantly, it led Cindy to do some Internet research, and that's where she saw a photograph of John MacDonald.

The photograph looked exactly like Howard Hughes.

Howard Hughes and John MacDonald side-by-side.

Notes

Hughes, Cindy. Interview with the authors. June 3, 2014.

Spiller, Jim. Interview with the authors. June 12, 2014.

TWENTY

HOWARD'S CHILDREN— JOHN

One of the rules of life is that no one gets to choose the circumstances of their birth, and another is that life isn't always fair. Sometimes these rules intertwine in curious and unfortunate ways. John MacDonald's youth is a good example. Fate took him through a lifetime of experiences by age six, and then, when he finally conquered his demons, came back at age sixty-seven to give him another jolt.

If one were to get all of the news from the society pages, the MacDonald family in 1940s Los Angles was doing very well. They had money, influence, and social standing. By all outward indications, being born into this family was a blessing. Unfortunately for John, by the time he was old enough to recognize his circumstances, the blessing had turned to a curse, one that would never fully go away.

The patriarch of the family and source of its wealth and social standing was John's grandfather, Archie MacDonald. Archie wasn't born into extreme wealth, but his mother did her best to give him and his siblings the best possible chance. She owned a couple of hotels in the oil field communities of Goldfield and Body, Montana. The local brothel also wore the MacDonald name, with the profits from these endeavors going to provide for her children's education at a Catholic boarding school in Helena, Montana. Although there is a certain irony in how their Catholic educations were financed, the ends apparently justified the means and Archie was trained as an accountant, a career that not only spared him from being an oil field roustabout but eventually led to substantial wealth (John MacDonald interview with the authors). His break came when he went to work for a man named Howard Hughes Sr. His timing couldn't have been better. Armed with his accounting skills, he arrived at the Hughes doorstep just before the creation of the Hughes drilling bit that launched Hughes Tool Company and became the foundation of the entire Hughes fortune. Amiable and skilled, Archie was dispatched to Los Angles to oversee finances for a myriad of smaller, oil-related businesses that Howard Sr. launched. There he rose steadily in power, influence, and wealth, becoming general manager of Hughes Tool at the age of thirty. He and his wife, Ellen, became parents to a son, Robert, in 1921, and with their money and connections to the burgeoning Hughes Empire they rapidly ascended the Los Angeles social ladder (Hull and Druxman 107–8).

"Archie was president of Hughes Tool at the time," John MacDonald told us. "I've got a note [in his files] that says where Hughes Sr. gave Archie a raise to $350 a month in 1921, and I have another one from 1924 when Hughes Sr. dies and he [Archie] loans Howard, Jr. $2,000 so he can marry Ella Rice." With the untimely death of Hughes Sr. in 1924, MacDonald kept the company on course while young Howard, still a minor and not legally allowed to run the company, fought in the courts for his emancipation and with his family for control of the company. Archie took good care of young Howard, and the two would maintain a solid business and personal relationship until Archie's death (John MacDonald interview with the authors).

The seat of power on the other side of John MacDonald's family was held by his maternal grandmother. Born Gaynell Wolfe, in comfortable circumstances in Akron, Ohio, her father died of a heart attack just as the family was moving to Los Angeles. Plunged into dire financial straits, her mother, Percy, remarried, hoping to improve their lot in life. It became a case of going from the frying pan into the fire. Her new husband turned out to be less than ideal. He was an abusive alcoholic, and mother and daughter suffered until Percy died in the flu epidemic that followed World War I (Hull and Druxman 40–2). This left young Gaynell vulnerable and looking for a fast means of safety and support. She longed for the privileged life she had as a young child. "Gaynell told me stories," John told us. "She came across country on the train in a private car, so she was used to that end of high living. There's no question about that, and I'm sure she wanted to get back to that after her mother passed" (John MacDonald interview with the authors). Gaynell made it clear she intended to marry into money, but she didn't have time to wait for the perfect, wealthy mate. Instead, Gaynell married the man she had been dating, a contractor named Lorenzo "Renny" Rockwell. Although he wasn't rich, he was handsome, a good contractor, and his business was successful. Soon after, business got much better when he hired a man named Nick Moretta.

In early twentieth century Los Angeles, the wealthy, the politically connected, and the underworld all traveled in circles that occasionally intersected. The wealthy accepted a little corruption if it was for their amusement, and the politicians and the mob thrived on it. Nick Moretta was a young, low-level, aspiring mobster who was connected to L.A. mob boss, Jack Dragna. As an underworld newcomer, Moretta wasn't pulling down the kind of money he needed to support his lifestyle, so he was forced to seek honest employment in the construction business. He landed at Rockwell Construction, and he and Renny Rockwell became great friends. It didn't take too long for Moretta to figure out that a little assistance from Jack Dragna—who was connected to the officials in Los Angeles City Hall who hired contractors for city building projects—could greatly improve the company balance sheet. Rockwell Construction apparently did good work at reasonable prices, but the inside track at City Hall certainly didn't hurt (Hull and Druxman 64–6). On the professional front, the money started rolling in like never before. Things were equally good on the personal front, when Renny and Gaynell became the parents of two children, Bob and Betty Ann. Things were looking good, especially for Gaynell, who believed she was on the verge of the affluent lifestyle she had long craved. Then suddenly, things fell apart. Renny was struck with tuberculosis, and after a hospitalization that drained the family's bank account, he died at the age of thirty. Gaynell was right back where she started— broke—but now she had two children to support (68–71).

John has great respect for his grandmother and remembers her as a strong and intelligent woman. Faced with still another disaster in her life, she gamely joined the workforce, toiling long hours for short money. She missed seeing her children, and it ate at her that she had missed her chance to be affluent and well-connected. Finally, in despair, she approached Jack Dragna to help her find work in the administration of newly elected Mayor Franklin Shaw. Shaw was as ethically challenged as Dragna, and the two men had a lucrative, under-the-table business going on. During the reign of Shaw, Los Angeles saw its most corrupt government ever, and as an insider, Gaynell knew whose pockets were being filled (74). Knowledge is power, and Gaynell became a very powerful woman. With enough money to ensure a roof over her children's heads and a certain amount of political influence, things were looking up. In fact, they got quite good when she acquired a new boyfriend who she was certain was the love of her life. There was a small problem, however. He wasn't rich. Gaynell was intent on having money and social standing, and the boyfriend could provide neither. Taking a pragmatic rather than romantic approach to her personal life, Gaynell set her sights on Ralph Applegate, an older, wealthy man she met at City Hall, and soon convinced him to divorce his wife and marry her. As it turned out, the money and social standing weren't enough (85). Gaynell missed her boyfriend, so she started an affair with him on the side. Applegate knew the marriage was in trouble, but was quite surprised to come home one night and find Gaynell and her lover in his bed. He left the house in a rage and was killed minutes later in a traffic accident (94–5). Gaynell inherited his money and was now free to marry her boyfriend, Nick Moretta.

Gaynell now had wealth from inheritance, love with Nick Moretta, and power through the dual realms of City Hall and the mob. What she still lacked was social standing, and it appeared she would not be able to acquire that on her own. Her daughter, Betty Ann, however, might be able to provide that through a good marriage. Gaynell had just the candidate.

Bob MacDonald was exactly what Gaynell was looking for in a son-in-law. He was handsome and about the same age as Betty Ann, but most importantly, he was the son of millionaire Hughes executive, and prominent social figure, Archie MacDonald. Gaynell had met Archie on numerous occasions when he was at City Hall on Hughes business, and she also met him socially while married to Ralph Applegate. At that point, it was just a matter of jockeying for position to get the young people together, which she eventually accomplished. Betty Ann and Bob were attracted to one another and began dating. As the story was told, the two slipped off to Catalina Island on a yacht owned by Howard Hughes, where Betty Ann became pregnant (121). Marriage and baby John MacDonald soon followed in the fall of 1941. As is common in marriages under these circumstances, marital bliss was short lived.

Betty Ann soon discovered that Bob had three hobbies that kept him from being the ideal husband: drinking, gambling, and womanizing. He wasn't very good at at least two of them, having been involved in a fatal drunk driving accident and repeatedly running up huge gambling debts to Jack Dragna. He paid off a $35,000 debt so he was allowed to run up another $50,000 marker before Dragna asked for his money (128). Bob told him he didn't have it. That was the wrong answer. Dragna sent a couple of thugs to see Bob and apply a little physical encouragement to cover his debt. After the beating ended, Bob emptied the family bank account to get Dragna half of his money. He went to his father for the rest of it, but Archie was tired of his son's vices and refused to give it to him (129). Betty Ann discovered that the bank account was tapped out, and an argument broke out in which Bob struck Betty Ann. Striking a woman was unconscionable. The whole family was mad at Bob, including Betty Ann's godfather, who just happened to be none other than Jack Dragna, an actual Godfather. Livid, Dragna now had two scores to settle with the young man. After carefully evaluating his domestic situation, Bob accepted a commission in the United States Army and went off to Europe to fight the Germans, which he apparently felt was safer.

While Bob was in the service, friends and family drew around Betty Ann for support. One of them was Howard Hughes, whom she had known for years through her mother's social power plays as well as her father-in-law, Archie. "My grandmother told me how Hughes was infatuated with my mom, quite a bit," John told us. Hughes and Betty Ann became close, exactly how close is not known, but the rumor mill churned (John MacDonald interview with the authors). Whatever her feelings for Howard, Betty Ann soon found a new man to occupy the empty spot in her heart. He was a stateside-stationed Army captain, and the two fell in love. Betty Ann sent Bob a letter notifying him that their marriage was over (131–2).

However Bob MacDonald may have felt about his marriage, it was pretty clear that his post-war life back home wasn't going to be a bed of roses. Everyone was mad at him, and he had a $25,000 gambling debt that he couldn't pay hanging over his head like a guillotine. His life didn't look much worth living so, as he later confessed to Betty Ann, he decided to end it in dramatic fashion. It occurred to him that if he died a heroic death in combat, it would make up for some of his former mistakes. He got his chance at a German town named Aachen when his unit was caught in a German ambush. After exhausting his rifle ammunition, Bob grabbed a satchel of grenades, hopped onto an old bicycle, and charged into the German position on a suicide mission. Throwing grenades in all directions, he inflicted casualties and broke up the German attack long enough for his company to escape. The heroic suicide mission was a remarkable success except for one thing: he didn't die, which is a pretty fundamental component in suicide. Instead, his act of bravery was recognized, and he was shipped home to recover. There he was honored with the Silver Star and Bronze Star for bravery as well as two Purple Hearts for his combat wounds (133–4). His war achievements, as hoped, had a positive effect on his family. They were proud of him and hoped this was an indication that he had changed his ways. He hadn't.

Betty Ann was faced with a personal crisis. Although she loved another man, her husband had returned home a wounded hero. Perhaps he deserved another chance, if for no other reason than maintaining his relationship with his son. Although she was still in love, she broke off the affair with the captain. Life was tolerable for a couple of years, and they even had another child, a daughter (138). Unfortunately, Bob had no real desire to work, and his drinking, gambling, and womanizing demons returned with vengeance. It wasn't long before Betty Ann was fed up with him and, perhaps worse, Bob owed Jack Dragna another twenty-five grand in gambling debts. He wasn't making any friends.

As if the story wasn't already strange enough, at this point mobster Bugsy Siegel enters the picture. Bugsy and his partner Meyer Lansky were part of the New York mob. As Jews, they couldn't be bona fide Mafia members, but as highly skilled crooks they were welcome partners in crime. In 1936, it was decided that Bugsy would set up shop in Los Angeles to establish a West Coast base for cross-country corruption. This put Bugsy on Jack Dragna's turf, which Dragna was grudgingly willing to accept (150). What he wasn't willing to accept was Bugsy's larger-than-life public persona. Dragna made his illicit living by keeping off of the public radar. Bugsy, on the other hand, was everywhere, courting celebrity in Hollywood and even appearing in a screen test to try his hand at acting. Dragna was unhappy, but kept his cool.

A decade later, there was a drastic change in the situation. Bugsy spotted a partially built casino-hotel in Las Vegas, Nevada, which, at the time, wasn't too much more than a wide spot on a dusty road. Bugsy had a vision that he could create a lush resort with top entertainment that would draw people from everywhere, but especially from Los Angeles. Best of all, gambling was legal there, so they wouldn't even be breaking the law for a change. He took his idea to partner Lansky, and the mob agreed to put up the money. Bugsy set to work on his masterpiece, the Flamingo Hotel (152–4). Unfortunately, Bugsy was more of a visionary than businessman. Along with his girlfriend, Virginia Hill, they ran up costs way beyond mob expectations, which caused some serious irritation among his East Coast partners. After a rocky start, the hotel stabilized and was even making money. This was the point where Bugsy was supposed to start shipping cash back east. He didn't do it. By then, even longtime partner Lansky was fed up. Bugsy had to go. The contract to take him out went to Jack Dragna.

Since Bugsy had been a thorn in his side for years, Dragna was probably not hesitant to take on the hit. All he had to do was hire a gunman, and it occurred to him that he had the opportunity to solve two problems at once. Bob MacDonald was still into him for $25,000 in gambling losses. It had also reached Dragna's ears that Bob had been beating his wife again, and the thought of someone touching his god-daughter, Betty Ann, enraged him. Dragna went to Bob and gave him three options. He could pay the $25,000 gambling debt immediately, he could cancel the debt by killing Bugsy Siegel, or he could himself be killed (156–7). Bob was broke, so that took care of option one. Option two didn't appeal to him at all, but option three was out of the question. So, on June 20, 1947, Bob took a WWII surplus .30 caliber carbine acquired for the occasion and drove to the Beverly Hills home of Bugsy's girlfriend, Virginia Hill. With an armed Dragna associate at his side to squash any second thoughts, Bob waited in the bushes until Bugsy came home and settled down in the living room to read the newspaper. Bob sighted in on his target and, after several careful trigger squeezes, Bugsy Siegel was no more (172).

The end of Bugsy Siegel, June 20, 1947.

Bob may have been out of his gambling debt, but that wasn't enough to turn him around. His life was spinning out of control, with his drinking and womanizing becoming even worse. Looking back on Bob's post-war behavior, John MacDonald believes that Bob's WWII combat experience left him with what was then called Combat Fatigue, or what we now call Post Traumatic Stress Disorder. Being forced to murder Bugsy apparently added to the problem. He became impossible to live with. Betty Ann reached her breaking point and announced she was getting a divorce. Bob reached his breaking point as well, but he also reached for the carbine, and on September 13, 1947, he shot Betty Ann twice before putting the barrel in his mouth and blowing his head off. Six-year-old John, watching in horror, was orphaned in front of his very eyes (John MacDonald interview with the authors).

Gaynell and Nick Moretta took in the MacDonald children and tried to give them a good home. Understandably, the murder-suicide caused great animosity between the Morettas and the MacDonalds. John told us he and his sister were caught right in the middle of the family feud, and it made an already tragic situation all the more unpleasant. Worse for John, he was left with a terrible memory. "And me witnessing what happened, I spent twelve years on the couch, almost. I should have a doctorate in psychology by now," he told us.

Still, there were good times. Nick Moretta cooked an Italian feast on Sundays, and they never knew who might show up. Jack Dragna was a frequent guest, as was mobster Johnny Roselli. Howard Hughes would also drop in occasionally. In contrast to the way these extended family members conducted their business, they were very kind to the children, and John has fond memories of them and a fondness for Italians in general.

John joined the Army at age seventeen, married, and raised children. Other than the unpleasant memories, they led a quiet life until John discovered the book *Family Secret* and saw a childhood picture of himself holding his puppy. He wasn't happy. He was sixty-seven years old and at peace, but now the whole emotional wound was being opened again. He tracked down author Warren Hull, who turned out to be his cousin, and the two of them compared memories.

After learning the bizarre family history, there was still one huge question: Where does Howard Hughes fit into this as a father? Even if Betty Ann and Howard had a fling during WWII, as rumored, John was already three or four years old. John was able to fill in the gap. "My grandmother said Howard and her [Betty Ann] were involved. She said Howard and her went out a few times. Bob was in college up in Santa Clara at the time my mother got pregnant. The boat going over to Catalina . . . that was Howard Hughes, that wasn't Bob."

It's an easy story to believe. When pictures of John and Howard at the same age are compared, they look like brothers. It also clears up another mystery. After Bob MacDonald's funeral, Howard Hughes added $10,000 to MacDonald's estate specifically for John. "I asked Gay [Gaynell] how come I have $10,000 more than my sister, and she said that Howard put it in. 'He owed it to your father.' $10,000 in 1947 . . . that's a piece of change."

Once again, John tried to put the past behind him and settle into retirement with his wife. It didn't last long. One day he got a message from a woman named Cindy that jolted him again.

"I think you're my brother."

Notes

Hull, Warren Robert, and Michael B. Druxman. *Family Secret*. Tucson: Hats Off Books, 2004.

MacDonald, John. Interview with the authors. June 4, 2014.

TWENTY-ONE

IT'S IN THE BLOOD

When Cindy sent us the picture of John MacDonald side by side with Howard, it got our attention. We had very little information about John at the time, but John told Cindy the story about his mother being with Howard while Bob was in school, and he undeniably looked like Howard, so it seemed worthy of further investigation. We were confident that Cindy was a Hughes child, and John looked like a Hughes child, so the next step was to arrange for a DNA test and see if we got a match. We did.

DNA stands for Deoxyribonucleic acid. The DNA molecule is a complex combination of proteins and carbohydrates, which form a nucleic acid. DNA is the instruction manual that all living organisms use to develop and function. An analysis of a person's DNA can give researchers and medical personnel insight into the core structure of that person's development and health. It also provides a historical record of the individual's heritage, which is what is important in the case of Cindy and John. Each parent provides half of the DNA to their children, and this process carries on from generation to generation, leaving a trail of markers that go back to the person's origins. This DNA record can reveal a person's ancestry and ethnic heritage. For example, for people in the United States whose forefathers immigrated to this country, DNA could provide information as to their country or area of origin. People whose ancestors came from Scandinavia would have different markers than those whose came from Italy, Russia, or anywhere else.

Needless to admit we are not DNA experts. Therefore, this analysis is kept simple and compares the alleles between Cindy's and John's DNA results. Since we have Cindy's mother's results, from a DNA test performed on her, we can eliminate her mother's contribution and therefore, leave only her father's, which are shown below. John's column shows both numbers, as we have no way of knowing which parent contributed which number. We are certain their mothers are not the same individual, therefore the common parent would be their father.

	Cindy (From Father)	John
CSF1PO	11	11, 11
D2S1338	23	17, 23
D3S1358	17	15, 17
D5S818	12	11, 13
D7S820	11	8, 9
D8S1179	10	13, 14
D13S317	13	11, 12
D16S39	13	10, 13
D18S51	18	16, 17
D19S433	14	12, 13
D21S11	28	27, 30
FGA	22.2	20, 24
Penta D	12	11, 13
Penta E	7	7, 7
TH01	7, 8	7, 8
TPOX	8	8, 8
vWA	16	16, 19
AMEL	X	X, Y

As can be seen on the chart, eight out of seventeen alleles are the same, which is certainly not random. By eliminating Cindy's mothers DNA, therefore leaving only her father's, there should be a near 50 percent match, assuming they have the same father. As exhibited above, with the seventeen alleles, is a 47 percent match between Cindy and John, revealing they have a much greater chance of having a common father than being randomly linked genetically.

There are rumored to be samples of Howard's DNA, but requests for data from the organization that has possession of the material have been declined. John's sister (or possibly half-sister) declined to participate in a DNA test. Obviously, if we had more data we would get a more accurate comparison. We'll let the numbers we have speak for themselves.

TWENTY-TWO

THE WITNESS

Human beings live in a constant cycle of absorbing, evaluating, and reacting to sensory input. We have been blessed with a highly functioning brain—at least in comparison to the other beings with which we share the planet—that allows us to take information from touch, smell, taste, hearing, and sight, and turn it into data to be processed by our brain in the interests of initiating a reaction that will be in our best interests. Sometimes emotion clouds our processing ability, but most of the time the analytical process works in our favor.

Our court system depends on this ability of people to analyze data. In an ideal situation, there will be one or more people present at the scene of an event who are able to recall what their senses told them at the time. The eyewitness provides the most reliable form of testimony. Frequently there is no eyewitness, and all facets of the event need to be independently investigated, like pieces of a puzzle, to form a judgment based on how these pieces fit together. This becomes a presentation of circumstantial evidence. Aside from the words of Eva, much of the first edition of this book was based on piecing together bits of circumstantial evidence. That has changed. We now have our eyewitness.

The story we are about to tell has been a carefully kept secret for thirty years. Some of the reasons for that will be apparent as we go on, but the primary reason was quite simple: Nik/Howard told the witness to say nothing so as to avoid putting herself in danger. She had seen enough by that point to know he told the truth and cared about her safety. Having read the first edition of this book, she decided to come forward with her story out of love and loyalty to Eva and Nik. She still has serious concerns about her safety, so we will not use her full name and refer to her only as Dee Dee. During our interviews with her, Dee Dee used the names Nik and Howard interchangeably.

Living in total seclusion has its drawbacks, particularly if one is getting on in age. Bodies fail, joints ache, and medicine cabinets begin to fill like rain gutters in a downpour. Neither Eva nor Nik were willing, or able, to make repeated trips into town. Eva went when necessary, but they arranged to have things delivered whenever possible. The local pharmacy in Troy, Alabama, was very accommodating to their needs and agreed to deliver all of their prescriptions. Shortly thereafter, a bright young college student named Dee Dee arrived on Nik and Eva's doorstep for the first of what would be many visits.

Dee Dee came from a family that would be considered old fashioned by today's standards. They believed that the place of a woman was in the home raising a family and that higher education and the workforce were the exclusive domains of the male. Dee Dee was a smart young woman with ambition, so she followed her dream without the full support of her family. Against their wishes she enrolled in college, but this decision to strike out on her own came with a financial burden. If she wanted to go to college she was going to have to pay for it. She was willing to work, and the pharmacy in Troy needed a worker. It was a good fit.

In 1981, as Dee Dee prepared herself for a career in the sciences, the pharmacy job provided her with more than just a paycheck. She was exposed to information on medicines and medical conditions, and the delivery job allowed her to visit the elderly and provide a moment of personal care and cheer. "I always spent a little conversation time with each client, not only to be sure the right person was getting the medication, but also to spend a little time with the elderly," she told us.

Getting the assignment to deliver prescriptions to the elderly couple wasn't hard. She was the only one who would do it. The other delivery girls who had ventured out there said that the old man was strange and made them uncomfortable. It wasn't like they thought he was dangerous, but the experience was uncomfortable enough that they had no desire to go back, and certainly had no intention of taking the time to chat the old boy up. Dee Dee didn't care. She had a simple formula for success. Job = money = education. It didn't matter to her whether he was a sweet old man in a bathrobe or a monster chained to a tree in the backyard. She was going to get the job done.

The first visits to the Nicely residence were quite uneventful. Nik wasn't there. To be more accurate, he was there, but he wouldn't come out. Dee Dee could see him taking the occasional quick peek from a distance, but he didn't show himself. Eva signed for his medication and was happy that Dee Dee was willing to spend a few minutes visiting with her. Dee Dee felt Eva was lonely, so she was happy to extend the amount of time she spent with her. As Dee Dee got to know her, she began to get as much from the visits as Eva did. Starting with topics like cooking and getting along with men, the conversations grew to include a broad range of subjects. Eva became a grandmother figure to Dee Dee and took great interest in her education. While Dee Dee's family frowned on her educational goals, Eva was enormously supportive. This wasn't just perfunctory encouragement. Eva was a commanding presence to the young woman and shared her wealth of knowledge with her.

"Eva was a very intelligent lady. I was in awe of her," she told us. Eva's travels, experience, and continuing self-education, probably mixed with things she had learned from Nik, were fascinating to a young woman whose family had sought to limit her horizons. Eva's tales of her work in Panama and how she met Nik sounded adventurous. Most of all, Eva represented the intelligent, strong, self-assured woman that Dee Dee was determined to become.

The grandmother-granddaughter relationship continued, with Dee Dee making more and more trips to the slightly run-down residence, regardless of whether or not a prescription needed to be delivered. Eva was now a friend, not just a customer. Nik— either because he began to trust the young girl or because he was tired of hiding in his own home—started to put in a few non-verbal appearances. While he looked a little rough around the edges, he was far from the ogre that had been implied might be lurking in the shadows. Eva acknowledged Nik could use a little polishing. "She would say things like, 'He may not appear to be gentlemanly now, but when he dresses up he's a dandy.' She would call him that . . . I loved that!" she told us with a big laugh.

A major portion of the bond between Eva and Dee Dee was the mutual need for intellectual interaction. Eva became a role model for Dee Dee, and Dee Dee became a sounding board for Eva. And one more important thing: Dee Dee was young and mobile. Through Dee Dee, Eva had access to the center of information in the area, the local library. Topics would come up in conversation, or out of Eva's private thoughts, and Dee Dee would be dispatched to find the answers. "She shared, she questioned things, she sent me to the library," Dee Dee told us. "'I'm dying to know . . .' [Eva would say]. She sent me to the library with . . . it was just a scrap of paper, I mean, it was on a brown paper bag, ripped off," Dee Dee told us laughing. "'See what you can find for me.'"

"The first thing she wanted me to look up . . . this guy . . . he had something to do with the LDS Church [Church of Jesus Christ of Latter-day Saints] and she wanted to look him up, check him out. He had something to do with airplanes. And I thought, how did she know [of] this man? From there she wanted to know immediately about Howard Hughes. The two things were connected. That's when I started to have questions." One answer appeared almost immediately. Dee Dee had never given any thought to Howard Hughes, but while doing Eva's research about him at the library, she saw his picture in the books. With the two men connected in her mind, everything suddenly made sense. She was stunned. That was the moment she knew Nik was Howard.

As the conversations and trips to the library progressed, it was apparent to Dee Dee that she was helping Eva conduct an organized and focused research project. Looking back, Dee Dee feels Eva decided to start digging after years of not asking any questions. Perhaps she had turned a corner in her life and wanted some solid answers, or perhaps it was access to a trusted and mobile friend like Dee Dee that finally gave her the first opportunity to reach out for answers. Whichever the case, Eva was on a mission for information and Dee Dee was along for the ride. Her questions and suspicions about the elderly couple were about to be answered through a life-changing friendship with Nik.

Eva needed to get away. She didn't say why, but whatever the reason, one day Eva told Dee Dee she needed to make a trip to Florida. She wasn't comfortable leaving Nik entirely alone for any length of time, so she asked the young woman if she would stop in on Nik, check on him, and make sure he got some decent meals. Dee Dee was happy to accommodate. Eva, rather cautiously, prepared Dee Dee for the full Nik experience. At this stage of the friendship, she didn't seem to know how much to reveal to her young friend. She told Dee Dee that Nik might say something "off the wall" and that she should "make light of everything." It didn't matter to Dee Dee. "I wasn't going to let [Eva] scare me away. I needed that job so bad." And so the deal was done. Dee Dee was launched into the Twilight Zone of Nik's world.

Nik most certainly would have had to agree to this in advance, which is interesting. He had resolutely avoided almost all outside human contact before and after the supposed death of Howard Hughes, but five or six years after the funeral, he seemed to have loosened up just a little bit. Some of this may be directly related to Dee Dee. Eva always said Nik had an eye for seventeen-year-old girls, and although Dee Dee was a few years older, the presence of an attractive young lady would certainly not be unwelcome. Eva had grown close to Dee Dee and had certainly shared her feelings with Nik, but there was also one more factor. Nik had medical needs and he, no doubt, trusted that the young woman had the knowledge to help him. After all, she was the one who delivered his medical supplies.

"He got this cream for his hands," Dee Dee told us. "He had a special cream because he had sensitivity to the touch. You didn't touch him. You didn't shake hands with him. You couldn't, it hurt him so bad." Nik appreciated Dee Dee's delicate touch when she applied the cream to his hands and feet. He felt compelled to explain the scars. "He told me he had survived a plane crash." Remembering Eva's remarks, Dee Dee had only one thought, a dubious "Yeah . . . right."

Dee Dee photographed by Eva, early '80s.

The Nik and Dee Dee relationship got off to a flying start from the first day. Dee Dee loved to bake and cook, and she was good at it. On the day of Eva's departure, Dee Dee showed up with a smile, a cheerful attitude, and a loaf of her homemade banana bread. A smiling, cheerful young lady will generally lift the spirits of an older man, but banana bread will definitely push friendship to a higher level. Nik was in heaven. He ate the entire loaf of banana bread before Eva even got out of the door. He was immediately comfortable with Dee Dee, and in no time he was calling her "kiddo" and teasing her about her love for Elvis Presley's music.

As with Eva, Nik was especially supportive of Dee Dee's educational aspirations. He would even help her study and was particularly helpful with her biology and chemistry studies. He had a very firm way of encouraging her. "You can do this," he would say to her, as though removing all choice in the matter. When he sensed she was low on money and needed books, he would quietly solve the problem. "He'd just call them up and pay for my books. I don't know the specifics of that. He would just tell me they were paid and I knew they were."

Education was another area where Nik was full of contradictions. He was obviously extremely intelligent with a broad range of knowledge on many topics, yet he told Dee Dee he lacked any advanced formal education and, in fact, was a very bad student. "He had trouble in school. It sounded like he had dyslexia, the way he said it. He didn't like to write. He couldn't spell. He had people read things to him. He was not dumb. I've thought about this." Regardless of his inability to read well, Nik had managed to absorb a great deal of knowledge and had the ability to analyze it and convey it to others.

Whether because Dee Dee had an interest in science and medicine, or he just felt comfortable with her and enjoyed talking to the attractive young woman, Nik opened up to her about his personal health issues. One of the most surprising statements was about the strangely opaque color of his eyes. "His eyes were blue. He said he had them changed. He went somewhere on the East Coast, the first place they ever did that." And "he had this weird pain . . . with sensations . . . I can't explain it, but he really had this weird disease of pain and it was caused by that plane wreck." Dee Dee told us that in addition to the medications she delivered, Nik received drugs in the mail, including an experimental pain medication. She knows where it came from, but even after all these years wouldn't reveal the source to us, only that there was another Hughes connection. "He liked that experimental stuff." She left it at that.

When Eva returned, their relationship continued, except in addition to the grandmother figure of Eva, Dee Dee now also had a grandfather figure in Nik. Dee Dee continued to help Eva and have fascinating conversations, as well as drive her into town. Nik loosened up a little more and started riding into town with them. It was at this point that he discovered the tractor supply store. For a man with a consuming interest in mechanics, the tractor supply store was a toyshop. He wandered through the place buying things he had no use for, and he loved every minute of it. "Eva got so tickled at him in tractor supply. We'd take the stuff back, or course." It was during one of these rides home from town that a simple event unleashed a torrent of information from Nik that Dee Dee kept secret for thirty years.

Dee Dee became family, and as such she became privy to the family secrets, or in this case, "the" family secret. There was no longer any smokescreen about aircraft maintenance supervision, or any other identity deception. Eva's research at the library and Nik's own words removed any doubt about his true identity. "By then, Eva and I knew he was who he said he was. We knew. We knew." Nik began to open up to the two of them. Whether he had a need to reveal things to get them off his chest, or his advancing age was affecting his judgment in the area of secrecy is anyone's guess. Sometimes he would be very focused and specific to Dee Dee as he spoke about things, but other times he would seem to drift off and almost talk to himself as he reviewed the events of his life in his mind. Dee Dee refers to these moments as "ramblings," not because they were incoherent or disjointed, but because they were monologues to no one in particular. He spoke out loud and even took on a different style of speech at these moments. The content was clear, focused, fascinating, and sometimes disturbing. The subject was always the same—the life of Howard Hughes.

It was on the way back from one of the trips to town when a simple item triggered something deep inside Nik. Dee Dee, as always, was driving and Eva sat next to her in the front seat. Nik was alone in the backseat where he had some room to stretch out his tall frame. On the seat next to Nik was one of Dee Dee's college books, a history book. Nik paged through it, got a bit riled up, and launched into a discourse that wouldn't end until the day he and Dee Dee parted company for the final time. Parts of history had been recorded incorrectly, he told Dee Dee, and he was going to straighten that out for her. "He wanted me to get my history right," Dee Dee told us. The thing that pulled Nik's emotional trigger was a term paper that Dee Dee had written and slipped between the pages of the book. The term paper was on Watergate.

We asked her if Nik said he'd been involved in Watergate. "Oh, my," she answered, followed by a long pause. With that, she repeated what Nik had told her about the contentious relationship with President Richard Nixon and the CIA that grew out of the bungled burglary. Nixon and Hughes were cut from the same bolt of cloth in many ways. In Nixon, Hughes saw a conservative, pro-business, pro-American ally who could push for the government research projects that interested him, particularly in the areas of aerospace and satellite technology. To ensure he got Nixon's undivided attention, he provided him with financial support both over and under the table. "My understanding from Howard was that he befriended people who he could manipulate with his money for research purposes. He preferred people who had come from no money and worked smarter, not harder, to earn it." In addition to his desire to secure government research contracts, Nik told her he had other reasons for needing people in high government places. His casual attitude toward paying taxes was likely to catch up with him sooner or later and that could be a very big problem. "Howard hoped to deflect the many [tax] litigations with a 'national security' shield. Satellites and the laser," Dee Dee told us. He wasn't clear if he meant to hide his profits under the cloak of "black" national security projects, or if he sought to get a special tax dispensation because of his national security work.

For Richard Nixon, the relationship with Howard Hughes was likely much simpler. Howard had money and power, the lifeblood of a politician. Nixon knew money and power were better than friends. He proved that time and time again. The Nixon-Hughes relationship worked well for many years, but when it came apart, it came apart quickly. Nik told Dee Dee the first major issue between Nixon and him was over nuclear weapons. "Howard said Nixon and he had a heated conversation over the testing of a bomb [using] the radioactive isotope Iodine 131. 'This isotope is 95 percent untreatable,' Nik said he told Nixon." As usual, he was right. In fact, he was even prophetic. Iodine 131 was a major health hazard from open air atomic bomb testing in the Cold War days, and became a major contaminate in both the Chernobyl reactor disaster in 1986 and the Fukushima reactor disaster in 2011. Howard was extremely afraid of an accident. The deaths from this could be in the millions, he feared, but he also reduced the problem to a personal level. He told Dee Dee he warned Nixon that something like that would destroy his re-election prospects, as well as cause problems for the Hughes organization that supported Nixon. Nixon said he wouldn't support the bomb testing, but reneged on the promise. Angered and in fear of radioactive germs, Howard left the country. Nixon was becoming an ex-friend.

The topic of Richard Nixon and the Watergate investigation was clearly one that raised Nik's ire. There was no question about that from the tone of his voice when he told the story to Dee Dee. Nik felt that Nixon had betrayed him. "They were investigating him because Nik had been fingered by Nixon. Nixon was trying to get off of what he had been involved in and all that. And he fingered some people and one of them was Nik."

Nik told Dee Dee he had been contacted by Watergate investigators because of what Nixon had told them and it infuriated him. He, perhaps with some amount of justification, felt he had provided the country with some great services in the areas of technology, defense, and espionage, and shouldn't be subjected to this kind of pointed inquiry. However, if they wanted a fight, Nik was willing to give it to them. He sent word back, asking how they would like to go before Congress and discuss everything he'd been involved in. "Nik told them, he just put it right in their faces and said, 'We'll put all of the cards on the table of all of the dealings I've had with the CIA,' but they didn't want to discuss that." The issue went away, but not Nik's anger (Dee Dee interview with the authors).

In his book, *The Ends of Power*, Watergate conspirator H.R. Haldeman states the famous eighteen-and-a-half minute portion of erased Oval Office tapes related to the Kennedy assassinations and Watergate, and that the name Howard Hughes was prominently mentioned. Nik confirmed to Dee Dee that he was mentioned in the deleted tape segment and knew "things" about the Kennedy assassinations, but firmly stated he wasn't involved and wanted nothing to do with anyone involved in the tragedies.

Nixon had two strikes against him with Nik at this point, and the CIA had at least one. Nik told Dee Dee about Project Jennifer, the *Glomar Explorer* mining vessel that had been a Hughes cover-up for a CIA operation to raise a Soviet sub. He was loud, emotional, and bitter as he spoke of the operation to Dee Dee, clear evidence of the personal investment he had in the mission, as well as multiple millions of his dollars. He felt the CIA had bungled the operation and deprived him of something he wanted. "Because they had let the world know—I don't know if it was Russia or Germany—one of the two knew, he wanted what was in Jennifer, why he was going after Jennifer. It was something like an [encryption device]. Yeah, he wanted that so bad. And it was like a secret mission and they exposed it to the world. He was done with all of them by then. He said he just wanted away. He just felt that they wanted to blow everything up. He had this thing against bombs. I mean, he hated the 4th of July. He was done with it [the CIA] after Watergate." The conversation ended on an educational note, with Nik insisting that she write her Watergate report with her newly acquired facts. "I wouldn't dare put them in my report," she told us with a laugh. "'No, no you write this report the way I say,'" he insisted, with his typically inflexible manner.

As time passed, Nik continued to provide Dee Dee with a new outlook on twentieth century history. Sometimes it was in face-to-face conversations and sometimes it was when she sat next to him in amazement as he drifted off into his eccentric monologues. Some of those conversations related to two of the most heinous assassinations of recent history, John and Robert Kennedy. His disclosures about the Kennedy brothers were chilling and another reason Dee Dee chose to keep what he told her a secret for so many years. The Kennedy assassinations continue to feed historical speculation and conspiracy theories. Perhaps the full truth will never be known, but Nik's revelations are an added source of information.

Nik was not a fan of John Kennedy or the fanciful Camelot mythology that was growing around him. This isn't surprising, since he took a much more conservative view of life and politics. It was Kennedy's escalation of the Vietnam War that angered him the most. However, it was curious that someone who had done so much for the Department of Defense and the Central Intelligence Agency would have such an aversion to war, and specifically to bombs, but Nik was steadfastly opposed to these weapons, conventional, and in particular, nuclear. From what he told Dee Dee, we have to surmise that the intent of his vast technological achievements in defense was exactly that—defense, not offense. It appears he wanted a strong national defensive position with which to ward off enemy aggression. However deeply his feelings on this subject may have run, he made one thing abundantly clear to Dee Dee; he was opposed to the Vietnam War and the bombing that was a part of it.

Nik told Dee Dee that he had another issue with JFK. He viewed Castro as a threat, but was uncomfortable with Kennedy using the Mafia with the CIA to overthrow him. It is interesting that he himself would do business with the mob by buying properties from them in Las Vegas, and would hire Robert Maheu, coordinator of the Bay of Pigs Invasion, as his right-hand man in the operation of those properties. Maheu, in turn, elicited the help of mobsters Sam Giancana and Johnny Roselli in both of those matters.

Eva mentioned several times in interviews that she believed Nik was involved in the assassination of President John Kennedy. She had no specific statements from him to that effect, but somewhere along the line he said something that gave her a hunch he participated in the plot. Nik, in his quest to give Dee Dee an accurate picture of history, revealed a high level of knowledge of the event, if not actual participation. "He was involved in that he knew the group of people who were involved in it, and he told me, 'Don't you believe anything you read in history on that one.'" As he told her what he knew and believed about the complicated plot, two names kept coming up. "He referred to two names, Frankie and Johnny . . . Frankie and Johnny always came up. He slipped one time and caught himself and I think he meant Johnny Roselli." Dee Dee doesn't know who Frankie may have been, but she is certain that he was connected to Vice President Lyndon Johnson. Johnny Roselli, on the other hand, was well known in underworld circles. He was Chicago Mafia boss Sam Giancana's representative in Hollywood and Las Vegas for years. Both Roselli and Giancana were implicated in the CIA plot to kill Castro, and there was strong suspicion they were involved with the Kennedy assassination. In 1975, Roselli testified before the United States Select Committee on Intelligence regarding the CIA–Mafia connection, and he was called to testify on the Kennedy assassination in 1976, but he didn't show up. Apparently there were some concerns about his ability to keep his mouth shut, and on August 9, 1976, his body was found in a 55-gallon drum in Florida's Dumfoundling Bay. He had been strangled, shot, and had his legs cut off. The process worked; he didn't talk. Giancana had also been called before Congress, but while cooking sausage in his kitchen on June 17, 1975, someone put seven bullets in him, rendering him equally silent.

Nik believed the assassination plot extended inside the Washington Beltway as well. "Howard believed LBJ [Vice President Lyndon Baines Johnson] had something to do with President Kennedy's assassination." There have been others to posit this theory, but Nik didn't elaborate to Dee Dee, so what he did or didn't know will remain a mystery. Nik also gave Dee Dee an added bit of speculation. "He was convinced they killed Bobby Kennedy, too. I believe [from his comments] it's the same group of people." The RFK connection is plausible. Giancana, through John Kennedy's father, Joe, had helped John Kennedy get elected. When President Kennedy appointed his brother, Robert, as Attorney General, and Robert immediately went after the Mafia, Giancana felt betrayed, especially after working with the CIA against Castro. A revenge murder of RFK is consistent with the way the mob handles problems like this, and it is especially probable if they had already killed the president. After a half-century, the whole truth remains elusive.

As the years passed, Nik continued to reveal the personal story of his life to Dee Dee. He spoke on a number of topics, shared facts and opinions, and had an unnerving way of making fast emotional changes. Dee Dee stated this was not any mental disorder. Nik decided how he wanted to act at any given moment and acted that way by choice. He could be a gentle old man or a snarling monster, but he did it when he wanted and for his own reasons. Teasing Dee Dee about Elvis generally came from the gentle old man character, but he was never without surprises. Howard knew Elvis and had even rented a house to him, but a curious business deal brought them together for a purpose that still isn't entirely clear.

The Hughes organization was a leader in satellite technology. Many of the cutting edge fruits of its satellite research and development division were housed under the "black projects" cover of the CIA and Department of Defense, but others went to support commercial ventures, such as satellite communications. Nik, apparently at the request of the CIA, decided to go into the entertainment business. The idea was to capitalize on the worldwide popularity of Elvis Presley with a special television broadcast to the entire world, via satellite. However, according to what Nik told Dee Dee, there was a little more to it than a fancy comingling of music and technology. "He wanted Elvis to do the satellite show because it had to do with . . . they were distracting the public from something. He [wanted to do] a satellite show around the world so people would be watching that and not know what was going on . . . what was really going on."

Ever thinking big, Nik teased Dee Dee with a joke about the location for the Elvis special. "He wanted to put him on the moon!" she told us, laughing. "Oh lord, Elvis on the moon!" His point was that he wanted a big distraction.

"Yes, it had something to do with the CIA." The result of this was the *Aloha from Hawaii* show that was broadcast live, worldwide on January 14, 1973. Why they wanted a distraction still appears to be an open question. Or maybe it was such a good distraction that they succeeded at hiding whatever clandestine operation they cooked up and we'll never know the answer.

It was about this time that the gadget-crazed Nik received a very special piece of equipment that he couldn't resist showing off to Dee Dee. She told us it was the size of a small suitcase and fairly heavy, about thirty pounds. Inside the case was a bewildering maze of electronics. Nik proudly announced that his new toy was a breakthrough in communications: a telephone that transmitted directly to a satellite. In the early '80s, cellular communications were just becoming available, but it would be many years before cell phone towers would reach the rural location of the ranch. However, with his new device, Nik happily demonstrated how he could wirelessly make phone calls by satellite. He was also amused by one other thing: He told Dee Dee that the frequency he communicated on was unknown to the federal government, so he had assurance that they couldn't be listening to him.

As a college student taking the lower division, fundamental liberal arts classes, Dee Dee was particularly attuned to what Nik had to say. "Everything made a lot of sense coming from him. I sure didn't get that information from my Democracy in America class. History could be rewritten." Nik told Dee Dee access to politicians was critical to his ability to operate his technology research and development programs. "I was entering the science world and found politicians are approached to back research. Howard was intriguing to listen to."

Nik, in his rambling monologues, would frequently go off into his thoughts and reveal people and information about his organization that he had previously closely guarded. Dee Dee remembers the names, but at the time she didn't always understand how they were connected. She made a conscious choice not to press too hard for information. "I never checked into any of these guys, because this is dangerous stuff." If she ever doubted that, events eventually made it clear to her.

Three names came up frequently in Nik's monologues, as well as in his discussions with Dee Dee. He gave her bits of information about the men, but would often move to the next topic before providing any clarity. At first he referred to the men merely as Bob, Bill, and the "Wingman", but over time he revealed their full names and a rough context of their relationships to him and one another. "They each had a different position with him . . . each had a different job to do." Although Nik generally referred to people by either their first or last name only, Dee Dee eventually learned that Bob was Robert Maheu, former FBI agent and CIA operative who was a driving force in the failed attempt to depose Fidel Castro in Cuba. Maheu was the chief of Hughes's interests in Las Vegas. Bill was Bill Gay, long-time chief aide and head of the staff of Mormon aides. "Bill replaced Bob, but I don't know why," Dee Dee told us. The dismissal of Bob Maheu was a contentious event, which eventually ended up in court. Whatever feelings Nik had for Bob Maheu were not shared with Dee Dee, but the "Wingman" was another story.

The "Wingman" turned out to be Jack Real, former Lockheed Aircraft executive and long-time confidant of Hughes. After leaving Lockheed, Real joined the Hughes organization and handled aviation-oriented matters. Not only did Nik speak of Jack Real fondly, but he communicated with him. "He mailed things to Jack Real, and I know because I posted them. Jack's went to Michigan. I thought it was pretty strange because I thought all of those guys were out in Utah or Vegas, but he [Nik] said that Jack had a boyhood home . . . he still got mail in Michigan." Biographical sources state that Jack Real was raised in Calumet, Michigan.

Another recipient of mail from Nik was one Dr. Lummis. Presumably this is Dr. Fredrick Rice Lummis Jr., son of Howard's aunt Annette Gano Lummis, who delayed her marriage to raise him for a year after the death of his mother. "That was the guy at the medical center . . . institute. Howard always called it the center," Dee Dee told us. The Howard Hughes Medical Institute is located in Chevy Chase, Maryland. "They didn't go where the center was at. They went to another P.O. Box somewhere near Philadelphia." After a few minutes of jogging her memory, Dee Dee remembered the city, Stroudsburg, Pennsylvania. "I don't know where they went from there. All I know is that they went to Dr. Lummis at a post office box there." The biography of Dr. Lummis doesn't specifically mention an association with the institute, but his brother, William, was a long-time trustee of the organization.

Even more intriguing is the fact that the post cards that she sent didn't have messages on them, at least, not messages in a normal sense of the term. All that was written was one or two movie titles. "It was weird," she told us. "It was like, I know this is some kind of code [but] I'm not going to question him [Nik]. Sometimes it would be one movie [title] or it would be two movies on there. But with Dr. Lummis it was usually one. It was very rare that there were two movies listed on there. But Jack Real, he always got two movies listed. And that's all he'd have on it." As if the cryptic messages weren't strange enough, Nik took the precaution of having Dee Dee drive all over the area to mail the postcards from different towns. "He did not want it postmarked from the same place all of the time." Dee Dee doesn't remember any of the movie titles after all of these years, but it likely doesn't matter. If Nik was going to use a code, he was certainly smart enough to use one that wasn't easily cracked. If you wanted anything from him, he was going to make you work for it (Dee Dee interview with the authors).

After years of listening to Nik, Dee Dee didn't have many doubts about the veracity of what he told her. If she did, they were pushed aside with the arrival of the "File Catcher," John Meier. The story of John Meier has almost as many twists and turns as the story of Nik/Howard. Meier worked for the Hughes organization for at least fifteen years, starting at Hughes Aircraft, and eventually working his way into a position where he claimed to have regular contact with Howard. His biggest project for Howard was a $20 million acquisition of gold and silver mines in Nevada and California. Some of these mines were located near Tonopah, Nevada, where Melvin Dummar states he picked up Howard by the side of the road. In fact, during the Mormon Will trial, a Nevada Deputy Attorney General read a letter into the court record stating that Meier told a man named Edwin Daniel that Howard was missing in the Tonopah area for two or three days during the time Dummar said he picked him up (Magnesen 103). Later, when he was being chased by the Feds for embezzlement and tax violations, Meier offered to provide proof that Howard traveled in and out of the Desert Inn and was actually picked up walking in the desert. The Feds would have to make a deal with him for the information, however. He wanted the charges against him dropped. Uncle Sam said no (210).

The mines were alleged to be worthless, although Meier claimed otherwise. He also claimed that the mining operation was part of a complex scheme on the part of Howard to get control of the Stardust Hotel by making payoffs in the guise of legitimate business transactions.

Throughout all of this, Howard remained loyal to Meier and rejected Maheu's demands that he be fired (209).

Whatever the truth really was, Meier was eventually sued by Hughes Tool Company, which received a $7.9 million judgment against him. In 1979 he was also indicted for tax evasion, fraud, and obstruction of justice, picking up a thirty-month sentence, of which he served twenty-one months.

Meier, by eyewitness accounts and his own biography, seems to have been everywhere, serving as a special assistant to Governor Paul Laxalt and advising Senators Hubert Humphrey and Robert Kennedy. He was involved in many environmental concerns, including working for Howard on his nuclear testing fears. When some of his actions caused him problems, he managed to acquire a diplomatic passport from the country of Tonga to keep the authorities at bay ("John H. Meier").

Meier clearly had his hand in many deals. One deal in particular hit the radar of Robert Maheu and set off alarms in the Hughes sanctum. Meier had developed a personal and business relationship with President Nixon's brother, Donald (Higham 240). The press had gotten wind of it, and Maheu was afraid the Democrats would win the 1972 election because information was believed to have gotten into the hands of Democratic Party operative Larry O'Brien. The president tried to reign in his rogue brother, and Maheu told Meier in the strongest possible words to cease and desist. The big question was what did O'Brien know? Nixon lieutenant G. Gordon Liddy was charged with damage control and devised a pretty straightforward plan. He would simply lead a team of burglars into the offices of the Democratic National Committee Headquarters at the Watergate Hotel, search O'Brien's files, bug his phone, and leave. Picking Memorial Day weekend as a reasonably safe, low traffic time for a burglary, they were fairly successful, except that the telephone bug didn't work. This turned out to be a great example of the old adage that it's better to do things right the first time. When they went back to fix the bug and photograph O'Brien's files on June 17, 1972, the police dropped in on them at 2:30 a.m. O'Brien was no longer Nixon's biggest problem (Drosnin 429).

Howard had already gone through one Nixon scandal when it was revealed he had "loaned" Donald Nixon $205,000 in the '50s, and he didn't need another one. Despite his aggravation with the president, Howard was still officially backing Team Nixon. He'd hedged his bets by making overtures to Democratic Party contender Senator Hubert Humphrey, with the stipulation that the Senator would be helpful in his quest to stop nuclear testing, but that was a back-up plan. The plan had one major flaw: Humphrey might very well not be the Democratic candidate. Despite years as a Democratic stalwart, Humphrey had daunting competition for the nomination from the young, vibrant figure of former Attorney General Robert Kennedy. Besides being wooed by his youth and charisma, many felt RFK was the worthy and legitimate successor to take up the mantle of his slain brother, John. Therein lay the problem for Howard. Robert Kennedy detested him. Whatever solution to this problem Howard may have considered is unknown, since fate solved the problem for him.

With the aid of Larry O'Brien and a dedicated team of young and energetic supporters, Robert Kennedy was riding a wave of success that grew bigger every day. He did well in the primaries, and in early summer of 1968 the smell of victory was in the air. The California primary was critical, so there was tremendous jubilation at the Ambassador Hotel in Los Angeles when RFK was the acknowledged winner. The celebration didn't last long. Just after midnight on June 5, 1968, Robert Kennedy was gunned down leaving the hotel through the kitchen.

Howard didn't wait long to launch another plan. The possibility that Edward Kennedy might enter the presidential race in Robert's place was not good for Howard. Edward would be equally troublesome. The safest action seemed to be for him to hire the entire RFK election team and take them off the market so they couldn't campaign for a competitor. Most went their own direction before Howard could make his move, but he did manage to hire Larry O'Brien. He might be useful in four years for a Paul Laxalt presidential bid (Higham 235). In the meantime, whatever secrets he had on Howard and Nixon would remain secret. As for Meier, after his resignation from the Hughes organization in 1969, there was an audit of the mining operation. Millions of dollars were unaccounted for, which would eventually lead to problems for Meier with both the Hughes organization and the Internal Revenue Service.

One day, as Dee Dee sat with Nik, Meier, the "File Catcher" arrived at the Nicely residence, and he was on a mission. After a perfunctory introduction, Meier got down to the business at hand. "He was moving files to a safe location," she told us. Dee Dee observed the work at hand, but knew enough not to talk to Meier or ask what it was all about. He was just taking files. "That's all I can really say." Meier had previously claimed to have secret files during the time he was under indictment, but the court didn't believe them to be genuine. Since Dee Dee doesn't know what was in the files, we can only speculate, but their removal had to be in the interests of both Nik and Meier (Dee Dee interview with the authors).

Given the acrimony between Meier and the Hughes organization, one might be surprised that he would show up at the ranch, but the link between Meier and Howard wasn't broken when he left the Hughes fold. Maheu was really the one who was pushing to move Meier out of the way. Howard, on the other hand, was still enchanted with having close ties to President Nixon through his brother, and he encouraged Meier to continue to entertain the president's sibling—but to do it out of the country, where the FBI wouldn't be lurking (Higham 240). Meier and Howard also maintained their mutual concern for the environment. Meier created the Nevada Environmental Foundation, with Howard as the financier ("John H. Meier").

Whatever was in those boxes was of mutual concern. Dee Dee identified a picture of John Meier as the man who took care of the problem.

Given his penchant for total secrecy, it is a bit surprising that Nik allowed Dee Dee to see Meier, and vice versa. However, it was the arrival of another guest one day that pushed Nik's alarm buttons. As he was sitting with Dee Dee, helping her with her studies, they spotted two men approaching from the wooded area behind the trailer, not from the long drive that led to the road. One was Meier, the other was blond with large, black-framed glasses. Nik went from being the kindly, grandfatherly Nik to the volcanic, demanding Nik in a heartbeat. "Get in your car and get out of here fast!" he shouted at her. Dee Dee was shocked by his sudden, emphatic tone but grabbed her books and bolted for the door. "Whatever was going on, he didn't want me to hear. He wanted me out of there before they saw me," she told us. Even though the glimpse of the man was fairly brief, it left a lasting impression on her. "[He wore] black-rimmed glasses. They were big. I didn't like him. He looked like a horned owl." As far as she knows, she managed to get off of the property before she was noticed, but the tone of anxiety in Nik's voice left a lasting impression on her (Dee Dee interview with the authors).

The greatest mystery of the Hughes legend is how, in his supposedly final years, he could be seen as a demented, ninety-pound collection of skin and bones with long hair and fingernails, and then in a matter of days or weeks be seen by and converse with others who found him to be articulate, well groomed, and in good health. The record is clear on this, but just how was it done? Nik explained it to Dee Dee, and it revolves around a man named Brucks Randall.

Researching Brucks Randall is a bit like chasing a shadow. The moment you shine a little light on him, he changes shape. It begins with his name. It is variously spelled Brucks or Brooks, depending on which source you quote. Randall is also spelled Randell in some sources. Where he came from is also a source of speculation. A December 1974 issue of *Playgirl Magazine for Women* quotes a January 24, 1972 article in the *San Jose Mercury* newspaper in which a Hughes employee, Gerald Chouinard, states that he hired a bit actor named Brucks Randall to impersonate the billionaire in 1957 and 1958 (Brussell and Carvana). One story, perhaps apocryphal, has the initial meeting, whenever it was, taking place in a bar where Randall was working as a bartender. As the story goes, Randall said he couldn't get acting work because he looked too much like Howard Hughes. That liability quickly turned to an asset. The physical similarity between the two men was close enough for Randall to successfully impersonate the billionaire, allowing

Howard to go about his business relatively unhindered. If people thought he was somewhere else, they wouldn't be looking for him where he was (Phelan 43).

We hoped to clear some of this up by hiring a private investigator in Los Angeles to gather as much information on our mystery man as possible. The search turned up nothing productive. A brief article in a 1955 Hollywood gossip magazine states a man named Brucks Randall was accused of defrauding people in a film financing scam. Is it the same man? It sounds promising, but we found no more information. A search of the records of the Screen Actors Guild does not produce a member by that name.

We are left to speculation, and this is our best guess: All sources state that Randall was an aspiring actor. It's quite possible that the name Brucks Randall was his screen name, particularly if the unusual spelling of the first name is used. If Randall was unsuccessful as an actor, which is apparently the case, he never would have been admitted to the Screen Actors Guild. Any official records of him, such as birth and death certificates, would be filed in his legal name, whatever it was. At this point in time it is likely the whole truth about him will never be known.

What we know for sure is the Randall–Howard ruse was successful. Since no one had seen the real Howard in years, the press and the curious public could only compare him to their memory of the man. When a diversion was necessary, it would be leaked that Howard was going to be in a specific place or city, and then, with all of the expected hustle and bustle, Randall would appear. Hughes aide Mike Conrad even arranged for a fake paparazzo photo. He planted Randall in a wooded area with several other men, with whom he appeared to be in earnest conversation. A photograph of the scene was taken through foliage with a telephoto lens, which subtly implied that the picture had been captured surreptitiously (44).

Nik told Dee Dee the arrangement with Randall started in 1957 and continued off and on for years as needed. Nik said he used Randall to "draw newsmen and others off his trail, not to mention, in later years, the government." The more Randall was seen, the easier it was for him to continue his research, he told her, as well as his other hobbies. "He allotted ability to go different places . . . sneak around." The arrangement continued until 1968, when Randall dropped out of sight, according to Chouinard.

Randall wasn't the only Hughes' double. At least two other names come up in this category, but one name is particularly interesting. Hollywood columnist James Bacon wrote that body double Vance Cooper, not Hughes, was actually the man who died on the flight from Acapulco. Long-time Hughes researcher Mae Brussell, co-author of the *Playgirl* article, also believed it was Cooper who died and was buried as Hughes. Not surprisingly, this theory has its share of critics (Bacon).

There was one very strong proponent of the dead body double theory, however: Nik. "He told me," Dee Dee explained to us, "this guy [one of his doubles] went home one night and got shot in the back part of his head. And someone had discovered him, luckily in time. He had some surgery . . . and that's where you got Howard Hughes the recluse. Because, you know, he let his hair grow long [to cover the gunshot damage]. It was the story I was told, anyway, by Howard. It was complicated because someone tried to kill Howard. They wanted to kill him. Howard felt obligated to take care of that man," (Dee Dee interview with the authors).

The story makes sense in many ways. It explains why Howard could undergo rapid physical and mental transformations, and also why he received a minimal amount of attention and, apparently, a maximum amount of drugs. It explains why the Howard character in England could be described by his doctor as, "Looking like a prisoner of war." He was a prisoner, of sorts.

In all of the conversation with Dee Dee, one thing is clear: Nik revealed a depth of understanding of these matters that was well beyond common knowledge. Living in virtual isolation in the pre-Internet era, what he knew had to come from experience, not research. His passionate joy and anger, depending on the topic, were clear evidence to Dee Dee that he had a strong emotional engagement in everything he told her. There is no question in her mind that Nik was Howard.

Notes

Bacon, James. *Hughes Tales: Hogwash.* The Deseret News, November 24, 1979

Brussell, Mae and Stephanie Carvana. "Is Howard Hughes Dead and Buried Off a Greek Island?" Playgirl Magazine for Women, December, 1974.

"Dee Dee." Interview with the authors. May 9, 2014.

Drosnin, Michael. Citizen Hughes. New York: Broadway Books, 1985.

Higham, Charles. Howard Hughes: The Secret Life. New York: St. Martin's Griffin, 2004.

"John H. Meier," http://www.meier.com/johnhmeier/About.html.

Magnesen, Gary. The Investigation. Fort Lee, NJ: Barricade Books, 2005.

Phelan, James. Hughes: The Hidden Years. New York: Random House, 1976

TWENTY-THREE

TRUTH

"What is truth?" Pontius Pilate mockingly asked Jesus at his trial. It seems like a simple question, and most people believe there is an absolute truth in most matters. However, a quick look at the news headlines or your local court docket will show that, at best, truth isn't always easy to find and, at worst, it can be reduced to nothing more than a convenient opinion. Where is the truth in this story?

Eva McLelland wholeheartedly believed she was married to Howard Hughes. That is the truth.

A man named Verner Nicely disappeared, and when he reappeared, his physical characteristics no longer matched those documented by medical records. Witnesses reported that his height, hearing loss, vision problem, burn scars, and phobias, among other things, match Hughes. They document that he looked and sounded like Hughes. That is the truth.

Witness sightings of Howard Hughes document him as being an emaciated, incoherent shell of a man one week, and a dynamic physical and intellectual personality a couple of weeks later. This extraordinary physical and mental metamorphosis is documented to have happened over and over again. That is the truth.

It is documented that Hughes had at least one body double, which allowed him to be somewhere other than where the world thought he was. That is the truth.

The Authors' Notes section of this book contains an overwhelming number of facts that indicate that Eva's husband, Nik Nicely, was really Howard Hughes. The authors join Eva in her belief that that is the truth. Readers are invited to look at the facts and determine the truth for themselves.

TWENTY-FOUR

REFLECTING ON LIFE, EVA

As I look back on my memories of living with Nik for thirty-one years, I feel I understood him better than any living person, but I still never really knew him. He was a mystery that still intrigues me. He was a very impressive gentleman: tall, handsome, and intelligent. I loved him very much, and he loved me. However, I can honestly say he would not allow me to get to know him. We had our share of problems; many of them were derived from his emotional instability. He was a very sick person, but he was also a genius who could discuss many subjects with the greatest of depth and go on and on and on, especially about aviation topics.

I never revealed his true identity. I felt it was my duty to front for him with true loyalty, and I really loved and respected him. Much has happened in the thirty-one years of our marriage; so much must be told about this story. I was his personal aide, doctor, secretary, mistress, nurse, lover, and cook. I was very proud that Nik chose me to complete his life.

I never had a home or a car bought for me, let alone late life security! Except for Nik's military disability retirement check, our living expenses were almost entirely paid by me, but if I had life to live over again, I would still take care of him to the end. On second thought, I don't believe he was in a position during his last few years to reject any financial arrangements.

If people could only have known how much and in how many ways we related to each other, there would never be any questions as to why we married. Nature's manifestations and its creatures meant more to both of us than anything else. He and I were made for each other! We seemed to like all the same things, and I will always believe our life together was predestined by higher orders.

How did I manage to emerge and survive from a lifetime of adversity? I believed in myself! If you cannot believe in yourself, don't expect anybody else to believe in you.

The fake funeral in 1976 was such a disgrace. After his death, Nik was cremated. According to his wishes, a portion of his ashes were strewn over the waves of the Gulf of Mexico near Navarre Beach, a location that held wonderful memories for us. The spreading of his ashes was a fitting end to a gentle, humble, caring person who would not hurt a living being of any kind.

I will not rest until I reveal the truth, having lived with the man called Verner D. Nicely for thirty-one years. If I should fail to correct some of the horrible mistakes of hearsay and gossip about his life, my ashes will be stirring forever in the "Restless Winds."

"Nik do you think they will ever believe me?" I would ask.

"No, they will never believe you," he would answer.

I think he is right!

Douglas Wellman, Eva McLelland, and Mark Musick, February 2009

Author's Note: Eva Renee McLelland died in November of 2009 at age 93, while living in the southeastern United States.

TIME LINE OF SIGNIFICANT EVENTS

1905   Howard Hughes was born either December 24 or September 24. Howard's maternal grandmother died in 1905.

1913   Howard's maternal grandfather, who lived on a ranch near Irving, Texas, died.

1916   Eva Renee Howard was born in Florida, May 4.

1921   Verner Nicely was born in Ohio, July 7.

1922   Howard's mother died.

1924   Howard's father died.

1925   Howard and Ella Rice were married in Houston, Texas.

1926–28   Howard's paternal grandparents died.

1929   Howard and Ella were divorced. Howard and Billie Dove (using aliases) resided in a shed with a dirt floor, working as farmhands in Nevada.

1933   During March, Howard and Glenn Odekirk took off from Glendale in an S-43 and flew to Houston to visit Aunt Annette. The route of flight went directly by or through the Grand Canyon, providing the opportunity for a little sightseeing.

        Later in life, Nik indicated to Eva he flew down the Grand Canyon, with a passenger aboard the aircraft. Nik never mentioned who the passenger was, just that there was a passenger with him during the flight.

1934   Howard Hughes won first place in the 1934 All-American Air Meet in Florida. Eva said Nik never initiated discussions of his aviation feats. However, when asked, he would comment about them. He was very modest about his accomplishments and did not brag about his notoriety.

1938   Howard took off on July 10 with a four-man crew and flew around the world in less than four days.

Nik talked about flying around the world in 1938, the ticker tape parade in New York City, and meeting President Roosevelt. He said that he was not a fan of President Roosevelt. Once, Eva mentioned a picture of him from a newspaper that she'd seen. It was of Howard Hughes shaking hands with President Roosevelt. Eva said, "Even though you did not like President Roosevelt, you shook his hand after you flew around the world, didn't you?" He said, "Well, that is different. I had to do that for the publicity."

1946   On July 7, the XF-11 Aircraft Howard Hughes was piloting crashed. It severely burned and nearly killed him. He had burns on his left chest wall, left ear and left buttock. Howard had extensive burns on his left hand, with cuts and bruises on his arms and legs. He hovered near death for several days. After the crash, Howard seared both hands to the bone while trying to open the Plexiglas cockpit cover.

Throughout his life, he was involved in fourteen airplane and automobile crashes, one resulting in the death of a pedestrian. His high-risk test pilot days resulted in several crashes, leaving him with massive injuries.

Eva relayed that Nik had burns on his hands (one more than the other), feet and scalp (one side more than the other). He also had some minor scars on his chest. She does not remember any on his back. There were no noticeable scars on his face. She thought that he might have had those addressed. Nik wore special-order boat deck shoes that were two sizes too big for him, so they did not hurt his feet.

1947 Terry Moore said she married Howard Hughes aboard his yacht in 1947. The records were subsequently tossed overboard.

In August 1947, Howard Hughes was called to testify before a Senate hearing. He stated, "If the flying boat fails to fly, I will leave the country and never come back."

On November 2, 1947, Howard Hughes flew the Hercules flying boat for one mile, for less than one minute, at a top speed of 80 mph.

Nik reminisced about building the Hercules or "The Spruce Goose," as the media called it, and also talked about flying it. Eva asked him, "Why were you so anxious to fly it?" Nik said, "Because they said that it couldn't be done. I wanted to prove a plane constructed of wood could fly." This seemed to be his pet project. Later, Eva asked him where the Hercules was located, and he knew exactly where it was— originally in southern California, then in Oregon. He said when it was being built, the workers were required to wear booties when performing work on it. He always called her socks "booties."

1949 Howard Hughes had quite a thing for Elizabeth Taylor, and he ordered his attorney to approach Liz's mother to approve an arranged marriage. If this could happen, Howard would give them $1 million for the arrangement. When Liz heard of the proposal, she laughed out loud.

1952 The last pictures of Howard Hughes were taken.

1953 The Howard Hughes Medical Institute was founded in late 1953.

1954 Robert Maheu started working for Howard Hughes. They never met face-to-face.

1956 Howard Hughes loaned Donald Nixon $205,000 for a failing business.

1957   Howard Hughes married Jean Peters on January 12 at the L
& L Motel in Tonopah, Nevada, in Room #33. The only
people allowed at the wedding were two of Hughes's aides and
the justice of the peace who performed the ceremony. Hughes
(age 51) and Peters (age 30) both used assumed names, and to
complete the masquerade, even the justice of the peace used
an alias when signing the marriage license. Hughes went
to Nassau to escape his new wife, and this was his last public
appearance. It was hardly a close marriage. Hughes traveled to
Montreal four months after they were married; however, Jean
did not go with him.

Years later, Nik talked to Eva about how much he loved
Canada.

1958   Hughes frequently went into total seclusion. Aide, Bill Gay,
did not see Howard from 1958 to 1973.

1960   News leaked of the Howard Hughes loan to Donald Nixon for
$205,000 just before the presidential election, possibly leading
to Nixon's narrow defeat to President Kennedy.

Don Nicely visited Verner in San Francisco. It was the last
time they saw each other. Verner went to Panama for a
classified task.

1961   The Bay of Pigs operation failed in Cuba.

Hughes investigated purchasing shares of Northeast Airlines.

1962   When Howard first attempted to buy Northeast Airlines in
1962, the Civil Aeronautics Board (CAB) would not
approve his ownership of two airlines, TWA and Northeast.
However, through Howard's covert financial support to
keep fuel flowing to the virtually bankrupt Northeast Airlines,
and legal maneuvering, he forced the CAB to reevaluate their
concerns.

1963   Hughes bought Northeast Airlines.

1966   Howard Hughes traveled by train from Los Angeles to Boston for an "eye problem" in July.

Nik related a story to Eva about a fight he was in, and she thought the location was in Africa. During the fight, he was hit in the eye and described the damage to Eva as if it was dislocated.

Jean Peters never personally saw Howard Hughes after 1966.

After solving the "eye problem," Howard Hughes traveled by train from Boston to Las Vegas in November.

1967   The Desert Inn Hotel became the official property of Howard Hughes in April.

Eva moved to the Panama Canal Zone after living in Georgia. On December 23, Howard Hughes purchased the Frontier Hotel in Las Vegas.

Between Christmas and New Year's 1967, Guido Robert Deiro flew Howard Hughes to the Cottontail Ranch north of Las Vegas.

December 29, Melvin Dummar picked up an individual on a desert road north of Las Vegas. The man said he was Howard Hughes.

1968   January 24, Hughes Tool purchased mines on the road where Howard was found in late 1967.

The Mormon Will was signed March 19.

A Soviet submarine sank in the Pacific Ocean.

1969   Nik told Eva that he arrived in Panama in September.

Eva met Nik for the first time in the Panama Canal Zone in October. In November, Nik disappeared.

* two month separation

1970   Nik returned to the Panama Canal Zone in January.

In April, Howard Hughes bought Air West Airlines.

Jean Peters formally filed for divorce in May.

May 13, Nik and Eva married in the Canal Zone.

Howard Hughes was reported to be on his deathbed in a Las Vegas hotel.

Eva traveled to Montgomery, Alabama, to visit her mother in November.

* separation for a few days

Howard Hughes was moved from Las Vegas to the Bahamas in November.

1971   Howard Hughes's and Jean Peters's divorce became final in June. Word became public about the Clifford Irving biography in December. Eva and Nik discussed the news of Clifford Irving's upcoming book.

1972   On January 7, Howard Hughes participated in a telephonic interview about the Irving book.

In February, Howard Hughes moved from the Bahamas to Nicaragua and began a three-and-a-half week stay.

On March 13, a healthy, commanding Howard Hughes met with the president of Nicaragua, flew to Vancouver, Canada, and walked into the hotel lobby as a normal person.

An emaciated Howard Hughes was moved to Canada.

Eva moved to Flagstaff, Arizona, in June.

* four month separation

Watergate was broken into on June 17.

Nik moved to the Veterans Hospital facility in Prescott, Arizona, in late July. Howard Hughes met with LaVane Forsythe and, possibly, John Meier in Canada in late August. They discussed the delivery of the Mormon Will after Howard's death.

An emaciated Howard Hughes was moved from Canada to Nicaragua in September.

On September 24, a commanding Howard Hughes met with Merrill Lynch brokers in Managua.

In October, an emaciated Howard Hughes was moved from Nicaragua to London.

Eva moved to Prescott, Arizona, from Flagstaff, Arizona, in October.

In December, Hughes Tool went public and was renamed the Summa Corporation. Eva and Nik moved to Camp Verde, Arizona, and lived on a horse ranch.

1973   A commanding Howard Hughes met with the Nevada governor and the Nevada gaming chairman in London on March 17.

Nik tried to choke Eva in May.

In early June, Eva traveled from Arizona to Alabama to take care of her ill mother.

* ten month separation

A healthy Howard Hughes flew a British aircraft in June and July.

On August 9, an emaciated Howard Hughes, "looking like a prisoner of war," fell in a London hotel and broke his hip.

Also on August 9, Eva's mother passed away in Alabama.

Immediately after the funeral, Eva moved to the West Indies and lived in a small cabin. The aides evaluated the possibility of operations from the island.

On December 20, an emaciated Howard Hughes moved to the Bahamas from the London hotel.

1974   Parts of the Soviet submarine were raised.

In March, Eva returned to Arizona from the West Indies. She

traveled on a plane to Miami, a bus to Troy, and an aircraft to Arizona. In April, Eva and Nik moved to the red house in Alabama. They made the trip in a 1947 GMC pickup. Eva returned to the West Indies, in May, while Nik stayed in Alabama.

* five month separation

In April, Dr. Norman Crane refused to write any more narcotics prescriptions for Howard. Bill Gay enlisted the aid of his brother-in-law, Dr. Wilber Thain, to take over supplying the drugs. Thain presented an extensive list of demands in exchange for his services, all of which the Summa Corporation agreed to meet.

Hughes's Romaine Street office was burglarized on June 5.

In August, Nixon resigned and left office.

Eva returned to Alabama in September.

In October, Nik relayed childhood events to Eva while they were located in Alabama. Eva thought Nik had kept the secret long enough, and he wanted the world to know.

In November, Eva and Nik moved to Florida for the winter.

1975   In March, Project Jennifer, the raising of the Soviet submarine, became public.

Nik received *True Magazine* in the mail and showed it to Eva in March.

In April, Nik and Eva moved from Florida to Alabama back into the red house.

1976   *On February 10, an emaciated Howard Hughes moved from the Bahamas to Acapulco.*

The emaciated Howard Hughes died as he was flown from Acapulco back to Texas on April 5.

On April 27, a short, stocky man (LaVane Forsythe) delivered the Mormon Will to Melvin Dummar at his gas station.

1979   On July 24, Howard's Aunt Annette Lummis died.

1982   Nik and Eva moved to the "ranch" west of Troy, Alabama.

2001   November 21, Nik died in Dothan, Alabama.

2002   A portion of Nik's ashes were spread on a beach in the panhandle of Florida where Eva and Nik lived in 1975.

* = times Nik and Eva were separated

Italics = Activities of Howard's stand-in

AUTHORS' NOTES

Comparisons between Howard Hughes, Verner Nicely, and Nik

Birth and Youth

Howard was born in Humble, Texas, in 1905 and raised in ranch country around Irving, Texas. His father was the inventor of an oil drilling bit. His father helped him build a motorized bicycle and paid the flying lessons for him. Howard played the saxophone with no particular skill. He was eleven years older than Eva.

Verner was born in 1921 in Franklin, Ohio, where he was raised. His father was a baker. Verner joined the military and apparently disappeared while working with the CIA in Panama in the late 1960s. He was five years younger than Eva.

Nik said he was from Irving, Texas, and his father was in the oil business. He told stories of life on the ranch with cowboys and did rope tricks for Eva. He never mentioned Ohio but told Eva of a motorized bicycle that he made as a youth and of learning to fly an airplane as a teenager. He mentioned attempting to learn to play the saxophone. He appeared to be considerably older than Eva, and he couldn't cook or bake to save his life.

Education

Howard was educated in a number of private schools without achieving any academic distinction. He never earned a high school diploma, although his father somehow managed to get him into some classes at Cal Tech and get him enrolled in the Rice Institute, a technical college in Houston.

Verner attended local public schools in Ohio and earned his high school diploma in his hometown. His son, Gary, reports that his spelling and writing skills were fine, and he never took any college courses.

Nik never spoke of his education except to occasionally mention that he had attended a technical college. His spelling and grammar were terrible.

Siblings and Friends
Howard was an only child, but he had a special boyhood friend, Dudley Sharp.

Verner had two brothers and one sister.

Nik said he was an only child, but he had a special boyhood friend that he missed.

Alcohol
Howard was not a drinker.

Gary Nicely remembers that his father, Verner, consumed alcohol.

Nik never touched alcohol.

Scars
Howard was severely burned in a 1946 airplane crash. He was left with prominent burn scars on his hands and head.

Verner Nicely had no burn scars the last time his son saw him in 1967.

Nik had prominent burn scars on his hands and head.

Physical Characteristics
Howard was six feet four inches tall with black hair and dark eyes. Howard went to Boston in 1966 for treatment for "eye trouble" and was not seen for several months. According to Jack Real, he had difficulty reading without a magnifying glass. He had a severe hearing loss.

Verner was five feet eleven with blond hair and hazel eyes. His vision and hearing were normal.

Nik was six feet three with strange, reflective bright blue eyes and dyed blond hair. He told Eva his hair was black when he was young. He could not read without a magnifying glass and turned his head to favor his right eye when he read. He had a severe hearing loss.

The medical records for Nik from the Alabama Veteran's Administration hospital from 1999–2001 match Howard, but not Verner.

CIA Connections

Howard had numerous dealings with the CIA, including building spy satellites and the ship *Glomar Explorer*, which was used in the clandestine recovery of a Soviet submarine. Howard was also indirectly connected to the CIA through his right-hand man for many years, Robert Maheu, a former CIA operative who worked on the failed Cuban Bay of Pigs invasion.

Both Verner's brother, Don, and his son, Gary, reported that Verner worked on classified projects after his military service was concluded and his health restored. The last time that Don saw him in the early 1960s, around the time of the Bay of Pigs invasion, he believed Verner was working for the CIA in a plot against Cuba.

Nik often spoke of his admiration for the CIA.

Personal Finances

Howard was rich.

Military records of Verner list him as a noncommissioned officer, a position with a modest salary. His CIA salary is unknown.

Nik seemed to have a great deal of money when he and Eva first met. He bought her lavish gifts and a $5,000 engagement ring, which was beyond the means of his aircraft maintenance supervisor's salary of roughly $9,000 per year.

Timing

By November 1969, Verner had been missing from his family for two years. His brother would never see him or hear from him again. In November 1969, Nik disappeared from Panama and Eva for two months.

Between the Christmas and New Year's holidays in 1969, Howard bought Air West Airlines and the Dunes Hotel and Country Club. The purchase of the airline and the antitrust implications of another Las Vegas hotel required his personal attention and a nudge to his friend Richard Nixon. He also fought with Robert Maheu over the dismissal of John Meier and engaged in a contract to build a spy ship for the CIA.

During this period, "Howard" was reported by Dr. Buckley to be six feet four inches tall and about 100 pounds with rotted teeth, paper-thin skin through which his shoulder bone protruded, long hair, a long beard, long curling fingernails, and was barely coherent.

Meetings, Conversations, and Travel

On January 9, 1972, Howard spoke by telephone to a number of journalists who knew him personally to refute the authenticity of the Clifford Irving biography. They reported it was definitely his voice and he spoke clearly and intelligently. Eva listened on the radio and also recognized the voice. It was Nik. He claimed to be calling from the Bahamas, but attempts to trace the call were unsuccessful. Since Howard owned a satellite communications company, he could have called from anywhere.

On February 15, 1972, a naked, emaciated "Howard" was carried aboard a chartered yacht by his aides. Skipper Bob Rehak commented on the spectacle of the man with the long curling toenails that poked out of his sandals and his long fingernails. He was taken to Nicaragua for a twenty-five-day stay.

Roughly three weeks later, in March 1972, Howard met Nicaraguan dictator General Somoza and United States Ambassador Turner Shelton aboard a Gulfstream II jet aircraft in Managua, Nicaragua. They reported he was charming, articulate, and well groomed. Howard continued to Vancouver, where he was seen by guests as he walked through a hotel.

Nik and Eva were separated periodically in Panama in early 1972, until Eva departed alone for Flagstaff, Arizona, in June 1972.

On September 25, 1972, two officials of the Merrill Lynch brokerage company met with Howard to arrange to take the Hughes Tool Company public to raise cash for a possible judgment against Howard in the TWA lawsuit. They reported he was businesslike, fit, and well groomed. During this period in 1972, Nik and Eva were separated.

On December 24, 1972, "Howard" arrived in Fort Lauderdale, Florida, aboard a private jet. Customs officials reported that he was emaciated, filthy, and nearly incoherent. Internal Revenue Service agents, who had been trying to catch him for years, determined there was no point in detaining the incompetent man.

On December 24, 1972, after a brief stopover in Fort Lauderdale, Florida, a drugged, incoherent, filthy "Howard," with long hair, curling fingernails, and toenails was flown to London.

On March 18, 1973, Howard met with Nevada Governor Mike O'Callahan and Nevada Gaming Control Board Chairman Philip Hannifin in London to discuss gaming licenses owned by Howard. They found him to be a well-groomed, "commanding personality" who was articulate, forceful, and knew exactly what was going on with his gambling properties.

On March 21 and 29, 1973, Howard met with friend Jack Real to discuss setting up a program for Howard to fly aircraft again. With Real and Hawker Siddeley test pilot Tony Blackman, Howard flew a turboprop aircraft on June 10 and 27, 1973, and a jet aircraft on July 17, 1973.

On August 9, 1973, "Howard" fell and broke his hip. He was attended by Dr. William Young, who reported he looked like a "prisoner of war" and had skin like parchment with long curling fingernails and toenails.

Eva and Nik were separated from June 1973 and remained so for the rest of the year.

On February 10, 1976, "Howard" was flown to Acapulco on a private jet. He was dressed in an overcoat and wrapped in a blanket. He was described by witnesses as "looking like a zombie." During this period, a Mexican doctor reported "Howard" to be little more than a living skeleton and was dying from neglect.

Shortly after arriving in Mexico, Howard contacted friend Jack Real and told him he wanted to buy more hotels and start flying again. On April 1, 1976, Howard had a long telephone conversation with aide George Francom, spoke philosophically about his life, and seemed depressed.

On April 5, 1976, "Howard" was loaded on a private jet to be flown to Houston, Texas. He died en route. The Hughes family prohibited photographs and an autopsy. On April 7, 1976, "Howard" was interred with little formality.

The Fortune

It would be strange that Howard would intentionally give up his earthly fortune after the passing of the "Howard" stand-in. The first item on the Mormon Will identified one quarter of his wealth to go to the Howard Hughes Medical Institute in Miami. Using the assumption that the Mormon Will might actually have been his intention, as former FBI agent Gary Magnesen hypothesized, a speculative plan began to form. Dr. Thain, Bill Gay's brother-in-law, was one of the insiders who would have known the entire truth about Howard's second life. Dr. Thain was given a lifetime contract, but he was also offered a high position at the Howard Hughes Medical Institute. Possibly, Howard planned that in some way he could gain access to a portion of his estate wealth through the medical institute and Dr. Thain. The Hughes family's successful challenge of the Mormon Will fouled up this plan, if it was true. Hence, Nik's comment, "I was screwed out of it by my relatives."

ACKNOWLEDGEMENTS

Gathering piles of data is one thing. Compiling it into a coherent book is quite something else. The authors gratefully acknowledge the contributions of the Writelife editorial team who guided us through the process with skill and professionalism.

Editor Paige Duke was instrumental in structuring the manuscript and pointing out areas that needed clarification or additional factual citations. This is a much better book because of her intellect and dedication.

Ellis Dixon was tasked with the difficult job of designing a cover that expressed the complex material in the book. She produced a number of great designs and it's unfortunate that we can only use one. We thank her for her hard work and artistic skills.

Alex Padalka has been our guiding light through this exciting project. The entire publication process was under his direction and he was absolutely instrumental in keeping us going in the right direction and on schedule. He was the "guy who knows everything."

We would also like to acknowledge our publisher, Terri Leidich, of Writelife/Boutique of Quality Books. Terri has been exceptionally supportive to us as well as all of the authors who publish under her imprints. Her guidance and professionalism are greatly appreciated.